Prostitution Policy

Prostitution Policy

Revolutionizing Practice through a Gendered Perspective

Lenore Kuo

NEW YORK UNIVERSITY PRESS

New York and London

NEW YORK UNIVERSITY PRESS
New York and London

Library of Congress Cataloging-in-Publication Data
Kuo, Lenore.
Prostitution policy : revolutionizing practice through
a gendered perspective / Lenore Kuo.
p. cm.
Includes bibliographical references and index.
ISBN 0-8147-4763-9 (cloth : alk. paper)
1. Prostitution—United States.   2. Feminism—United States.
3. Prostitutes—Legal status, laws, etc.
4. Prostitutes—United States—Social conditions.   I. Title.
HQ144 .K86 2002
306.74'0973—dc21   2002007814

New York University Press books are printed on acid-free paper,
and their binding materials are chosen for strength and durability.

Manufactured in the United States of America
10 9 8 7 6 5 4 3 2 1

Contents

Acknowledgments		vii
Preface		xi
	Introduction	1
1	Contextualizing the Discussion: Feminism and Policy Analysis	15
2	A Sexually Charged Context, the Feminist "Sex Wars," and Prostitution Defined	36
3	The Intrinsic Character of Heterosexual Activity and Prostitution	44
4	Sexuality and Prostitution as Conceptual Constructs	51
5	The Practice of Heterosexuality and Heterosexual Prostitution	62
6	The "Ideal" Character of Heterosex/Intercourse and Prostitution	111
7	Evolving a Policy—Legal Status	119
8	The Feminist Debate	138
9	Prostitution Solution: Policy Recommendations	152
	Notes	171
	Bibliography	199
	Index	208
	About the Author	214

Acknowledgments

Numerous people, organizations, and institutions have provided generous support over the many years it has taken to complete this book.

First and foremost, I thank my dear friend Frank Anechiarico, who encouraged me from the outset to research my passion—gendered public policy—and whose unwavering support throughout this project has been truly remarkable. I also express my deepest gratitude to my ex-husband, James Kuo, without whose consistent encouragement I would never have begun this voyage, and to Dena Whitebook, without whose wisdom I could never have remained afloat.

Among the many individuals who shared their specialized knowledge with me, I particularly thank Petra Baas, Stefi Barna, Kein Beekman, "Bridgit," Robert DelCarlo, Melissa Dittmore, Cyrille Fijnaut, George Flint, "Gena," Kelly Holsopple, "Jo," Carole Leigh, Alberta Nelson, Ellen Pillard, Rene Romkes, "Pepper," Sari van der Poel, Marieke van Doominck, Lucie van Mens, and Jan Visser. In addition, I am most grateful to the staffs of the various organizations and collections that were critical to researching this topic, especially those at COYOTE—San Francisco; the Foundation against Trafficking in Women (STV)—Utrecht, The Netherlands; the Global Alliance against Trafficking in Women—Thailand; the HAP Foundation—Utrecht; the IIAV (Internationaal Informatiecentum en Archief voor de Vrouwenbeweging)—Amsterdam; the Mr. A. de Graaff Foundation—Amsterdam; PONY—New York; the Red Thread—Amsterdam; the University of Nebraska at Omaha Library (especially Carole Larson); the University of Nevada Reno Library; and VENA—Leiden University, the Netherlands.

I am also most indebted to those who read earlier drafts of all or part of this manuscript and provided valuable suggestions, including Frank Anechiarico, Jean Anyon, David Butcher, Anne Donchin, Karen Falconer-

Al Hindi, Nanette Funk, and Nancy Holmstrom. In addition, I thank Elizabeth Ring and Richard Werner for their helpful comments on this project.

Research for this study was supported in part by numerous faculty research grants from the University of Nebraska–Omaha. I also thank the Center for the Study of Women and Society of the Graduate College of the City University of New York and the Institute for Research on Women, Rutgers University, New Brunswick, New Jersey, for providing me with a sense of community and the resources required to complete this work.

I want to express my heartfelt gratitude to generous friends who have challenged me intellectually, supported me emotionally, provided a genuine community, tolerated my sometimes obsessive preoccupation with this project, and convinced me that I could complete this manuscript—really— including Mary Anne Lamanna, Mary Anne Krezmian, Beverly Walker, Karen Falconer-Al Hindi, Missy Kubitschek, Martin Rosenberg, Dale Stover, and the faculty of the Women's Studies Program at the University of Nebraska–Omaha. And especially, my thanks to Mary Zeleny, who, in addition to being an extraordinary friend, has taught me by example what it is to remain tenacious and courageous in the face of great adversity.

I also want to thank Despina Papazoglou Gimbel, Managing Editor at NYU Press, for her skill and patience.

Preface

During the summer of my senior year of college, I took a job waitressing at the Dangle Bar, a go-go joint in Madison, Wisconsin. Until then, though my refusal to be 'discreet' about my relatively tame sexual life caused the occasional raised eyebrow, I had always been treated as a 'good girl'—"the kind of woman a man can take home to his mother," the *sort of woman* with whom men had to 'mind their manners'.[1] But at a place like the Dangle, men felt free to express traditional patriarchal contempt and devaluation of 'bad girls', and, ultimately, all women without subtly or charade. The simple fact of my working at such an establishment was sufficient for me to be reclassified as a 'bad girl'—making this a decidedly educational summer. Although, on the surface, most of the customers treated me with courtesy, I was aware of a prevailing misogyny which was palpable in an environment, in which in 20th century U.S. culture, women danced, nearly naked, before a group of men.

One evening, an unfamiliar customer pointed to a $50 bill he had laid on his table and asked if I was interested. I fully understood the question, and, in a polite tone, simply answered "no." From that point on, nothing unusual transpired between us. He was equally polite, apparently respecting that the conversation was closed. He left a normal tip, indicating neither resentment nor embarrassment.

I remember very well the conversation I had afterwards with the bar's bouncer. I remember laughing, expressing incredulity and amusement that anyone would pay what was then a fair sum of money for sexual services when, with little effort, he could have found a co-ed who would have had sex with him for free. (I was very naive!) The bouncer insisted, rather offendedly, that I was dismissing the compliment the customer had paid me—that his offer of money indicated that he found me attractive enough to 'pay for me'.

The bouncer's interpretation, had an extraordinary impact on me; I knew his claim was false, indeed screamingly false, though I did not, at that time, understand why. Understanding why, understanding the general presumptions and power relations implicit in both my conversations with the customer and the bouncer, has, in a sense, been a recurring focus of a good part of my personal and professional life. In many ways, this book is the completion of a circle, of a lengthy internal dialogue which began with that incident.

Introduction

So all this time she has been considered only "ass," "meat," "twat," or "stuff," to be gotten a "piece of," "that bitch," or "this broad" to be tricked out of money or sex or love! To understand finally that she is no better than other women but completely indistinguishable comes not just as a blow but as a total annihilation.[1]

This book is intended to answer the question "What adult heterosexual prostitution policy should U.S. feminists support?" In a variety of respects, it radically departs from the current feminist and nonfeminist literature on prostitution policy and from public policy analyses in general.

This analysis is based on research whose focus is far broader than other public policy approaches because it takes as pivotal aspects of prostitution not usually considered in policy assessment. In addition to an extended overview of current prostitution practice, my approach treats both the conceptual construction of "the prostitute" and feminist ideals regarding prostitution as critical considerations in evaluating any potentially effective resolution to the current situation. As I briefly argue, failure to consider the conceptual construction of the prostitute can and has led to policies that are devastating to prostitute and nonprostitute women alike, while lack of concern for ultimate ideals condemns us, at best, to eternal crisis management. Because heterosexual prostitution is minimally tainted by the same destructive and contradictory phenomena as mark current heterosexual practice in general, this book also contains explicit discussions of the conceptual construction, feminist ideals, and current practice of heterosexual activity as they bear directly on the question of prostitution policy.

This work further maintains that if policy recommendations are limited solely to legal solutions, they cannot hope to be adequate or even especially helpful. The various governmental extralegal activities, including economic, educational, medical, and social service supports, that may be conjoined to possible legal approaches are so critical to an effective policy that unless they are spelled out in sufficient detail, they may be constructed so as to pervert altogether the goals of the proffered legal policy. For this reason, Chapter 9 includes a lengthy and detailed discussion of extralegal supports required for a coherent and credible prostitution policy. Similarly, because, given the nature of the industry, prostitution cannot be addressed independent of prostitution facilitation (ie. acting as an agent for the sale of prostitutes' services such as pimping and brothel management), Chapter 9 also contains a detailed discussion of a legal and extralegal prostitution facilitation policy.

Additionally, my analysis contains a unique perspective on the relationship between prostitution and pornography. Contrary to the implications of U.S. law, which permits the production and dissemination of most pornography while outlawing prostitution, and contrary to current feminist approaches that lump pornography and prostitution together as "sex work," I argue that pornography is a far more devastating and misogynist practice than prostitution, one that not only needs far greater legal restrictions than prostitution but that also must be restricted specifically for the protection of prostitutes.

This discussion constitutes a radical departure from previous American feminist approaches. Of particular importance, my evaluation has not been based solely on the social science data currently available on U.S. prostitution, because this research clearly misrepresents the industry as a whole. American statistical studies of prostitution have focused almost exclusively on streetwalking. But, except for trafficking, streetwalking is unquestionably the most exploitative, violent, and abusive form of prostitution. Given that streetwalking is estimated to constitute only 10 to 20 percent of prostitution activity, any analysis based solely on U.S. data becomes inexcusably skewed toward a negative assessment of the industry as a whole. This work attempts to overcome this bias by looking carefully at international social science data, especially from the Netherlands. As a result, my overall analysis is considerably more positive toward prostitution as an industry than that of most American feminist works, arguing for a policy that is directed not at ultimately abolishing the practice but at radically transforming it. In effect, I argue that women will never be normalized until sex is normalized, and sex will never be normalized until prostitution is normalized. Furthermore, in light of the available international research, my perspective is far more sympathetic to the voices of anti-abolitionist prostitutes than virtually all other American feminist policy analyses. Thus this work is also unusual in incorporating these prostitutes' perspectives extensively in the policy recommendations.

The recommendations that emerge from this approach represent a blend of the prevailing U.S. and international feminist perspectives. While speaking to the many problematic aspects of prostitution, they also are intended to provide the greatest possible protection and autonomy to women choosing to enter or continue in the life. But beyond simply considering the needs of women in the industry, these recommendations are constructed so as to improve the lives of all women by undermining the conceptual construction of "the whore," a representation that inflicts extraordinary damage on the lives of all women, both as individuals and as members of a gender class.

What Is a Public Policy?

Questions such as "Should we permit abortions and, if so, when?"; "Should consenting adults have access to pornographic materials?"; and "Should we devote 15 percent of our national budget to cancer research?" are questions of public policy. Public policy positions are ones that argue what, *all things considered*, a society or, more strictly, a state ought to do about any particular class of behaviors or activities.

In considering "social or public policies," people tend to think in terms of some generalized conclusion, for example, "Consenting adults should have access to pornographic materials if these are viewed in private and if they depict only the behavior of consenting adults" or, to the contrary, "Pornographic materials should be banned." Often in arguing about public policies we presume we are referring only to the broad legal policies to be adopted by the state in order to deal with a particular issue. When I describe the topic of my research, I am often asked, "What is your position? Do you think prostitution should be legalized?" But equating a public policy with a legal policy necessarily renders any policy analysis inadequate and is especially dangerous for women. The complexity of serious social problems generally requires the provision of state-funded supports, of social, medical, psychological, educational, and political elements as well as legal "solutions," in order genuinely to address the issue. For example, a policy outlawing natural surrogacy contracts is likely to drive many such arrangements underground, where the child produced through surrogacy will have even fewer protections than under a legalized surrogacy policy. What protections might be put in place to lessen the likelihood of this outcome? Should we initiate public educational programs designed to question the value of biological connection as the ultimately desirable custodial parental relationship? Should we expend resources to facilitate easier adoption of children in this country and abroad?

It is not just that extralegal supports are necessary to the success of proposed legal solutions; failure to specify such support elements leaves a policy vulnerable to being conjoined with apparatuses that actually undermine the intended outcome of the legal solution. For example, if we pass a law outlawing discrimination against those who are physically disabled but the available governmental transportation and education support services isolate the physically disabled in buses and classrooms solely for their use, then the "support" services will actually be oppositional to the goals of the legal solution. In this case, government support services would continue to stigmatize the physically challenged and thus encourage de facto discrimination.

Additionally, and of particular concern to feminists, the failure to specify necessary support services along with a legal approach as part of a larger proposed policy package often results in the government abdicating responsibility for the provision of such services. The responsibility then ends up falling to nongovernmental organizations (NGOs). But as Mary Hawkesworth notes, leaving to NGOs the nonlegal aspects of policies, particularly those relevant to "women's issues," has led to a host of problems, including the privatization of women's lives and needs, effectively removing us from the public agenda and making women dependent on the largesse of charitable organizations for our survival. We are once again disfranchised of the protection and financial support of the state. Not only has this been a persistent problem globally,[2] but in the United States the problematic result of assigning women's needs to the private arena is amply exemplified in the case of domestic violence, where the vast majority of social services for victims of battery are provided by NGOs. Indeed, only in the past decade have state-supported battered women's shelters emerged, and as a result we still have thoroughly insufficient facilities to address the burgeoning need. And while prostitution is illegal in most U.S. jurisdictions, the state offers no shelters for prostitutes who are attempting to leave the practice.

My goal, therefore, is to provide a fully developed policy that includes consideration of whatever governmental activities should be brought to bear in attempting to address prostitution.

Political Context, Feminist Commitment

As the title of the book indicates, this analysis of prostitution emerges from a gendered perspective, that is, one that recognizes and is sensitive to the significance of *patriarchy*. Very broadly, patriarchy is the social organization that systematically and unjustifiably assigns subordinate status and power to women,[3] relative to their male counterparts.[4] Feminists both recognize patriarchy as a fundamental organization of current human civilizations and, further, believe that it must be eliminated.

This view, however, describes a diverse array of nuanced and at times contradictory perspectives. Early second-wave feminisms emerged as competing perspectives, generally arguing for a primary or original site of women's oppression. Thus, while early liberal feminists held that women's subordination was attributable to legal and customary constraints, radical feminists ascribed women's domination to biological differences from men, especially reproductive and sexual differences. Marxists held that women's oppression should be understood as an outgrowth of capitalism. Such either/or approaches are far less common nowadays.

In what follows, I do not argue for any of the particular feminist theories that have shaped my feminism; to do so would require a separate book. But to understand and assess my work, readers, particularly feminist theorists, will find it useful to know what my specific feminist commitments are. Like most contemporary feminists, I view women's subordination as located in a complex of interrelated sites and sources of oppression. The physical body may be the primary source of domination for a woman in a particular culture at a particular time in her life, but economics, legal and social controls (including forced gender roles), conceptual and linguistic subordination, medical and educational bias and barriers, and disparities in the distribution of institutionalized political power may all be sites of primary control in other cultures, or at other moments of, or in different arenas of an individual woman's life. At the same time, feminists are nearly universally sensitive to the implications of identity theory and politics, recognizing that there is no "Woman's" experience but rather, diverse experiences based in part, on a complex of the individual's positions relative to other hierarchies of power, such as race, ethnicity, sexual orientation, and economic privilege.

When I was first exposed to feminist theories, I was most powerfully drawn to radical feminism and socialist feminism. I was and remain deeply affected by the work of Shulamith Firestone, Ti-Grace Atkinson, and Juliette Mitchell. In the 1980s, I was strongly influenced by the works of Catharine MacKinnon and Andrea Dworkin, though also by Elaine Rubin, Carole Vance, and other feminist "pleasure and danger"[5] theorists. I am altogether committed to the view that women's bodies, including and especially our sexual and reproductive functions, are a crucial site of women's subordination. I am also certain that capitalist economies are crucial sites of women's oppression. I was forced to radically reconsider my feminist views and perspective when multicultural feminism emerged within the larger feminist debate; I particularly found the works of bell hooks and Angela Davis profoundly compelling. Similarly, the emergence of global feminism, which demands even greater inclusion of diverse populations of women as well as a comprehension of the ramifications of colonialism, has unalterably changed my perspective. The works of Cynthia Enloe and Charlotte Bunch have especially affected my approach. Finally, the views of feminists such as Sandra Bartky, Susan Bordo, and Shannon Bell, who work to deconstruct texts, including the body as text, have expanded my conception of patriarchy and especially of the methods employed not simply to institutionalize power based on gender class but to make it structurally and psychologically systemic.

A feminist analytical perspective, particularly one incorporating these diverse approaches, has become fundamental to how I experience and know the world. And it is this perspective that largely informs the thinking and arguments in this book.

In 1989, I began writing on issues of public policy of particular concern to women. I have found that I am especially drawn to issues involving women's bodies and the state.[6] I am convinced that eliminating the state's control over women's bodies, including the state's power to transfer the control of women's bodies to specific men, is an essential element for the destruction of patriarchy. This book is, to some degree, a natural extension of that conviction, for the question of prostitution policy is a question of who shall determine how people, especially women,[7] use their bodies sexually.

My concern with women's bodies as a focus for my research has clearly been influenced by my many years of exposure to the realities of domestic violence and rape. In the late 1970s, I volunteered to work for Haven House, a shelter in Pasadena, California for women attempting to escape domestic violence. I was trained to answer their hot line and to provide appropriate counseling to those seeking information and aid. I ultimately was employed as a shelter worker for the organization while I completed my doctoral dissertation. When I moved to Omaha, Nebraska, in 1985, I volunteered to serve on a crisis hot line, this time for Women Against Violence, a crisis intervention and referral service for victims of domestic violence and rape. I continued to work for them until 1994, when my responsibilities as coordinator of the Women's Studies program at the University of Nebraska at Omaha made my continued service impossible.

In addition to the rewards of doing this work, I have found working with and for victims of domestic violence and rape both educational and humbling. The training I received to assist individuals in crisis, and sometimes in imminent danger, has been an invaluable tool for me in general and has provided me with many of the skills and approaches I have used in my qualitative research for this book. Techniques such as active listening have been invaluable in my qualitative field research—in my interviews with prostitutes, brothel owners, medical support staff, police, anti- and pro-prostitution advocates, and others. Further, counseling victims of domestic violence and rape has repeatedly taught me the dangers of overgeneralizing and the unwisdom of classifying individuals as simple types—for example, as "victims" (simpliciter)—and of presuming that either my theoretical understanding or my past experience will necessarily be a useful, let alone dependable, indicator of the realities and experiences of my next client. I have come to believe that social phenomena and the dynamics of social practices are not only crushingly complex but also sufficiently diverse to make really broad generalizations about individuals or policies of little use. It is my sincere hope that this analysis avoids such pitfalls by consistently respecting the complexity and diversity of prostitutes and prostitution.

The Political and Academic Context of This Study

Women's Studies

The history of Western thought has exhibited a consistent tendency to pursue "knowledge" within the confines of ever narrower and more specialized disciplines and approaches. Early Greek philosophers sought answers to questions that now would be raised by physicists, biologists, mathematicians, metaphysicians, political scientists, and psychologists, among others. Over time, developing technologies and intellectual discoveries have enabled us to evolve different methods of inquiry, different ways of addressing questions, and, with them, different disciplines. Historically, we have made great strides in human knowledge by seeking answers within the confines of narrowly defined disciplines, with narrowly defined (and gendered) methodologies and standards. But we have begun to recognize that meaningful answers to a large host of questions can be achieved only through an interdisciplinary approach (while those in Women's Studies are also seeking nonpatriarchal approaches).

The academic movement toward interdisciplinary research has now become so well recognized that "interdisciplinary studies," along with "multiculturalism," has become a ubiquitous catchphrase in the rhetoric of most U.S. university and college administrators and in their "strategic plans"—ones that far too often, however, are never translated into any actual changes in curriculum or organization. Happily, a purely rhetorical commitment to an interdisciplinary approach has not blighted the emerging "identity studies" or "disciplines of the oppressed,"[8] for such fields are, by definition, interdisciplinary. To pursue Women's, Gender, or Feminist Studies is in part to pursue knowledge of how women have experienced objective discrimination and psychological oppression in *all* aspects of human life and culture in which this has occurred . I cannot begin to understand "women's situation" unless I understand a variety of women's experiences in and contributions to the law, politics, art, philosophy, religion, sociology, society, culture, education, psychology, literature, and so forth. Not only are all of these relevant to women's situation, but they cannot be isolated from one another; what occurs in one aspect of life has ramifications on others. We know, for example, that prevailing cultural views of women's maternal roles are the basis for legal constructs (including laws) and practices. How the criminal justice system treats individual women reflects these cultural perceptions of women as a class, as mothers. Conversely, how the criminal justice system treats women alters prevailing cultural views of women as mothers, as a class.

In addition to a commitment to interdisciplinarity, Women's Studies has come to recognize and generally to take seriously that one cannot understand "Woman's situation" since there is no "Woman" but rather a multiplicity of women with differing experiences, which are significantly, though not exclusively, affected by particular memberships in the various structures of subordination/dominance. Race, ethnicity, age, sexual orientation, religion, and economic class, for example, all have major impacts on a woman's experiences and on the specific perspective those experiences generate. The life of a rural teenage Thai woman is sufficiently different from my own that generalizations about "women" based solely on either of our experiences constitute both bad scholarship and bad faith.

Since public policies must function for the whole citizenry, effective public policy analysis requires a genuinely multicultural approach. Similarly, the lives of human beings do not fit into any one discipline but are, by their very nature, interdisciplinary. And because public policies are directed at controlling, altering, and, one hopes, improving human lives, their analysis should be interdisciplinary.

Philosophy

I received my original academic training not in Women's Studies but in one of the most esoteric and formalized disciplines in modern academia, Anglo-American analytic philosophy. Not only does this tradition presume, canonically, a world of objective truth, but its very discourse, including a highly technical vocabulary and literature that regularly translate a propositional sentence into one of the many possible formal systems of logical calculi, ensures its inaccessibility to those outside the field. Although I find helpful many of the skills and concepts I developed through this education, over time I came to reject much of that tradition. I am, however, convinced that those trained in philosophy have an invaluable contribution to make to policy studies.

The question of what constitutes "philosophy," as a discipline and activity, is itself a subject of controversy in the field, but what is uncontroversial is that doing philosophy is doing theory. In Jane Flax's words, "The most important characteristic of theory is that it is a systematic analytic approach to everyday experience."[9] Doing theory is constructing a story, a coherent, systematic explanation, to account for certain "facts" that have been uncovered.[10] Conversely, as specific facts are incorporated into prevailing theories, they are better understood and take on new meanings. In addition to constructing theories, philosophers are increasingly engaged, particularly in ethics, in applying those theories to specific problems and policy questions. Very generally, this is my approach. Specifically, I analyze prostitution by applying feminist and traditional ethical and political theories (including emerging theories of public policy analysis).

Additionally, much of traditional philosophy involves discussion of both specific ideals and meaning. While feminist philosophers view the issue of ideals somewhat differently from the traditional approaches, contemporary philosophy has also been deeply influenced by semiotics, poststructuralism, deconstruction, and, most recently, postmodernism and critical theory (now Cultural Studies). These theories have rejected the traditional post-Enlightenment philosophical assumptions that meaning is static, synchronic, ahistorical, and definitive. They argue that meaning, like other things, is a contingent, historically specific cultural construction that often serves the political function of covertly supporting the continued empowerment of members of dominant, privileged classes and the continued disempowerment of members of subordinate classes. In Chapter 1, I argue that any satisfactory social policy must include consideration of both the meaning—or, more strictly, the current conceptual construction—and the ideal of the activity that is the subject of a policy analysis. If I am correct in this claim, then philosophical analysis is a necessary component in the development of specific public policies.

Finally, the value of philosophy to public policy rests on its (supposed) tradition of complete and systematic analysis and evaluation. Philosophers are, at least in theory, trained to look at all the data—economic, social, psychological, and so forth—in coming to our decisions.[11] Philosophical methodology is particularly suitable to the consideration and balancing of the diverse and sometimes competing values and concerns of different disciplines. Philosophers are trained to weigh the information from diverse disciplines, including the various consequences posited by them, and come to some generalized conclusion about what "ought to be the case," what "ought to be done." This, of course, is the point of public policy studies.

While I believe that philosophy as a discipline has failed to be adequately interdisciplinary in its approach to developing policy positions, public policy analysts in other fields have tended to ignore the potential contributions of philosophers to policy debates. It is my hope that this work will help clarify the value of philosophical methodologies for those engaged in public policy development.

Intended Audience

In writing this book, I am motivated by a variety of concerns. First and foremost, I intend this book to be part of the ongoing dialogue among feminists on heterosexual prostitution policy. From a feminist perspective and commitment, I am proposing a heterosexual prostitution policy that I believe should be adopted at this point in history in the United States and in similarly situated nations. I realize that this statement is immediately likely to raise some objections—for instance, whose feminist perspective and commitment do I have in mind? Because I am aware that there are probably as many nuanced feminisms as there are feminists, I have chosen to make my own feminist influences and commitments explicit. Minimally, however, I contend that the policy I advocate is the most likely to improve the lives of women immediately, and that in the long run it will help undermine an important rationale for subordinating and controlling women in the United States (and in many other cultures).

Thus this book is not intended as a purely theoretical discussion but will, I hope, have political import and application. Rather than being a philosophical treatise, I see it as part of a lifelong feminist activism and a commitment to ensure that scholarship in the interdisciplinary field of Women's Studies retains its focus on making a practical difference in the lives of women and girls. Put simply, it is my hope that this discussion will contribute to our understanding of prostitution and thus influence the decisions we ultimately reach, as a community, on the state's and society's treatment of the institution as well as the individuals involved in the practice. In this regard, I attempt to speak to a broad audience—to social policy theorists within and outside academia and across academic disciplines, to feminist activists, and, ultimately, to anyone interested in public policy that consciously recognizes and speaks to the institutionalized class oppression of women.

I also intend this book to contribute to the growing interdisciplinary feminist dialogue in public policy studies. Like many feminist scholars, I find myself wading in uncharted waters in this emerging scholarship, where canons of style, methodology, and form have yet to be established, leaving the researcher with a heady and, at times, paralyzing freedom. The drive toward a more personal account, one that does not presume an objective world with objective, universal answers and respects both the insight of identity perspective and postmodern theory, is becoming standard in this evolving field. Beyond this, however, the stylistic and theoretical approaches of Women's Studies are something of a crapshoot. In Chapter 1, I briefly suggest methodological changes that need to be made in public policy studies if it is to accommodate a more multicultural and interdisciplinary perspective.

Finally, both "social policy ethics" and feminist theory emerged as defined subfields in academic philosophy only in the latter half of the twentieth century. Because their emergence requires significant departures from traditional philosophical approaches, distinctions, and assumptions, it is my hope that this book will contribute to some of the technical philosophical discussions that must be addressed about doing feminist policy ethics.

Global Context: Emphasis on the Dutch Model and Data

Because the goal of this book is to determine what, from a feminist perspective, would be the best policies on heterosexual prostitution and prostitute facilitation for the United States to adopt at the beginning of the twenty-first century, I consider the different legal positions that can be taken toward each. In the broadest sense, there are three options: criminalization, legalization (which permits an activity only with special regulations), and decriminalization (which permits an activity without specific regulation).[12] While I look at models of each of these options as they exist in a variety of countries and cultures, I draw the majority of my data from U.S. and Dutch studies. My reason for reliance on U.S. data should be apparent. I note, however, that although the United States has, depending on jurisdiction, a variety of criminalized and legalized[13] prostitution policies, no U.S. jurisdiction has decriminalized prostitution.

The Dutch, by contrast, after separating the activity of prostitution from prostitute facilitation, have experimented with a variety of decriminalized systems of prostitution since early in the twentieth century. In this regard, they offer an interesting and established alternative to U.S. experience. But another factor has made the Dutch experience of particular value to this dialogue: their courageous approach to dealing with social problems. When I visited Maastricht in 1995, I was told of a common Dutch saying: "You can obtain anything you really want anywhere in the world, if you look for it hard enough. The difference between other cul-

tures and the Dutch is that in the Netherlands, we show it on TV."
Though I expect this is literally true, it is certainly metaphorically true. In
all my experiences in the Netherlands, I have been astounded at the degree to which the Dutch, as a nation, are not willing only to recognize that
"ugliness" exists but also to examine it, to hold it up to the light without
sentimentality or prejudgment. This openness to the examination of
human behavior (and especially to the examination of their own behavior) has been combined with "Dutch tolerance," an almost pure commitment to a traditional Millian "liberal" insistence on limiting individual
liberties only if they cause harm to others. Although as individuals the
Dutch, who are predominantly Calvinist in the north and Catholic in the
south, often disapprove of "seamier" activities, they are generally loath
to proscribe behavior that has no direct effect on others (i.e., what are
loosely termed "victimless crimes").

As a result, many activities that are forced underground in places like
the United States are tolerated, although not embraced, in the Netherlands. This combination of cultural aspects has produced truly fertile
fields for social science research and policy examination. When one adds
to these factors an economic wealth that allows both private and public
funding of research institutions and archives, the result for policy examination is truly gratifying. I cannot begin to express the debt I owe to the
Internationaal Informatiecentrum en Archief Voor de Vrouwendeweging
(IIAV), a Dutch government-funded research center and archive on
women, and to the Mr. A. De Graaf Foundation, a thirty-year-old center
for research on prostitution, for their efforts to access and collect global
information on prostitution. In addition, the Dutch political and social
climate has led to rather extraordinary studies that would be virtually
unimaginable in most contexts. An excellent example of this is the work
of Ine Vanwesenbeeck, which is heavily cited in Chapter 5.

These factors, combined with the astonishing generosity of Dutch
scholars, social workers, public officials, and others in sharing their findings (and making their research available in English), have led me to focus
significantly on the Dutch experience in developing my analysis. Clearly,
given cultural differences, it would be unwise to use the Dutch experience
with prostitution as a blueprint for a U.S. approach. But the information
available because of the intellectual, legal, political, and social climate in
the Netherlands must be given serious consideration in offering a full
analysis of prostitution policy.

Limitations of This Analysis

Finally, I do not believe the policy I advocate is the complete or final version of a feminist position on prostitution policy. I expect that it will require emendation based both on the need for inclusion of some perspectives I have failed to consider adequately and on the need to alter policies, once implemented, in response to unforeseen and unanticipatable consequences. Most important, in what follows I have limited my discussion of prostitution policy to a discussion of heterosexual prostitution.[14] Although the most common practice of prostitution occurs between nontranssexual, nontransgendered males and females (and with three notable exceptions involves men as customers and women as prostitutes),[15] there is a large and significant practice both nationally and internationally of male, transsexual, and transgendered prostitution for male customers. (There appears to be very little lesbian prostitution.) My analysis, however, does not directly address nonheterosexual prostitution practice. This is not because I see other forms of prostitution as unimportant but rather because I am convinced that I am not the appropriate person to develop such an analysis. My analysis of heterosexual prostitution has emerged in light of my expertise regarding what are classified as heterosexual acts (e.g. reproduction) and heterosexual theory including the conceptual construction of heterosexual acts as well as from my knowledge of feminist analyses of patriarchy. This background includes an awareness of and, I hope, a sensitivity to heterosexism. But because I am not an expert on the structuring and dynamics of power in homosexual, transgendered, or transsexual relationships, I consider it irresponsible for me to proffer a prostitution policy that could be assumed to cover non-heterosexual prostitution practices. Hence one requirement for adoption of the policy I advocate herein is that it be emended to include and reflect these other perspectives.

1

Contextualizing the Discussion
Feminism and Policy Analysis

In 1992, I traveled to Europe for the first time, with a friend who was attending a conference in Amsterdam, and so found myself one evening walking around the city with four U.S. academicians who were attending the same conference. When we walked through the infamous red-light district, I was truly overwhelmed. The neighborhood is romantically beautiful; located in the oldest part of the city, it is filled with lovely old leaning Dutch buildings, some reputedly dating back to the eleventh century; canals often draped by trees; and bridges whose curved arches are lit with white lights that reflect off the water. On a pleasant June evening, the narrow streets fill with throngs of tourists and men seeking prostitutes.

The ground floors of most of these buildings are single narrow rooms containing a bed, a sink, and sometimes other "amenities." All have large commercial windows overlooking the street. Female prostitutes sit in the windows or occasionally stand or sit outside, usually dressed in "tacky" "revealing" outfits. In general, the women are clumped in ethnic groups: South American women are located near the tram station; African women are more centrally located, by the Old Church; nearby are Asian (usually Thai) women; and so on. As I was later to learn, Amsterdam alone has 430 such windows, rented for two to three separate shifts daily. Men approach the women and bargain for specific services and prices. When an agreement is reached, the customer enters the establishment, a curtain is drawn across the window, and the contracted services are provided.

At my first exposure, I found the dynamics of window prostitution truly disturbing and remarkable, but I was equally struck by the behavior of the men in the many bars that dot the area. With the bar windows open, it was easy to observe the physical play and raucous conversations of the customers. It appeared that large numbers of men were getting reasonably drunk and engaging in contemporary "male bonding" behavior (high-fiving, patting one another on the back, and the like).

After we had walked in the area for perhaps ten minutes, one member of our party asked that we leave. I still remember my frustration, perhaps most of all with my own acquiescence to the middle-class professional conceptions of courtesy that constrained me from objecting and with my succumbing to the middle-class gendered timidity that initially prevented me from continuing on my own, unescorted, through such a bizarre atmosphere. It was an extraordinary spectacle of women, most of them non-Dutch and many nonwhite, on display while crowds of gawkers, foreign and native sightseers, and potential johns swirled around them. The air was filled with contrasting and conflicting sensations—the physical beauty of the environment juxtaposition with layered emotions of excitement and rawness, thrill and sadness, falseness, desperation, anticipation, and brittleness emitted by the women in the windows and the people in the crowd. I was overwhelmingly assailed by a deeply visceral sense of being subsumed by the raucous crowd transformed to body, an entity, a being funneled through the narrow streets in a human stream—a feeling akin to losing oneself to the ephemeral unity of a crowded, warm dance floor. It was nothing I could ever have envisioned, neither its organization nor its intensity. I was furious and frustrated at having to just walk away, failing even to attempt to absorb something of the reality of so many women's lives.

The experience was pivotal to my decision to research prostitution policy. I had no idea what I was taking on. I had no suspicion of the diversity of the practice, of the dynamics of the differing forms and the myriad aspects that needed to be accounted for. I was unprepared for its ability to confound, to contradict, and sometimes to my perspective and presumptions.

Although my methodological approach evolved over time, from the outset I was committed to analyzing prostitution through a gendered lens, with an insistent awareness of how the power dynamics of racism, economic classism, homophobia, ethnic and religious bigotry, and especially patriarchy shape and impact on the practice. After reading a variety of American feminist legal and philosophical treatments of prostitution, I returned to the Netherlands in 1993, looking for data to support the prevailing American feminist view that prostitution was an exploitative practice that embodied the violation of women, their dignity, and sexual acts as a source of emotional intimacy. I was altogether unprepared for the differences in empirical information and feminist perspectives I would encounter.

I spent my first day gathering materials at the IIAV. Over dinner that evening, exhausted but curious, I began flipping through the literature I had gathered that afternoon—and became riveted by the complexity and conflict exhibited in the relatively small number of materials I had perused. Even in one fundamentally anti-prostitution brochure that had collected various articles on international prostitution, particularly on trafficking, sex tourism, and sexual exploitation in underdeveloped nations, I found contradictions. On one page was the testimony of a prostitute from Cameroon, who stated, "I am a woman who enjoys life . . . and I don't hide the fact by any means. I get on with people—tourist or otherwise. What matters to me is simply that the customer pays enough." Juxtaposed against this was an article containing what remains one of the most grotesque statements I have encountered in eight years of research. Despite the fact that prostitution is illegal in Thailand and prostitutes and former prostitutes are socially and legally stigmatized there, that country has for some time been a center for sex tourism and trafficking in women and children.[1] Boonchu Rojanasathien, former vice premier of Thailand ("and internationally well-known banker"), in a veiled reference to prostitution, stated in 1980:

> Within the next two years, we have need of money. Therefore, I ask all governors to consider the natural scenery in your provinces, together with some forms of entertainment that some of you might consider disgusting and shameful because they are forms of sexual entertainment that attract tourists. Such forms of entertainment should not be prohibited if only because you are morally fastidious. Yet explicit obscenities that may lead to damaging moral consequences should be avoided within a reasonable limit. We must do this because we have to consider jobs that will be created for the people.[2]

By the time I looked up to discover that it was 3 A.M., I had come to understand the inappropriateness of any broad, generalized policy claim about what is a genuinely diverse, complex, and nuanced industry. From that short exposure, I realized that I would have to disabuse my analysis of presumptions of values, such as that of a natural or ideal connection between sex and intimacy, which, I was quickly recognizing, emerged from the perspective of white privileged American scholars but was unlikely to be shared by women in underdeveloped nations, whose primary focus was survival of themselves and their children. One evening was enough to convince me that it was essential that I globalize the discussion. Prostitution does not respect national boundaries. The lives of Thai prostitutes bear directly on the lives of U.S. prostitute and nonprostitute women alike.

As I also quickly came to understand, I could not limit this research solely to the question of the governance of prostitution. Given current practice, I needed to consider how the three-way relationship between prostitute, facilitator (pimps, brothels, etc.), and client impacts both on prostitution and on the larger society. Ultimately, this has led me to conjoin a prostitute facilitation policy with a policy governing prostitution activity.

Feminist Public Policy Analysis—Basic Methodology

Those working in traditional disciplines generally pursue their inquiries by following established methodologies in their respective fields. The problem for the public policy theorist is that there is no clear paradigm, no system of rules that tells us how to go about doing policy analysis. What sorts of questions must be addressed to determine a reasonable public policy? Who needs to be considered? How must different concerns be weighed? The problem is only exacerbated for the feminist policy analyst. How do we ensure that women's voices and lives will be pivotal in the determination of policy? Which voices and lives are relevant to U.S. policy? How can we evaluate what is *really* in "women's" interest when the available data are already so skewed by patriarchal power?[3]

When I first began this project, I found myself rather intuitively reading materials from incredibly diverse disciplines. I sensed these various resources somehow fit together, and I was regularly brought up short when a social scientist would express puzzlement about my concern with ideals or a philosopher would be perplexed by my insistence on interviewing individuals working in the field. In explaining the breadth of my concerns to them, I began better to understand the mosaic of information I have come to believe is critical to policy analysis in general and to prostitution policy in particular.

Having been trained in philosophy, I could not come to a position on prostitution without understanding how that decision was being made.

Was the method I was using sufficient to justify a legitimate policy decision? But because public policy questions have no preexisting, defined rules or structures for arriving at answers, let alone feminist ones, I felt it was not enough to offer strong reasons and arguments in favor of my proffered policy. The structure of my analysis and many of the standards and strategies I apply are original and constitute my contribution to emerging methodologies of public policy analysis that are contesting traditional gendered "rhetorical spaces."[4] Hence I want to make explicit the structures and principles of my evaluative analysis for the theorists in my audience. This discussion, however, particularly the portions on methodological contextualization and data gathering in this chapter and Chapter VII, may not be of interest to readers who are concerned solely with the question of prostitution policy. Those individuals may choose to skip over the discussion in these sections of the more theoretical issues (save for the summary conclusions).

Whose Voices? Including Anti-Abolitionist Prostitute Voices

One of the most revolutionary influences of feminist and postmodern theories has been their contribution to undermining traditional epistemologies. Whereas historically and in mainstream contemporary Anglo-American analytic epistemology the concept of "objective" truth and knowledge has been virtually deified, postmodern and feminist theorists like Lorraine Code, have argued that there is no such thing:

> The dominant epistemologies of modernity . . . have defined themselves around ideals of pure objectivity and value-neutrality. These ideals are best suited to govern evaluations of the knowledge of knowers who can be considered capable of achieving a "view from nowhere" that allows them through the autonomous exercise of their reason, to transcend particularity and contingency. The ideals presuppose a universal, homogeneous, and essential human nature that allows knowers to be substitutable for one another. . . . The project of remapping the epistemic terrain that I envisage . . . abandons the search for—denies the possibility of—the disinterested dislocated view from nowhere.[5]

Instead, feminist epistemologists argue that, minimally, "subjectivity contributes to the production of knowledge," where "subjective" means roughly "pertinent to the locations and identities of knowing subjects."[6]

In such an epistemic framework, the need to recognize the perspectives of innumerable populations is apparent. Most contemporary feminists have abandoned any attempt to offer a universalized account of the "woman's" point of view, because it is clear that features such as race, ethnicity, sexual orientation, and economic class, as well as differences in individual lives, are part of the subjectivity that contributes to the production of knowledge. Most feminists have therefore attempted to be as inclusive as possible in the perspectives that inform their research.

One obvious exception to this approach occurs in the work of many, particularly U.S., feminists on prostitution, where it has been deemed acceptable, indeed necessary, to exclude prostitutes' voices in the development of prostitution policy if those voices defended prostitution as a legitimate option for women. Having classified all prostitutes as victims, when U.S. feminists encounter prostitutes who defend the right to prostitute, many maintain either that this view represents an extreme minority position or that such a position comes from a false consciousness—and therefore can and should be dismissed.[7] This view has, until recently, justified excluding anti-abolitionist prostitutes from participation in various forums, including UN Conventions, directed at developing prostitution policies.

Some feminists, especially from Europe and, more recently, from the United States, have rejected this approach. Indeed, its rejection is a recurrent theme in Shannon Bell's eloquent *Reading, Writing and Rewriting the Prostitute Body*. She states, "Postmodern Feminism has shown that the three dominant feminisms [liberal, socialist, and radical] can oppress women of difference through the appropriation or occlusion of their spaces and the silencing of their voices."[8] And Gail Pheterson, whose edited volume *A Vindication of the Rights of Whores* and organizing of the First and Second World Whores Congresses constitute a backlash against the silencing of prostitute voices, maintains, "Never have prostitutes been legitimized as spokespersons or self-determining agents, not by those who defend them against male abuse and not by those who depend upon them for sexual service."[9] Various prostitutes' rights organizations, both in the United States and globally, have insisted on inclusion in prostitution policy decisions. For example, the Network of Sex Work Projects, a global sex-workers' rights organization, has maintained:

The dominant ideology about prostitution within the United Nations is that prostitution is a form of sexual exploitation which should be abolished. This view has been legitimized and passed into resolutions and laws at conferences such as Beijing with no input at all from sex workers themselves. Many sex workers feel that it is time to demand that we are heard in such a significant international forum. More than being simply heard it is essential to form some resolutions which reflect our demands for human rights, and have those passed rather than the resolutions which lead to repressive measures to abolish prostitution.[10]

Similar statements appear throughout the position statements of Coyote, the most visible U.S. prostitutes' rights organization; De Rode Draad (The Red Thread), the most prominent Dutch prostitutes' rights organization; and various papers issued by the World Whores Congresses.

I have found this silencing of "anti-abolitionist" prostitutes' voices one of the most difficult features to reconcile in traditional U.S. feminist approaches.[11] When I have discussed the phenomenon with prostitutes, their responses invariably evoke bell hooks's description of her experience with early second-wave white feminism:

When I participated in feminist groups, I found that white women adopted a condescending attitude towards me and other non-white participants. The condescension they directed at black women was one of the means they employed to remind us that the women's movement was "theirs"—that we were able to participate because they allowed it, even encouraged it; after all we were needed to legitimate the process. They did not see us as equals. They did not treat us as equals. And though they expected us to provide first hand accounts of black experience, they felt it was their role *to decide if these experiences were authentic.*[12]

My approach in researching this book has been to rely as heavily on the testimony of working prostitutes as on other relevant sectors of the community. This means I include the voices of prostitutes who are what I call, for lack of a better term, "anti-abolitionist." These are generally women who feel prostitution is a legitimate option, believe that prostitution is not always more or as exploitative as other options open to women, and, although they are aware of how abusive prostitution is for some women in the industry, feel that their own experiences and the quality of their lives as prostitutes is to be preferred over their alternative options. Many of these women view prostituting as, under some conditions, an act of feminist resistance. Mostly these women do not see prostitution as purely an outgrowth of patriarchy, although they often understand how patriarchy impacts on the practice.

In earlier drafts of this discussion, I referred to these voices in the singular as "the anti-abolitionist prostitute voice" because, although I am aware of the multiplicity and diversity of these voices, anti-abolitionist prostitutes have, I think, done an extraordinary job of developing a global lobby that attempts, as far as possible, to speak as one policy voice. Whether one looks at the suggested policies of U.S., Thai, or Dutch prostitutes' rights organizations, one finds the basic structures and approaches, as well as many of the specifics, remain the same. There is also an impressive level of sanity and sophistication in their recommendations and their arguments for these. For this reason, I have put great weight on their views. But because my doing so is highly controversial, at least among some U.S. feminist groups, and because I believe anti-abolitionists' inclusion in this debate is crucial, I suggest here some further justifications, in addition to the eloquent arguments of Bell, Pheterson, Kamala Kempadoo and Jo Doezema, and others, for insisting on the inclusion of prostitutes' rights voices in feminist policy discourse.

The claim that prostitutes' rights positions represent only a small minority view can be dealt with briefly. First, even were this the case, it would not justify dismissing inclusion of their perspective in prostitution policy development. Feminists are supposed to be committed to including *all* legitimate perspectives, no matter how small the group that asserts them. Second, as is discussed in Chapter 3, it is far from apparent that this view represents a *minority* perspective, let alone a small one. So the real question becomes whether such a position represents a legitimate perspective—whether it arises from an authentic subjectivity whose experiences contribute to the production of knowledge about prostitution.

Sometimes, rather than simply dismissing anti-abolitionist prostitutes as dupes of "the organized commercial sex industry," the silencing of these voices is justified by pathologizing them—an approach that is relatively easy both because prostitutes have traditionally been viewed as depraved and diseased and because, more recently, social science research has indicated that a disproportionate number of the prostitute population who have been the subject of scholarly study are child sexual assault survivors.[13] These voices can be and are pathologized as the product of a false consciousness arising from childhood victimization. The same phenomenon of silencing occurs in the treatment of girls, particularly "delinquent" ones:

> The pervasiveness of the tendency to pathologise girls' problems is no more apparent than in the way in which knowledge about the extent of sexual abuse among girls has been incorporated into practice. . . . Insinuations of sexual abuse are invoked in ways which pathologise her problems, constitute her as a victim and obscure her agency, and limit the range of options considered. . . . For example, expressions of anger or multiple sex partners are explained as a consequence of abuse. The possibility of the anger constituting a legitimate emotion in the context of existing circumstances, or of her sexuality being dealt with in terms of health and safety issues, are understandings or explanations for her anger less likely to be considered.[14]

Evidence of the frequency of childhood sexual abuse in adult prostitute populations is used to justify lumping all prostitute voices into a simplistic category of "victims" and to designate anti-abolitionist prostitutes as victims masochistically seeking continued abuse, which apparently justifies dismissing their positions and testimonies.

Let us assume, as current evidence indicates, that a disproportionate percentage of women who prostitute are adult survivors of childhood sexual assault. Logically, this in no way suggests that they are not credible or insightful regarding prostitution policy. When I worked as a domestic violence counselor for Haven House, one of the studies I found especially interesting demonstrated that 75 percent of those involved in the anti–domestic violence movement had themselves been exposed to domestic violence in their homes, either as adult or child recipients of abuse or as observers of domestic violence. But this fact did not suggest it was appropriate to dismiss the voices of anti–domestic violence workers in policy development; rather, it was viewed as giving these voices special authority. Although I have been unable to locate similar research on those working with sexually abused children, I suspect that a disproportionate percentage of activists in this arena are also childhood sexual assault survivors or in some way were witnesses to childhood sexual assault. Thus the fact that a disproportionate percentage of prostitutes appear to be childhood sexual assault survivors in itself proves nothing about the value of anti-abolitionist prostitute voices in the development of prostitution policy—unless one presupposes that all prostitution is harmful to women and that prostitutes' voices are never credible when they defend prostitution as a legitimate alternative. A history of childhood sexual assault in no way justifies discounting the prostitute's voice, whatever her position.

In addition, contextualizing the lives of women who are sexual assault survivors makes it clear that the decision to begin or remain in prostitution cannot simply be dismissed as a matter of pathology, as the direct result of a history of childhood molestation. Rather, female sexual assault survivors often become prostitutes or remain in prostitution due to economic need. Many young women leave home to escape abuse or neglect and turn to crime to survive. Women's criminal choices, like our other life choices, are narrowed by patriarchy. Most adult women are arrested for "trivial offenses," such as larceny, theft, fraud, disorderly conduct, drunkenness and drunk driving, and prostitution.[15] Since prostitution is one of the few forms of profit-making criminal behavior women engage in and childhood abuse a common cause of criminality among women, a correlation between prostitution and childhood experience of abuse is not surprising. Rather than opting for prostitution as the result of pathology, survivors of childhood molestation often prostitute because of poverty. So rather than simply dismissing the voices of prostitutes as being tainted by pathology and psychological disease, feminists in particular should consider that their voices may provide the greatest insight into the social and economic factors that precipitate the decision to enter or to remain in "the life."

In a somewhat different vein, some (especially U.S.) theorists hold that *all* prostitutes are currently victims of sexual exploitation—that there is no distinction between "forced" and "free" prostitution. Thus any prostitute who maintains she is opting to prostitute can only be doing so from a false consciousness. For example, in 1991 a working group of the Coalition Against Trafficking in Women drafted the "Convention against Sexual Exploitation" (CASE), which held that

> sexual exploitation aggravates the harm of other existing inequalities, often taking the form of sexual slavery, torture, mutilation, and death. The proposed Convention recognizes that sexual exploitation takes the form of denial of life through female infanticide, murder of women by reason of their gender, including wife/widow murder, woman battering, pornography, *prostitution*, genital mutilation, female seclusion, dowry

and bride price, sexual harassment, rape, incest and sexual abuse, and torture, including sadistic and mutilating practices.[16]

If one defines prostitution as equivalent to practices such as infanticide, battering, and sexual abuse, it follows that the voices of prostitutes who defend prostitution are deluded, representing the perspective of the "happy slave" who fails to recognize that her "decision" was, in fact, coerced. Several responses to this "logic" must be considered.

First, even if we assume that all prostitutes are victims of sexual exploitation, this does not make their voices, even the voices of those who defend the practice, irrelevant to policy determination. Prostitutes can acknowledge their victimization, their exploitation, but, as the discussion of current practice in Chapter 3 demonstrates, rightly maintain that sometimes prostitution is a legitimate option for those in a patriarchal, capitalist, racist, imperialist society. COYOTE's National Task Force on Prostitution maintains:

> Voluntary prostitution is the mutually voluntary exchange of sexual services for money or other consideration; it is a form of work, and like most work in our capitalist society, it is often alienated, that is the worker/prostitute has too little control over her/his working conditions and the way the work is organized. [Whereas f]orced prostitution is a form of aggravated sexual assault.[17]

The *World Charter for Prostitutes Rights* avoided using the term *voluntary* because it held that "truly voluntary choices for women were uncommon at best and that especially poor women in poor countries had few or no alternatives."[18] Rather, the First World Whores Congress unanimously agreed that prostitution is a "legitimate work decision for adults, be it a decision based on choice or necessity."[19]

A position that maintains all prostitution is forced or all prostitution is sexual exploitation (or, more accurately, that it is more sexually exploitative than other kinds of labor or heterosexual interactions currently available to women) paints with too broad strokes. There are many types of prostitution and prostitution arrangements. Sweeping generalizations that maintain all prostitution is forced fail to recognize the complexity and diversity of both the experiences of prostitutes and the motivations for prostitution. This failure may arise partly because social science data emerge within a legally repressive system. The only prostitution studied extensively in the United States, as well as in most other nations, is streetwalking, which, although the most visible, is estimated to constitute at most 20 percent of the practice.[20] Streetwalking is also universally recognized to be the most abusive and risky form of prostitution, and the one with the largest percentage of vulnerable personalities who enter it. Using these data as indicators of the practice of prostitution overall is like determining the nature of marriage by viewing only instances of those in abusive relationships—an analysis that may represent some, but certainly not all, married women.

Furthermore, in a variety of ways the exploitation of prostitutes is partially attributable to features that can be eliminated by feminist activism. Because prostitution is illegal in the United States in all but a few counties in Nevada, prostitutes' exploitation is facilitated; they are "outlaws" who lose their basic rights. As Pheterson eloquently states:

> Basic denial of citizenship status to prostitutes cuts across all other rights. Whore-identified women are not considered citizens. . . . That's clear from the Human Rights Convention of the European Community, for instance, wherein a whole list of human rights conclude with the sentence: "That none of these rights hold if one is considered a moral offense to society." And obviously, prostitutes are always included in that clause. . . . The laws that forbid prostitutes to travel [known prostitutes are not allowed to visit or emigrate to the United States], to raise their own children, to have homes, to have associates, lovers, or even to live with their families without the families being called pimps are laws which affect all women and which restrict us, control us, justify violence against us.[21]

It is also clear that community stigmatization of prostitutes facilitates their exploitation. Lack of community response to known instances of the abuse of prostitutes, including the murder of prostitutes—the lack of outcry and concern when such instances are reported in the media—encourages those who would abuse and exploit women to seek out prostitutes for victimization and exploitation. They are acceptable targets.

Both the legal status and the community stigmatization of prostitution are patriarchal constructs intended to strengthen the good girl/bad girl dichotomy and to justify punishing the "bad" girl by marginalization and dismissal. But, given these insights, it is difficult to understand why some feminists are willing to accept the patriarchal bifurcation of women and dismiss the voices of the "bad girls," the unrepentant prostitutes' voices, while assuming "our" voices (the voices of "good girls") are "accurate" and "untainted" and appropriate judges of prostitution policy. Therefore, I heartily agree with Bell's conclusion that, "ethically, there can no longer be a philosophy of prostitution in which there is an absence of prostitute perspectives and prostitute philosophers,"[22] and I have included, to the greatest extent possible, anti-abolitionist prostitutes' voices in my analysis.

Methodological Contextualization

A variety of disciplines, most notably philosophy and legal theory, have long-standing traditions of analyzing and assessing social policies by considering the policies "in the abstract." We are charged with evaluating the relationship between the proposed policy and other abstract (legal and moral) principles and standards, and we are expected to anticipate the "*theoretical* consequences" that would, in general, be likely to follow (in "any" society) if such a policy were adopted. Dovetailing their approaches with the mainstream epistemic commitment to "objective truth and knowledge," philosophers and legal theorists have historically asked such generalized questions as "Is abortion (morally or legally) justifiable?" with the expectation of arriving at an objective, neutral, universal answer that is not relative to any culture, historical period, or individual but that captures some timeless moral or legal "truth." Thus, for example, John Rawls argues in the contemporary classic *A Theory of Justice* that what is morally right can be determined by "placing oneself" behind a "veil of ignorance," a conceptual apparatus in which the thinker is supposed to imagine him- or herself to be ignorant of personal identity, history, and life. The veil of ignorance is presumed to allow one to judge from the position of "every*man*," which, like the "view from nowhere," is supposed to permit the individual to make an unbiased judgment of the moral and legal acceptability of any act.[23]

Contemporary feminist theory has, on the whole, rightly rejected such traditional approaches and methodologies and their justifying presumptions, insisting that social policy theorists acknowledge the relevance of perspective and context in determining acceptable moral actions and legal policy.[24] Contemporary feminist theory recognizes that both the meaning and the consequences of adopting any specific policy do not occur in an abstract or valueless world but are implemented in specific spatial-temporal contexts in which there is not a "level playing field." Social science data overwhelmingly demonstrate that people's lives are deeply and unrelentingly impacted by their membership in hierarchical classes; the circumstances under which the individual who belongs to a subordinated class acts are significantly different from the circumstances under which dominant-membership individuals act, and this difference will unfailingly alter the meaning and consequences of their behavior. As such, the very notion of an objective and unbiased moral perspective is a confusion.[25] Feminist theorists therefore insist that the specific context of a proposed policy be carefully considered in determining the acceptability of enacting the policy *here and now*. In addition, or perhaps simply stated differently, as Catharine MacKinnon's work on sexual harassment (which the Supreme Court accepted) clearly demonstrates with regard to a variety of issues, membership in a subordinated class can constitute an authoritative standpoint in determining the acceptability of specific behavior. What has finally been acknowledged is that, for example, it is the "average woman's" view that must determine what constitutes "sexual harassment"—not the perspective of the "average man." With regard to a variety of behaviors, feminists rightly maintain that it is not the intention of the agent but the impact the act has on others (its "recipients") that must determine its legal (and moral) status.[26]

One of the difficulties, then, of constructing a feminist prostitution policy is fundamentally a question of contextualization. We need to determine how to ensure that the policy choices we make respond accurately to how sexism is actually playing out, here and now. But it is far from obvious how to go about doing this. Part of what is required is a willingness to focus on social science data far more time and attention than traditional approaches in law and ethics have encouraged; but more is needed. We need to discover methodologies and principles that will enable us to contextualize the discussion in a way that is coherent and defensible.

Gathering the Data

A particularly fruitful approach to take to contextualize public policy discourse is to break the relevant activity down into four separate aspects:

A. its intrinsic characteristics
B. its current conceptual construction
C. its current practice
D. its ideal practice

A. Intrinsic Characteristics

In discussing policies that regulate specific human activities and practices, we cannot hope to provide a workable analysis unless we recognize and acknowledge aspects of the relevant behavior that are "intrinsic" to such actions. Intrinsic characteristics are those that belong to the activity as defined, regardless of culture or time (unless technological intervention is applied). In speaking of intrinsic qualities, I in no way intend to suggest, defend, or advocate for traditional "essentialism," the view that things are what they are because they have a "true essence" that is irreducible, unchanging, provided by nature (as opposed to culture), and that makes them the sort of thing that they are. My sympathies lie more with "constructivism," the view that meaning and the categories on which meaning are based are not the result of natural facts but rather are socially constructed; "knowledge" (epistemic constructions) or perceptions of reality are produced within cultures and cultural institutions and often "reflect and reinforce the disparate power of ruling elites."[27] I do not believe, however, that positions that ascribe nature to biology and those that ascribe nature to culture are mutually exclusive, nor do I believe that constructivist views require the rejection of *all* natural facts. In a decidedly qualified sense, I suggest that some characteristics of human activity are intrinsic, in part because that activity involves the body, an organism that is, among other things, involved in biological causal relationships. (In making this claim, I intend to speak to Carole Vance's concern that if we overstate the degree to which sexuality is socially constructed, we risk disembodying sexuality altogether, and to Susan Bordo's critique of postmodern and poststructuralist theorists for tending to treat the body as pure text rather than recognizing its physicality and the "authority of our own experiences."[28]

Instances of biological causation—biological "facts"—are not immutable, since often technological options can prevent or significantly lessen them. Still, if we intend to develop policies regulating activities that may involve biological causation, we must take this intrinsic factor into account. Doing so may involve no more, for example, than acknowledging the likelihood of such outcomes; conversely, it may result in the development of lengthy and sophisticated regulations for employing technological means to prevent these anticipatable outcomes. In this sense, all policy decisions must acknowledge and speak to the intrinsic aspects of an activity, that is, to the characteristics that are a part of any practice as a simple result of biology, whatever the meaning or particular form of practice being considered.

In addition, some features are intrinsic to activities because they are logically implied by the description of the action. If I am developing a policy to regulate the sale of china figurines, part of what I need to consider is that the act of selling anything in a capitalist economy always carries with it the possibility that the seller can make a profit. So any policy regulating sales should at least speak to possible profits, since this outcome follows logically from the definition of "selling."[29]

B. Current Conceptual Construct/Meaning

The process of determining "meaning," or what philosophers call "conceptual analysis," has been one of the most common activities of philosophy since the time of Socrates. Philosophers recognize that sometimes the solution to complex problems lies totally or in part in confusions regarding the meaning of specific terms in which the problem is couched. The current conceptual construction of a term denoting a human activity includes the ways in which a culture thinks about the activity and about those involved in it—both our conscious beliefs and the values and power assumptions that the culture attaches to the activity, including both political and linguistic "representations."[30] Although there are many ways in which determining meaning or conceptual construction may be pivotal to answering a host of practical questions, for the present purposes I am concerned with two.

(1) Definition (lack of clarity, ambiguity, vagueness)

Often when we are not clear on how we are using a specific term, we cannot provide a coherent answer to any question in which the term is embedded. Because the term *prostitution* is highly ambiguous even in its nonmetaphoric uses, in Chapter 2, I designate a specific definition for it, to ensure that readers understand the precise set of activities which are the subject of this study.

(2) CONCEPTUAL CONSTRUCTS AS BEARERS OF POLITICAL MEANING AND VALUE

One of the most influential theses of modern philosophy, linguistics, art, and literary theory is that language mirrors and reinforces the values, dynamics, and organizations of power in the society. Language is, at least in part, a political practice; by analyzing specific terms, we can uncover the system of thought in which a term is embedded, including its assumed political structures and social institutions.[31] Indeed, this insight is the basis for the now horribly maligned call for "politically correct" terminology—a call to avoid terms that historically and conceptually imply, and thus reinforce, pejorative judgments of members of oppressed classes.

The recognition that words have important social and political value is not limited to those in the humanities or fine arts but is part of the research focus of many individuals in the social sciences. Yet, despite this, it is not unusual for discussions of social policy, especially among social scientists, to ignore consideration of the significance of relevant terms. Nevertheless, the stigmas attached to such varied behaviors as illicit drug usage, prostitution, and lawyering often have significant ramifications on the activity and especially on the psychological well-being of the agent, and these need to be addressed when developing any relevant social policy. Conversely, we need to recognize that the constructions of social policies, the choices that are made to govern any behavior, also have meaning, including political import. Although any human behavior implies a value system and perspective,[32] this is emphatically the case in the activity of creating public policy. "Organizations reproduce or react against the societal or national culture in which they reside. . . . Metaphors are present not only in poems but also in policy and professional language, where they are linked to ways of seeing and understanding."[33] Thus policy makers need to consider not only the meaning of the activity they are attempting to govern but also the meaning their proposed policy will transmit and reproduce.

To develop a useful and defensible social policy, it is necessary to expend the time and energy required to provide an analysis of our concept of the activity being governed, both to clarify the specific behaviors the policy is directed at and to understand the political and social power arrangements that underlie or are promoted by the activity in the prevailing culture. Additionally, a coherent and defensible social policy requires that policy makers analyze and evaluate the policy they advocate on the basis of the meanings it conveys. I use the term *conceptual construction* to cover all these various, interrelated features of definition, social and political meaning, and value of both the activity and its proposed legislation and governance.

C. Current Practice

The most familiar discussions of public policy are those that focus on the current practice of a particular activity in a specific society. Current practice tells us how the activity is actually lived—the various social science, legal, medical, and other data available on the activity as well as the conventions, the necessary and sufficient conditions for, and the impact of such actions on individuals engaged in the activity and on society as a whole. (We obtain most of our information on specific practices through social science research, although the natural sciences are also important contributors.)

In the discussion of prostitution practice that follows, I demonstrate that, more often than not, both the public and the professional conception of current prostitution practice are deeply inadequate and based on generalizations that fail accurately to represent the actual majority behaviors of prostitutes, reflecting the current conceptual construction rather than actual practice. We must radically alter our conception of current practice and thus our perspective on what social policy is needed to deal with the practice as it actually exists.

D. Ideal Practice

A significant portion of philosophical inquiry has been and remains directed at determining what, with regard to any particular thing, an ideal form would be. Ideal practice describes what we believe an activity would look like in an ideal world, one in which sexism, racism, homophobia, economic classism, and the like did not exist.

In my discussions with social scientists, I have come to understand how foreign talk about ideals is to many who work on public policy. The presumption appears to be that talk of ideals is merely an abstract enterprise, without political or practical import. This view seems to be at the heart of many problems that occur in current public policy development;

for if I can construct a coherent analysis of what an ideal policy for a practice would look like, I can use this conception as a goal toward which current policy should be directed. How can I know which of several options ought to be instituted today unless I have some real sense of where I want to be (at a distant) tomorrow? I cannot, for example, know if I should adopt a policy of aggressively educating the populace on the use of condoms unless I know my long-range goals. Am I concerned simply with lowering the spread of STDs, or do I want to lower the rate of sexual intercourse altogether? When policies are developed without a clear sense of the ideals toward which they are directed, they become no more than a hodgepodge of measures which merely provide crisis management. Instead of being intentionally directed toward supporting and promoting a long-term vision of the most desirable outcome, public policies often become no more than an unrelated conglomeration of Band-Aids instituted to speak only to currently obvious problems. This may result in adopting policies, or more commonly pieces of policies, that directly contradict what would, if we troubled to conceive it, be our long-range goal.

At the same time, it is critical to recognize that our visions of an ideal practice reflect our understanding of the current practice, conceptual construction, and intrinsic characteristics of an activity. Ideals are formed in part by reflecting on and responding to what we judge to be the positive and negative features of these other three aspects. Additionally, we need to remember that constructing social policies by focusing *purely* on idealized forms of an activity is pragmatically worthless. In developing social policies, we are not starting from a blank slate. Understanding the ideal form of an activity tells us what to shoot for, but taken alone it will do nothing to tell us how to get there. For a policy to be successful, it must explicate, in sufficient detail, the measures necessary to transform current practice into the ideal.[34]

Conclusion

Policy theorists must recognize both the distinctions among the intrinsic qualities, conceptual construction, current practice, and ideal of an activity and the ways in which these overlap and interact. It is most important to understand the difference between how a concept plays out in a given society and how its corresponding activity is actually lived. Similarly, we must maintain the distinction between "intrinsic qualities" and "current practice" in order to understand what can be altered or re-formed; that is, we must distinguish qualities of the practice that are in-evitable without technological intervention, due to the intrinsic charac-ter of the act, from those that are conditional on the particular spatial-temporal location in which the act is constructed and performed. When these lines are not maintained, the cost can be substantial. If I mistakenly ascribe the source of a problem to the act's intrinsic character rather than to its conceptual construction, I will falsely believe that the problem can be eliminated only through technological intervention and will mis-direct my efforts to eradicate it or will give up attempting to do so on the assumption that "nothing can be done." Most feminists familiar with the history of theories of sexuality and gender are painfully familiar with this error. Far too often traditional theorists have misascribed gender roles as "natural and immutable" rather than as created by practice and conceptual construct, and virtually always to the disadvantage of women. Therefore, it is especially important for feminist social policy theorists to keep these factors separate.

We must also recognize, however, that although they may be concep-tually distinct, these four features impact on one another. None of them exists in isolation, nor is it fruitful to focus entirely on one as though it were isolatable in reality. The intrinsic characteristics of an act shape our conception, practice, and ideal of it. Conversely, because technological intervention can change the causal impact of intrinsic characteristics, an ideal or practice using such devices will alter the causal consequences of the intrinsic characteristics. There is a constant interplay between cur-rent concept and current practice. They become causally interactive—practice rewrites conceptual construct; conceptual construct limits and shapes practice. And as noted, our conception of an ideal is largely a re-flection of current practice, intrinsic character, and current conceptual construct—that is, a response to the known. Conversely, our judgment of practice and conceptual construct is informed by our sometimes un-conscious conception of an ideal. Because we are not starting from a blank position, evolving an ideal policy is useless unless we know enough about the other three aspects to develop a coherent plan to get us there, and in sufficient detail to ensure approximation of the ideal. Thus, in analyzing any social policy, one must consider all four distinct aspects of an activity; however, in considering any one aspect, the policy analyst must be sensitive to the ways in which the specifics or alteration of one aspect may impact on or alter the specifics of a different aspect.

Social policy theorists must also recognize that individuals' lives are affected by both the social-cultural organizations of power and by their individual life scripts. Insofar as policy is intended to change the lives of those in a practice, it must honestly appraise the variety of experiences of those involved, including the variations due to an individual's membership in one or more oppressed classes. Insofar as an activity impacts on the larger population of those who are not engaged in the activity, as both theory and practice, it is important to undermine harmful conceptual constructions, including those that reinforce class oppressions, by either eliminating the practice or demanding its conceptual reconstruction. At the same time, it is vital to ensure that those outside the practice are not directly and literally harmed by a suggested revision of current policy.

It should at this point be apparent why this method of organizing one's analysis ensures that the discussion will be at least partly contextualized. The requirement that we look at the current practice and current conceptual construction of the activity requires some inclusion of the life scripts and values played out by the activity in a particular spatial-temporal context.

In the four chapters that follow, I describe the intrinsic characteristics, current practice, conceptual construct, and ideal of contemporary heterosexual prostitution.

2

A Sexually Charged Context, the Feminist "Sex Wars," and Prostitution Defined

Our "society,." . . if it's not deflected from its present course . . . will hump itself to death.

—Valerie Solanas[1]

Prostitution, particularly in its worst forms, can embody some of the most devaluing and dehumanizing presumptions of patriarchy. I cannot imagine it possible to read about, let alone research, this topic without being deeply and often painfully affected by one's findings. Our sexuality and sexual activity are integral to where we live, who we are. We identify ourselves significantly in terms of these features. In academia and in minority politics, one's sexuality including sexual orientation are considered significant features in one's perspective. But in the larger culture their meaning and impact are enormous and, for women as well as gay men and transgendered and transsexual individuals, often destructive, if not devastating. In the past quarter century, U.S. women as a political class have done relatively well on some fronts in improving the quality of our lives. We have greater economic freedom. Cultural values regarding rape and spousal abuse have significantly improved, even if the number of women brutalized by these practices has not decreased. Women have had an impact on medical research and represent a political force that can affect election outcomes; social pressure and constraints on women with regard to marriage and family have lessened. But we have also paid for our advances. One arena of significant backlash in the United States is that of sexuality. Whether female or male, lesbian, gay, or straight, transgendered or transsexual, we live in a culture that has come to view sex as virtually monolithic, the (self-) defining feature, a deity. The most significant aspects of who we are have increasingly been defined by intercourse and sexual activity. Our most significant relationships are *supposed* to be determined by sexual "partnership," as opposed to procreative, economic, emotional, familial, or social relationship—hence the emergence of the "significant other," a term that attaches solely to a regular sexual "partner," though the presumption that this individual is significant, let alone *the* significant individual in one's life, surely begs the question. We are encouraged to view our individual identities through the conceptual framework of "sexual being," understood as sexual actor or participant. We are encouraged to focus significant time, energy, and angst on our sexual attractiveness to others.[2] Culturally, we now define being physically healthy, emotionally healthy, and psychologically well with great, if not complete, attention to issues of sexual activity and attitudes. More and more, sexually relevant features function as the basis for self-evaluation and judgment.

Both sexuality and prostitution are institutions—the institution of heterosexual prostitution clearly being derivative of the institution of heterosexuality and heterosexual activity. Heterosexual intercourse is, as Ti-Grace Atkinson noted more than thirty years ago, itself an institution, constituting a "form of activity specified by a system of rules which defines offices, roles, moves, penalties, defenses, and so on and which gives the activity its structure."[3] Like other, similarly structured relationships and organizations, heterosexuality supports and disseminates existing cultural values, including those of patriarchy, so effectively that all even nonheterosexual ones, become infected with these values. One may argue that individual relationships and acts exhibit patriarchal values to a greater or lesser degree, but few who understand the extent to which patriarchy is endemic to sexuality as currently constructed will contend that any sexual relationship or act can be altogether free of these values, including misogyny. None of us is capable of stepping that far out of our socialization, no matter how good or sincere our will. And because the worst forms of heterosexual prostitution embody the most misogynistic aspects of heterosexuality, expressing those values bluntly and unequivocally, to study them tends to make one aware of how these values reverberate in one's own sexual life, no matter how hard one may struggle to eliminate them. This may explain the relative paucity of feminist materials on prostitution as a lived behavior rather than a metaphor. Where one would expect reams of theoretical and empirical scholarly feminist materials on the actual practice of prostitution, surprisingly little such discussion has occurred. I suspect this is partially because understanding how patriarchal sexual constructs impact on prostitution requires one to understand, far more bluntly, how they impact on one's own life, that is, on that of the "normal," "good" (read "nonprostitute") woman. And this is a degree of understanding that must be repugnant to all women.

The Feminist Sex Wars

A discussion of heterosexuality[4] in the context of current feminist thinking is certain to be controversial. Although societal interest in and theorizing about sex and sexuality have a long history, it was in the work of deconstructionist theorists such as Michel Foucault that sexuality and sexual acts began to be interpreted as deeply socially constructed political (power) phenomena. Indeed, even in speaking of heterosexuality we find the problematic presumption that there are two "opposite" sexes. Whether human beings express a true sexual dimorphism is itself highly controversial; on the basis of neither physical nor chemical structures can human beings be neatly classified into one of two binaries. And although biologists are able to point to several features that generally differentiate these exceedingly rough classifications, the question remains: Even if we could make sense of them, would these "binaries" describe a biologically rather than culturally significant difference? Are the designations of male and female more culturally constructed than natural?

Unfortunately, as most feminist philosophers of sex acknowledge, feminist discussions of sexuality have resulted in what are sometimes referred to as the "feminist sex wars."[5] On the one hand is the view that heterosexuality is the central source of female subordination, and thus sexuality is power. MacKinnon holds that "as work is to Marxism, sexuality is to feminism."[6] This view, often classified as "radical feminist,"[7] is at the core of Andrea Dworkin's *Intercourse*:

> And men had an affirmative obligation to use the fuck to create and maintain a social system of power over women, a social and political system in which the fuck, regulated and restrained, kept women compliant, a sexually subjected class. [8]

Radical feminists tend to present heterosexuality and heterosexual acts as unremittingly bleak and dangerous for women,[9] positing that "normal" sex has been constructed on a continuum of violence with rape, murder, and other sexual abuse.

Several feminist camps have criticized this perspective. Minority, especially black, feminists object that the radical feminist perspective is race-blind and fails to recognize that sexual violence, coercion, and brutality contextualize differently in communities with a history of slavery and colonialism, where women "have been subject to specific racialized forms of patriarchal oppression and sexualized forms of racial oppression."[10] Multicultural feminists reject a radical feminist perspective as presenting a unitary, monolithic view of Woman's sexual experience.

Other feminists argue that the radical feminist view places "too much emphasis . . . on sexual danger at the expense of sexual pleasure."[11] Shannon Bell, for example, contends that MacKinnon and Dworkin, imaging all sex as penetration and violation, hold that "women who not only engage in but enjoy heterosexual intercourse are assigned only one position—that of the collaborator."[12] She maintains that this analysis reads all sexual interaction as negative and destructive and is "blind to the potential for anything but disempowered female sexuality. . . . MacKinnon leaves no room in the masculinist regime for multiple truths or dissenting truths: the truth and reality of female sexuality is the construct of male desire: female sexuality is defined by men and forced on women. Homosexuality is no less gendered than heterosexuality, all sexual subjects reproduce the dominant order."[13] "Woman is nothing but a prostitute, and the prostitute is nothing but a hole, a passive object of the omnipotent phallus."[14]

Sex radical feminists, by contrast, analyze sex as (potential) pleasure commingled with danger, holding that women's sexual liberation involves both "woman's personal pursuit of sexual agency and self-definition and . . . the sexual liberation of women as a class."[15] This view, described in terms ranging from "sex radical feminist" (so called by its sympathizers)[16] to "feminist with a libertarian perspective on sexuality"[17] or "sexual liberal" (by its critics),[18] holds that radical feminists fail to consider or to place sufficient value on the role of minority sexualities (e.g., lesbianism and sadomasochism) or to recognize that these may constitute a form of resistance to patriarchy. In maintaining that all sexual desire is (totally) constructed, radical feminists ignore the existence of many desires and acts that do not conform to the requirements of the masculinist system.[19] Sex radical feminists hold that one cannot paint all sexuality with the same brush; one cannot "assume a unitary women's experience which is derived out of critiquing the unitary male point of view . . . ignor[ing] . . . the margins of sexuality and difference and construct[ing] woman exclusively as a hegemonic category."[20] Sex radical feminists often emphasize sexual oppression rather than gender oppression and argue for the (re)erotization of "outlaw" sexualities.[21] Under this broad umbrella, positions vary widely, ranging from views that argue simply that power itself can be a legitimate source of eroticism[22] to those that defend "cross-generational relations" with children.[23] In turn, these views are sometimes criticized for ignoring the fact that many "outlaw" sexualities reproduce existing destructive cultural hierarchies.

Historically this debate has unfortunately tended to presume an absolutist position, but in recent years has seen growing recognition that heterosexual acts and heterosexuality cannot possibly be understood on this strategy. Several current feminist works have called for a blending of these positions.[24] For example, Stevi Jackson and Sue Scott contend:

> While we have been critical of libertarian perspectives, we believe that the pursuit of pleasure is a positive goal for feminists. In pursuing this goal, however, we need to retain a critical stance on the ways in which our desires have been constructed within a heterosexually ordered patriarchal society, and remain aware of the material constraints which limit the pleasure we can currently attain. The polarization of the debate between libertarian and anti-libertarian feminists has made it difficult to theorize a space between these two positions in which we can explore both power and pleasure and their interconnections.[25]

Indeed, this polarization suggests a fundamental error in the conceptualization of sexuality and sexual acts. If we genuinely want to understand sexuality in the current embedded context, it is essential that we recognize, first and foremost, that it is an extraordinarily complex, diverse, and at times contradictory concept and range of behaviors. The assumption that there is *a correct* analysis of heterosexuality has been belied by multicultural and global perspectives. Whereas earlier theorists argued for an analysis of female sexuality, most contemporary writers recognize that women's experiences vary significantly according to culture, race, ethnicity, economic class, and other factors. Indeed, even the significance of heterosexuality in a specific woman's experience varies greatly over her lifetime, affected by her culture's response to female age

and sexuality. Furthermore, any analysis of heterosexual acts and heterosexuality as purely a political, a cultural, or a psychological phenomenon
is inadequate: Heterosexuality is all of these and a good deal more. And
surprisingly often, heterosexuality involves deeply contradictory or conflicting values and meanings, even for one individual within a single act
at a particular moment. Heterosexuality is an extraordinarily complex set
of experiences, constructed meanings, biological propensities, political
values and arrangements, and social behaviors. To view heterosexuality
under a single lens or perspective or to claim that it constitutes a straightforward and unmixed phenomenon, even under a single subjectivity or
perspective, necessarily involves a grotesque oversimplification of reality.
A competent analysis of heterosexuality cannot be offered based purely
on an understanding of what it is under patriarchy, for it does not exist
only there; it also exists under and is constructed by such systems as colonialism, racism, classism, capitalism, ageism, and heterosexism. Of equal
importance, sex involves aspects that are not political or social or cultural
but, among others, biological (not an apolitical context but one in which
the "-isms" converge around existing life-forms) and experiential (i.e., related to the sensation rather than that which arouses it).

In *Loose Women, Lecherous Men: A Feminist Philosophy of Sex*,
Linda LeMoncheck argues for an analysis that attempts to interweave
and wed these two differing feminist stances. And in the introduction
and first chapter of their anthology, Jackson and Scott argue for an
analysis that clarifies why we need to consider both "camps".[26] Because
a full analysis of heterosexuality requires a book-length discussion, I
cannot hope to present one here, but in the sections below, I offer
thumbnail sketches of those features critical to prostitution policy that
emerge on a "blended" analysis.

Prostitution Defined

> The flesh-and-blood female body engaged in some form of sexual inter-
> action in exchange for some kind of payment has no inherent meaning
> and is signified differently in different discourses.
>
> —Shannon Bell[27]

There are innumerable, sometimes inconsistent legal, social, and moral
definitions for "prostitution," and a good deal of ambiguity surrounds

the use of the term generally.[28] Its ubiquitous use as metaphor further muddies our understanding of the term. But since it is impossible to offer a coherent analysis of, let alone develop a policy regulating, prostitution without a definition limiting the scope of the discussion, I here demarcate my precise focus. (To keep this discussion as brief as possible, some technical distinctions of importance particularly to legal and philosophical theorists are confined to the notes.)

By "prostitution," I first mean the practice of selling, explicitly and contractually, the private performance of specified acts of a sexual nature (where "sexual" is intended to be read broadly as any act that causes sexual arousal in the client). To constitute prostitution, the sale must involve a contract specifying the items of exchange (both the cost and the services to be provided). The prostitution contract includes both implicit and explicit agreement regarding access to the body[29] (or specific body parts)[30] of the seller in a private setting.[31] This definition is intentionally narrow in scope. I am concerned, first, to distinguish prostitution from other forms of sex work. Although many feminist analyses equate the two,[32] because the current practice, intrinsic qualities, conceptual construction, and ideal of prostitution are significantly different *in kind* than those of other forms of sex work, including differences in their legality, potential physical vulnerability, and "propaganda" value, I consider it critical to distinguish these activities. Conversely, it is necessary to distinguish prostitution from a large number of instances that common usage and legal contexts view as the antithesis of the practice in that they involve sexually exclusive arrangements with, for example, wives, girlfriends, and mistresses, who may be paid in a variety of ways (basic maintenance, dinner, jewelry, etc.) for sexual services.

Importantly, the expression "the sale of sexual services and access" was chosen to deny, contrary to both metaphoric and nonmetaphoric uses, that prostitution is equivalent to the sale of either the person or her vagina. A prostitute does not literally "sell herself." She does not take money in exchange for servitude or enslavement. The notion that a prostitute sells herself is a metaphoric or religious one, in effect maintaining that a woman sells her soul, or at least her moral character, through prostitution. This perspective, which equates a woman's moral value and character with her sexual activity, is antithetical to any feminist analysis. Feminism must insist that, unless she is harming another, a woman's sexual activity is not relevant to her moral character or moral value.[33] Nor is the prostitute literally selling her body or parts of her body. One can literally sell a kidney while alive or sell rights to one's body after death, but prostitutes are clearly doing nothing of the sort.

If one can momentarily ignore the sexual nature of the act, it becomes apparent that the prostitute is selling a service not unlike that of a hairdresser, physical or massage therapist, chiropractor, or a variety of physicians and other medical personnel whose services include and sometimes require body-to-body contact. Nor are hands the only parts of these service providers' bodies required for the provision of services: Massage therapists, for example, regularly use their forearms and elbows in massage,[34] and chiropractors sometimes use their knees and nurses their hips (to move patients).[35] Some may hold that prostitution is not like these other services because prostitutes' bodies are penetrated, unlike the bodies of the other service providers; but heterosexual prostitution often does not involve penetration, and in the relatively rare instances of heterosexual prostitution by men for female customers, it is the client's body that is most likely to be penetrated. Further, it is far from apparent why being penetrated, whether orally, anally, or vaginally, would suggest that the prostitute is not actively engaged in the provision of a service. Nor, for that matter, do we always find it problematic to sell access permitting (nonsexual) physical penetration; we allow people to be paid as test subjects in medical studies when it requires penetration of body cavities, whether oral, anal, or vaginal. (Perhaps here a difference is perceived because the purchaser is not supposed to be experiencing pleasure?)

The tendency to deny that prostitution simply involves the sale of a service and physical access appears attributable to the stigma attached to sexual activity and to the political power dynamics traditionally attached to heterosexual arrangements under patriarchy. But these concerns only demonstrate that prostitution is the provision of a deeply tainted and highly charged service and physical access that may, under patriarchy, have significant ramifications not shared by nonsexual service providers.

Finally, it is important to remember that prostitution, like other sexual activity, involves more than just a physical service; a significant psychological and cultural component constructs the physical behavior and is as much a part of the client's purchase as are purely physically defined activities. The client is paying for sexual gratification in accord with his specific erotic desires and sexual identity.

3

The Intrinsic Character of Heterosexual Activity and Prostitution

Intrinsic Qualities of Heterosexual Activity

Most feminists emphatically reject the view that sexual activity is purely biologically determined—that anatomy is solely decisive in the specifics of how, when, and with whom human sexual acts occur. We disagree, however, over the extent to which nature versus nurture (especially social construction) are determinants of individual and cultural sexual activity.

Save for the issue of sexual orientation,[1] in my view biology determines sexual activity in the very narrow sense in which sexual activity falls under the description of pure physical movement. For example, biology is central to understanding the act in which semen is released, through penile penetration, into the vagina of a fertile woman during ovulation. The concept of "sexual activity," however, is significantly broader than that of physical movement, and on this broader conception, while biology is one of the sources of (or contributors to) sexual activity, its role is nowhere as decisive as is commonly believed. Most of the qualities of sexual activity traditionally traced to biology are never *purely* biological but are propensities shaped and determined by culture.

In general, there appears to be a natural biological drive for sexual activity itself, for sexual "outlet" or release, though even this drive is highly acculturated. Sex therapists maintain that the drive for "sexual relief" occurs "naturally" only a fraction as often as it is experienced by the average American—that everything from the pervasiveness of sexual imagery to adequate food supplies affects the extent of sexual desire.

Sexual desire also has visceral aspects that I argue are, in part, intrinsic. For example, I have been aware for some time of how important scent is to my sexual desires. I am not here referring to commercial scents but to the natural body smells of my partners, which have attracted or repelled me. And it has been especially true that I have been drawn to (and missed) the scent of partners with whom I have felt happy and satisfied. I am hardly alone in this; the response is sufficiently typical that women in literature, film, and in popular culture in general are often depicted doing things like smelling the shirts of their partners when ironing or simply when their partners are away. I do not intend to suggest that this is a totally unacculturated phenomenon; in current U.S. culture the reaction to natural body scents is highly socialized, with exorbitant amounts of money invested by personal hygiene product manufacturers to convince us that "body odor" is sexually unappealing. But the response to scent in general and the preferences that occur within the range of odors that are culturally acceptable surely suggest some nonsocialized biological component of sexual desire.

Similarly, I believe that the pure feel and touch of another may be part of what triggers a positive sexual response in human beings. We know that nonsexual contact with other organisms, including physical contact with dogs and cats, has clear positive effects on human beings, for example, in lowering blood pressure. It seems likely that additional physiological changes occur when one experiences sexual acts or arousal with another human being, as opposed to purely masturbatory experiences. But again, the response to physical touch I refer to is not experienced as an unacculturated phenomenon. The preference most individuals in current U.S. culture demonstrate for soft skin, muscularity, and the like in their sexual partners is surely socialized, as these are neither acultural nor ahistorical aspects. Still, it seems highly probable that human beings are "hardwired" to prefer having some of our sexual experiences with other beings over solitary ones. And I think the need for heterosexual intercourse for species survival makes it highly probable that at least some individuals in the species have a biological drive toward sexual encounters that include (though not necessarily exclusively) the desire for, or at least no decisive aversion to, encounters with those of "the opposite" sex.

Surely intrinsic to heterosexuality as pure physical movement and bodily state is the capacity to cause pleasure and orgasm, though which movements, if any, will do so and under what circumstances and with whom appear to be determined by culture and individual.[2] There are, therefore, intrinsic, visceral aspects to heterosexuality that, though acculturated, are necessarily part of the overall experience and must be taken into account in any analysis of it. Though this claim may seem to be obvious to many readers, its statement reflects my concern that we keep the body *as body* in our account of heterosexuality. It is also an important recognition in understanding why, in later discussions, I reject some suggested feminist solutions to the problems of heterosexuality and prostitution.

In addition to these visceral elements of heterosexuality are specific biological causal relationships that are intrinsic to any act of heterosexuality and especially to heterosexual intercourse. The propensity that our and many other cultures have to wed sexual activity with intimacy, which I discuss at length below, can be attributed in part to the fact that heterosexual acts in general, and particularly acts of heterosexual intercourse, make the participants vulnerable to a variety of risks and dangers, regardless of issues of acculturation. And although much of that vulnerability arises from heterosexuality and heterosexual acts as constructed, at least three features are intrinsic to heterosexual activities.

First, many heterosexual acts involve the possibility of contracting a large variety of sexually transmitted diseases (STDs). This risk is of particular concern in the contemporary context, in which we are confronted with the presently fatal acquired immune deficiency syndrome (AIDS). Although the risk of contracting an STD is, broadly, intrinsic to heterosexual encounters, particularly to acts of oral and anal sex and heterosexual intercourse, this risk can be significantly lessened by technological intervention, particularly through the use of condoms, and by visual examination of the genitals and surrounding areas. It is important to specify, however, that even in instances in which an individual uses condoms after "screening" a partner for visual evidence of infection, there is no certainty that infection will be prevented, although the likelihood is significantly diminished. Some STDs are not preventable through condom usage; condoms sometimes break; and visual screening is not useful for diseases that have no identifiable appearance. Furthermore, prevention of infection from STDs necessarily requires the cooperation of one's partners, particularly with regard to the use of condoms.

Second, there is significant vulnerability involved in engaging in any close physical activity with another human being who is large enough to cause physical harm. Some of this risk is intrinsic to acts of heterosexuality, particularly in instances of unintentional harm: One can unintentionally twist the wrong way, exert too much force, and so forth. However, the risk of physical injury from one's partner is significantly increased because sexual acts are considered to be appropriately "private"—that is, they are rarely performed in the presence of nonparticipants. Because, in general, we have the luxury of relatively private bedrooms, and because sexual activity is usually confined to these or similarly isolated physical spaces, the likelihood of intentional physical injury, including vulnerability to rape, is greatly increased. And because (as is discussed in Chapter 4) violence is eroticized as part of or the embodiment of sexual activity in contemporary U.S. culture, this risk becomes decidedly serious. I contend, however, that this is due to the manner in which our culture constructs sexual behavior; there is no reason to suppose either that genetic or biological factors make human sexual activity necessarily private (since they are not for many nonhuman species or for all human cultures) or that violence is intrinsically or biologically wed to sexual activity. As such, the *intrinsic* likelihood of injury during sexual activity may actually be rather low. For this reason, I pursue this issue in the section on heterosexuality as constructed.

Both of these vulnerabilities are intrinsic to acts of heterosexuality, including, but not limited to, heterosexual intercourse, and fall disproportionately on women. Women are more likely than men to be infected by STDs (including HIV/AIDS) through sexual activity, particularly through intercourse. And because women are, on average, physically smaller than men and usually have less "brute strength,"[3] we are at greater risk for physical injury.

Third, all fertile women face the intrinsic risk of unintended pregnancy from heterosexual intercourse. As with STDs, technology has greatly lessened this risk. Short of radical surgical intervention, however, no method of birth control, including tubal ligation, can altogether guarantee prevention of pregnancy—all have some rate of failure. But the probability of unintended pregnancy can be reduced by the use of more than one (compatible) method of birth control,[4] though some of these, especially the condom, require the cooperation of the male partner. Significantly, many currently available methods of birth control carry medical risks to women users. Recent social and social policy changes have limited women's access to birth control technology, particularly to abortion, and thus unintended pregnancies remain a real risk for fertile women engaging in heterosexual intercourse.

Intrinsic Value of Heterosexual Activity

Is heterosexuality intrinsically objectionable? If an action is intrinsically objectionable, it will remain so under any instantiation; no version of it, no matter how "morally sensitive," can altogether eliminate its negative value. One may come to perform such acts as "the least of all possible evils" but the act itself will always be problematic. So the first question that must be asked is: Are heterosexual acts intrinsically negative?

Virtually all actions, even breathing in a polluted world, carry some degree of risk, so in evaluating actions we need both to determine the severity and probability of potential risks and then to weigh them against possible benefits.[5] But the severity and probability of the three risks described above are tremendously context-dependent. The probability of spreading STDs and of unintended pregnancies is directly a result of the technologies available, public dissemination of information about them, and social pressures encouraging or discouraging their use. In the case of both pregnancy and nonfatal STDs, the "severity" of the risk is also deeply context-dependent. In cultures with adequate food supplies, unplanned pregnancies are not always viewed as a hardship; without cultural stigma, having genital herpes is no worse than many other annoying (and sometimes painful) syndromes. The vulnerability of close physical contact is a risk due in part to cultural norms requiring that sexual acts be performed in private, as well as those encouraging rougher sexual activity. And that risk is significantly enhanced by the eroticization of female helplessness and accompanying strong cultural discouragement of training girls and women in activities that increase "brute strength."

Is there, however, any sense in which heterosexual acts are acontextually objectional? Andrea Dworkin's work at times seems to suggest this. In *Intercourse* she states, "[Victoria Woodhull] . . . simply understood that women are unspeakably vulnerable in intercourse because of the *nature of the act*—entry, penetration, occupation."[6] Dworkin maintains that intercourse is always a violation of female physical privacy, penetration of the vaginal hole being equivalent to entry:

> By definition, . . . she is intended to have a lesser privacy, a lesser integrity of the body, a lesser sense of self, since her body can be physically occupied and in the occupation taken over. By definition . . . this lesser privacy, this lesser integrity, this lesser self, establishes her lesser signifi-

cance: not just in the world of social policy but in the world of bare, true real existence. She is defined by how she is made, that hole, which is synonymous with entry; and intercourse, the act fundamental to existence, has consequences to her being that may be intrinsic, not socially imposed.[7]

This passage is among some feminist writings that seem to suggest heterosexual intercourse, in and of itself, makes women necessarily and acontextually vulnerable to male dominance, as it involves the loss of bodily autonomy and physical occupation of one gender class by another. If these power relations were intrinsic, it would indeed be difficult to argue that any instance of heterosexual intercourse was morally acceptable[8] or that there could be any ideal form of it. But the qualities of "entry, penetration, occupation" are not truly intrinsic to heterosexual intercourse but are critical to how the act is conceptually constructed. As Dworkin notes elsewhere in the book, heterosexual intercourse could as easily be conceived and constructed as the female engulfment of the male penis, the capture and imprisonment (occupation) of the penis by the vagina. One may also envision heterosexual intercourse as a "coupling," "meeting," or "uniting," that is, as an activity in which neither participant (nor either gender) is assumed to have dominance. There is therefore *no intrinsic* reason for a subordination/domination dynamic in heterosexual acts, and thus no obvious reason to view heterosexual intercourse as intrinsically and therefore necessarily objectionable.[9]

Intrinsic Character of Heterosexual Prostitution

Since heterosexual prostitution involves the sale of heterosexual acts and access, its intrinsic characteristics are, in part, simply derivative of those of heterosexual activity in general, including the capacity for pleasure and orgasm; visceral elements of desire related to scent, touch, and the like; the risk of sexually transmitted diseases and other physical injuries; and sometimes the risk of unplanned pregnancy. Further, because prostitution involves an economic, contractual aspect, it has the intrinsic features common to the sale of any service; because prostitution, by definition, involves a contract, the parties to the contract will either meet or fail to meet their contractual obligations. In addition, and of particular importance for our purposes, prostitution, like the contracting of other services, may involve a third party (or parties). There is therefore the logical and practical possibility of separating the delivery of services from the facilitation and sale of services. Thus the prostitution contract can involve more than two people, including a pimp or brothel owner. (Indeed, it is not uncommon for a brothel owner to contract with a pimp for a prostitute to work in his or her brothel.)

Is the act of prostitution, the sale of sexual services and access, intrinsically objectionable? As in the case of heterosexual acts, including intercourse, it appears to me that it is not. Barter in a capitalistically organized economy is often morally problematic because it creates significant power differentials that can be, and often are, used exploitatively. This certainly infects prostitution, where in the majority of instances the purchaser has an undue degree of power over the seller/prostitute. But in many instances this power differential is reversed. Indeed, who has what degree of power in the prostitute-client relationship is a complex formulation that derives from a variety of organizational and individual factors. Furthermore, prostitution can and has existed in virtually all economies, however organized. Therefore I reject the view that prostitution is *intrinsically* objectionable due to the power relationships intrinsic to its economic character, because I see these issues as arising from prostitution as contextualized under capitalism and not as intrinsic to any acts involving barter of sexual services and sexual access.

There may also be those who wish to object that "sexual acts (including sexual intercourse) are intrinsically intimate," and thus their sale is a violation of their "nature." I deal with this issue at some length in Chapter 6; however, it should suffice to indicate here that in speaking of "intrinsic" aspects of actions, I am discussing those aspects that *necessarily* attach to the behavior, without technological intervention. And given current heterosexual practice, it should be painfully evident that heterosexual acts are not *necessarily* acts of intimacy in any coherent sense.

4

Sexuality and Prostitution as Conceptual Constructs

> Modernity through a process of othering has produced "the prosti-
> tute" as the other of the other: the other within the categorical
> other, "woman."
>
> —Shannon Bell, Reading[1]

Heterosexuality as Constructed

Most feminists recognize that sexual behaviors, including sexual acts, are the product of culture—that is, they are constructed. Characteristics as diverse as the ability to orgasm, the age of sexual activity, the sexual roles assigned (including degrees of aggressiveness and passivity), the acts actually performed, and the significance of sex and sexuality have been demonstrated to vary by culture. As Foucault's groundbreaking work revealed, a good deal of what counts as sexuality, including sexual acts themselves, is socially constructed and maintains and reinforces the existing cultural power arrangements. Contemporary feminist literature is filled with discussions of how the constructions of sexuality and sexual acts maintain and reinforce sexism. In what follows, I offer only a thumbnail sketch of the specifics of this dynamic—focusing on those aspects I believe to be central to prostitution.

On the prevailing U.S. construction, heterosexual activity is imaged as highly contradictory, containing both extremely positive and extremely negative values. To understand prostitution, it is crucial to recognize the romanticized and positive aspects of heterosexual activity as current hegemonic constructs. Although positive values that attach to heterosexual acts are often overlooked in feminist discussions, it is worth mentioning at the outset two positive values that U.S. culture preponderantly includes in their construction. Heterosexual acts, especially intercourse, are constructed as intimacy, indeed, as the ultimate form of intimacy, as well as the source of the ultimate physical pleasure—the orgasm. One cannot understand why people, particularly women, would choose to engage in heterosexual activities unless these aspects are recognized.

In contrast are those features that emerge in feminist works deconstructing hegemonic views of heterosexual activity, particularly stigma, highly unequal gendered power relationships, and the related bifurcation of women into the roles of "madonna" and "whore."

Heterosexual acts are, under current U.S. construction, virtually universally tainted, always the possible subject of "dirty" jokes, of gossip and of harm. Even sexual acts in marriage are not normalized but are considered off-limits for discussion in "polite" society and, minimally, are likely to raise smirks or discomfort if openly acknowledged. Despite the so-called sexual revolution, all forms of sexual activity remain a source of stigma as well as fascination. The major change brought about by the sexual revolution is that stigma now also attaches to *not* engaging in sexual activity.

Whether a feminist believes, as traditional radical feminists have held, that sexuality is *the primary* site of women's oppression or alternatively that it is simply one of several sites of women's oppression, one would be hard pressed to find any feminist who did not acknowledge that sexuality, and particularly heterosexuality (including heterosexism and homophobia), is a significant feature of most, if not all, contemporary sexism. The current conceptual constructions of heterosexuality and heterosexual activities are antithetical to conceiving of women as human beings; women are merely the objects of sexual desire and repulsion, often constructed and judged almost solely on the basis of our heterosexuality (as opposed to, for example, the products of our market labor or our performance of the traditional roles of wife and mother). Indeed, most of the terms used to denote heterosexual intercourse automatically construct the male in the active role, while the female is always passive—a thing that is harmed.[2] Patriarchy has been most effective at creating women's false consciousness; we have been sold subordination as erotic—the most personal truly is political.[3]

The traditional bifurcation of all women as "madonnas" or "whores" has remained a constant of our cultural experience, despite the so-called sexual revolution. (Any review of popular culture reveals the degree to which this bifurcation continues, significantly unabated.)

These classifications are often the sole basis for determining the moral status of a woman as moral agent/human being. Women classified as madonnas are accorded an "honorific" status. They are "put on a pedestal" and deserve male chivalry and protection. This status, of course, is not to be confused with the full moral agency generally awarded to white, middle- or upper-middle-class, able-bodied males. The madonna, though "honored," is still woman—at best an individual with significant moral value but without the capacity for full moral agency or autonomy, an individual requiring protection, one whose "tender heart" prevents full rationality. The whore, by contrast, is "nothing but a whore," an individual without moral value. She is beneath contempt and "gets what she deserves."

It is critical to understand the slippage built into this system of bifurcation. Put simply, it is difficult indeed for a woman to retain the madonna status. Not only is a single act of sexual intercourse sufficient, in many instances, to change a woman's status from "madonna" to "whore," but wearing "improper" clothing, going into bars without a male escort, or "failing in one's wifely or maternal responsibilities" may be the basis for the judgment that one is "nothing but a whore." Even being the victim of rape (or gang rape) is sufficient in the eyes of many to earn a girl or woman the "whore" classification. A woman's husband or significant other may deny her the status of madonna because he has, presumably, "had her" and thus knows that she is indeed "nothing but a whore."[4] This bifurcation has, if anything, been exacerbated by the sexual revolution because women have been acculturated to believe that we can enjoy our sexuality, including sexual acts, making us ever more vulnerable to the "whore" classification.[5] This ease of slippage is the reason the current construction and treatment of "the prostitute," the ultimate embodiment of the whore, reverberates so powerfully in the lives of *all* women; her fate is ultimately the fate of all women. The political power of these concepts is breathtaking.

The reason the work of many radical feminists is compelling to many women is that it makes sense of sexual experiences which women otherwise find bizarre, and anomalous. While rejecting radical feminists' claim that sexual exploitation is *the* distinguishing characteristic of women's exploitation, I certainly consider it to be a significant one. Through unpacking patriarchal constructions of sexuality, women's "personal" experiences are comprehensible as part of a universal structure of power. Heterosexuality, including heterosexual intercourse, constitutes an embodiment of men's misogyny, a repulsion toward and possession and occupation of women. Women are made inferior through the construction and imaging of our bodies as dirty—through dirty jokes, dirty words for our bodies and body parts and for things done to those parts, and the like. Women's genitals are associated with urine, mucous, slime. Men's repulsion toward women reflects, contrarily, a repulsion toward the very object they desire. They pursue sexual contact that ameliorates this negative moral dimension by having sex with "degraded" women, the socially "inferior" (e.g., prostitutes or the "racially inferior"). Nonwhite women are special targets for sexual abuse and exploitation, including in prostitution and sexually motivated rape, because men want to do something "dirty." Racially motivated rapes are noticed only when they occur on a massive scale and are combined with the killing of men (as in the recent Bosnian holocaust). This construction leads to the invisibility of women's humanity. Male desire for that which is necessarily inferior constructs an impersonal something, an object, not human. Women can then be examined and exploited but not loved as individuals.

When women are imaged as sexually "possessing" men, as agents rather than passive recipients of sexual acts, they are inevitably also imaged as magical, evil, or sex-obsessed "sluts," whereas for women, "being possessed" in heterosexual intercourse is pedestrian, indeed, eroticized. It symbolizes and accords with our possession and ownership by men as objects, laborers, wives, and so forth. The construction and eroticism of heterosexuality as the male possession of women becomes internalized, narrowing a woman's capacity for and vision of possible experience. "Experience is chosen for us, then, imposed on us, especially in intercourse, *and so is its meaning.*"[6] We are likely to experience sexual intercourse as "being taken." A particularly useful insight provided by both Dworkin and Robert Baker is that intercourse is constructed as the penetration and covering over of women (if done "properly") but could equally have been imaged as the vaginal engulfing of men.[7] While *constructed* as women's surrender to and possession by men, intercourse could, logically, have been constructed as men's surrender to and possession by women (Indeed, he comes out smaller and shrunken.) As constructed, when the "fuck works," it is experienced by the woman as surrender and possession and amounts to annihilation of the self. Even woman's sexuality is not truly her own but focuses on her capacity to arouse desire in someone else.[8] To be female is to be carnal and accessible, that is, to be whore.

Heterosexism, the assumption that the world is and should be heterosexual, is central to constructed heterosexuality and a major weapon of gender oppression—as is homophobia, "the fear of homosexuality in oneself or others."[9] Lest it be thought, however, that women can escape sexual surrender and possession in lesbian relationships, it should be recognized that they, too, are constructed as echoing the gender disparity in heterosexual relations ("Which one's butch?").

Preclusion and force are part of the very meaning of sex and therefore of arousal. One of the most destructive aspects of constructed heterosexuality is the normalization and eroticizing of violence, especially of male sexual violence against women. Women are not just sexual objects; we are "naturally masochistic sexual objects."[10] Heterosexuality includes sexual terrorism, the "system by which males frighten and, by frightening, control and dominate females,"[11] through rape, spousal battery, incest, pornography, harassment, and the like.[12] Even mainstream media consistently depicts women as desiring violence, degradation, and subordination, as being "turned on" by these.

Despite its imaging as the source of female vulnerability to invasion, heterosexuality is imbued with the contradictory value of female power—the power of making men lose control, thereby justifying male distrust and misogyny. Men experience enormous rage toward women because, as currently constructed, heterosexuality gives women the power to dominate and manipulate men through their sexual desire—women's very powerlessness is seen as generating a desire for revenge, which is played out sexually. Since "nice girls don't" or at least don't nonmonogamously, sexual access to women becomes, in the broadest sense, marketable. Women are socialized to use men's sexual desire to obtain men's money, power, approval, and submission. While patriarchy ensures female dependence, intercourse provides attachment to and a "hold" on men. Men must be wary of women they greatly desire, lest the women use this power destructively. On the current construction of sexuality, men cannot control their sexual desires but simultaneously are repulsed by their lack of control. Sexual desire and activity are experienced as stigmata, carrying with them the value of one who is "defined by fucking,"[13] who is unable to control or reject his (or her) carnal character. Thus it is not just women but sexual acts themselves that are stigmatized.

Dworkin suggests two potentially positive outcomes of heterosexual intercourse or other sexual activities: "communion" and "skinlessness." Communion is a state outside civilization and its constructs, including self. Time and space cease to exist, and the self/other distinction is lost. All that exists is the physical sensation, touch without experienced or conceptual boundaries. It is intense and alive—neither alienated nor abstract. "Two become one" in a space where nothing but visceral pleasure exists. One can find redemption, a place where one's vulnerability will not be betrayed.

Dworkin's "skinless" sex is the exposing of the self to the elemental human condition, fragile and delicate. Personality, individuality, and mentality are lost; the skin "melts." "[It] forces one to live wholly in the body, in the present without mental evasion or self-preoccupied introspection or free-floating anxiety."[14] But because society interposes itself through its constructs, the loss of identity is ultimately impossible, creating a painful tension. "[Women become] the escape route from mental self-absorption into reality: they are the world, connection, contact, touch, feeling, what is real, the physical, what is true." But men desire both "fucking without barriers" and, contradictorily, the preservation of self, which leads to overwhelming loneliness and, ultimately, violence.

Through communion, one may confront the fear of total commitment, of being loved. Through it, one's deepest emotions are expressed. But this requires that one live with the fear of abandonment and rejection. Those capable of self-knowledge must conquer their fear of these. Intercourse can then evolve into communion, "a sharing, mutual possession of an enormous mystery—the intensity and magnificence of violent feeling transformed into tenderness. . . . Fucking as communion is larger than an individual personality; it is a radical experience of seeing and knowing, experiencing possibilities within one that have been hidden."[15]

Dworkin's descriptions of communion and skinlessness closely resemble the views of a variety of sexual theorists who hold that heterosexual acts can and ideally do involve "true intimacy," a view that has become ubiquitous in twentieth-century American culture. Where, formally, the only morally justifiable acts of sexual intercourse used to be those between legal husband and wife (and, according to some viewpoints, purely for procreative purposes), U.S. educated middle-class majority opinion now holds that it is morally acceptable to have intercourse with someone you "truly love and feel intimate toward." I fully agree with Dworkin and others that this view is central to the concept of heterosexual intercourse as currently constructed. Indeed, I think it is a major factor behind the view that prostitution is bad, undesirable, or outright immoral. For this reason, and because I believe that the corresponding normative claim that heterosexual intercourse *should* ideally, be an act of intimacy with an intimate partner is not only wrong but politically self-destructive, I return to this issue at some length in the discussion on ideal heterosexuality in Chapter 7.

Prostitution as Constructed

What is prostitution, as a conceptual construct?[16] The simple answer is that "prostitution" refers to the activities of prostitutes, for this concept is the most fundamental unit of meaning. Activities such as archery, attending college, and raising funds for a worthy cause are not presumed to be, in any respect, inextricably tied to the character and nature of the agent, whereas teaching college courses or raising funds for the Young Republicans are presumed, in a general sense, to be somewhat so tied. But for some small number of activities an inextricable connection to the character and nature of the actor is presumed to exist. I can think of no instance where this is more obvious than in the case of prostitution.

A significant part of the reason for this virtual equating of actor and act emerges from the overwhelming importance of the concept of the whore-prostitute as a paradigm and facilitator of patriarchy. Because, if classified as "whore," one becomes "nothing but a whore," being a prostitute-whore becomes *the* definer of the persona and personhood of a woman. It is critical to understand that the madonna/whore dichotomy is more than a binary; it is a rigid hierarchy. Where to be "other" is to be less than, to be "other of other" is to be nothing, worthless. So whereas the voice of the madonna may legitimately be dismissed within patriarchal hegemony, the prostitute has no voice at all, not even when interacting with the madonna. Whereas the "good woman" is viewed with contempt, the prostitute is beneath contempt.

Depending on context, there are differences between the uses and meanings of "whore" and "prostitute."[17] I use the terms as follows: In general, all prostitutes are whores, though not all whores are prostitutes. The term *whore* is used to describe any female viewed as sexually available, sexually assertive, or simply morally imperfect. I use *prostitute* more narrowly to describe those who contract to perform sexual services for explicitly agreed-upon material payment. "The prostitute," however, embodies the archetype of the paradigm "whore." "The whore as prostitute or sex worker is the prototype of the stigmatized woman."[18] Because the long-term consequences of being classified as "whore" are so life-altering, the whore-prostitute paradigm becomes a significant weapon of patriarchy, another form of sexual terrorism. As such, the prostitution policies feminists develop need to address two separate questions: (1) How does the conceptual construct of "The prostitute" impact on the lives of both prostitute and nonprostitute women? (2) How will any proposed policy affect and alter this conceptual construct?

The modern conception of the prostitute, including its emergence as a discursive domain, began with the Victorian period, when prostitution was institutionally codified as deviant and illicit by the British Royal Commission on the Contagious Diseases Acts and thus became an explicit target of medical, political, and therapeutic intervention.[19] The dominant, especially medical and legal-moral, male discourse produced two prevailing images of the prostitute: one as the ruined, damaged, or destroyed victim, the other as a diseased victimizer who "spreads and rots the body politic."[20] It was also during this period that the prostitute became mere paradigm and metaphor; she ceased to be a person and became a disembodied stereotype.

By the mid–nineteenth century there was a propensity among some respected theorists to wed class bias with sexism by equating the prostitute with the working-class woman. In general, prostitutes were constructed as degenerate, physically unclean, disease-prone, and the source of disease and pollution, including moral pollution. Their "personality profiles" included such diverse traits as being husky-voiced or raucous and shrill, mentally inconstant, angry, and "sexual perverts" (often understood as lesbian). The prevailing wisdom of this period held that prostitution was motivated by financial need, vanity, laziness, sinfulness, or love of pleasure, including material pleasure. Interestingly, although the ease of slippage from madonna to whore appears to be a historical constant, these theorists focused primarily on slippage in the opposite direction. The prevailing construction was that of the prostitute as a working-class woman who would leave prostitution and blend back into the working class: "By far the large number of women who have resorted to prostitution for a livelihood, return sooner or later to a more or less regular course of life. . . . The better inclined class of prostitutes become the wedded wives of men of every grade of society, from the peerage to the stable."[21] Because this was perceived as a serious threat to the community, it was decided that prostitutes must be regulated to keep them free from disease.

In contrast, feminist discourse in the repeal movement, (a lobbying effort to repeal the Contagious Disease Acts) and, later, in the Progressive Era constructed the prostitute solely as a passive victim who was capable of being reformed and recovering female "dignity and virtue," allowing her to become an "honorable wife and mother."[22] Although the unreformed prostitute was depicted as depraved and polluted, this was maintained to be the fault of her customers; the prostitute remained redeemable. In accord with the chaste/unchaste dichotomy of the period, repeal feminists held that prostitutes were really asexual, chaste women forced into prostitution solely by monetary need, while in the Progressive Era it was contended that "white slavery" coerced women into prostitution. In both instances, feminists held that prostitutes were innocents who "fell into" prostitution; prostitution was so degrading that no woman would freely choose it. Nineteenth-century feminists exaggerated prostitution's magnitude and coerciveness. They "not only failed to challenge this oversimplified and condescending explanation of prostitution, but also made it central to their understanding of women's oppression."[23]

From 1890 to 1910, the views of Sigmund Freud and Havelock Ellis held sway in the formation of the concept. Ellis held that some women are born prostitutes, born criminals, and biologically destined to degeneracy, maintaining that they are prone to masturbate (which he considered positive) and to lesbianism (which he considered perversion). Freud, in contrast, held that prostitutes are psychologically immature and lack the "civilized" view of sexuality. On Freud's view, however, this was a perversion all women were capable of, particularly "uncultivated" (i.e., poor or uneducated) women. His Oedipal analysis, including the male's realization that his father has sex with his mother, was held to cause a wedding of the "mother" "whore" constructions in the male unconscious. The concept of "the prostitute" combines with the oppositional concept of "the mother"; "the madonna" collapses into "the polymorphously uninhibited sexual woman and the woman lacking sexual integrity."[24]

The modern construction of the prostitute is clearly rooted in these traditions, embodying and reflecting their contradictions. The construction remains one of a woman who is diseased and dirty (the dirt magnified if she is nonwhite), poor or working-class, a sexual deviant, and a symbol of the disintegration of society. At the same time, she embodies "the mother": warm, kind, helpful, nurturant (remember *Gunsmoke*'s "Miss Kitty"). But the prostitute is further bifurcated—into a victim who would do anything rather than prostitute (if not for the needs of her family, threats, drug addiction caused by another, etc.), one who awaits a savior and redemption, or into a victimizer, a criminal, heartless, morally bereft, greedy, altogether untrustworthy thing—a dishonest seducer. Jo Doezema notes how the traditional bifurcation of prostitutes into victim and victimizer has been given an interesting twentieth-century spin. In the current discourse, the popular "forced" versus "voluntary" prostitution distinction leads to the bifurcation of the modern prostitute into that of the Western woman—the guilty sexual transgressor who freely chooses a life of sin—and that of the non-Western (usually Asian), young, innocent (read "virgin") woman who is forced into prostitution (by poverty, trafficking, etc.) and who is or will soon become the passive diseased woman.[25] Or, as Linda LeMoncheck describes it, feminists who adopt this perspective, "regard sex workers as either victims of an overpowering patriarchy or collaborators in collective brainwashing."[26] The voluntary/forced dichotomy reproduces the whore/madonna division within the "prostitute" category. "The distinction between voluntary and forced prostitution, a radical and resistive attack on previous discourses that constructed all prostitutes as victims and/or deviants, has been co-opted and inverted, and incorporated to reinforce systems that abuse sex workers rights."[27]

Importantly, living, embodied prostitutes continue to be reduced to mere paradigms and metaphors; a prostitute continues to be a disembodied stereotype, a one-dimensional object without individual identity—"nothing but a prostitute." Hegemonic wisdom holds that her life and reality can be understood totally through "the prostitute" construct.

According to the current conceptual construct, the prostitute victimizer is an appropriate target for violence, including, though not limited to, sexual violence, since she is *pure* moral degenerate who would "do practically anything for money." Acts normally viewed as criminal are not crimes if directed against the prostitute victimizer. Criminal behavior requires a victim, and the prostitute victimizer cannot be a victim; victimization requires personhood, moral status, and identity. The prostitute victimizer is not simply "the other of the other"—she is the end of the continuum. She is the *appropriate* target of misogyny and "deserves what she gets—what else could she expect?" That the prevailing conceptual construct of the prostitute promotes her (or him) as an acceptable target for violence is evidenced not only in cultural artifacts but also by accepted practice. Mass media do not see fit to cover extensively, if at all, the assaults or even the deaths of those known to prostitute, unless the bodies are beginning to stack up (in which case the stories are often made lurid and salacious); as a pure sexual object, even the prostitute's death is "sexy"). In these cases the media rarely see fit to provide the victim's name (or they wait until the end of the article to give it). "The prostitute" is faceless. Stigma, illegality, and lack of community interest if she is victimized ensure that she will remain so.

Police and other public officials demonstrate little interest in pursuing crimes against prostitutes, since the prostitute victimizer does not warrant the time or the cost to the community. In 1975 this tradition sparked a two-month-long strike and the occupation of a church in Lyon, France by prostitutes protesting the lack of concern and efforts by the Lyon police to solve the murder of several prostitutes and to provide prostitutes with protection while the murderer was still at large and active. In 1989, Norma Jean Almodovar, a former Los Angeles police officer turned prostitute, maintained, "We have serial murderers, with eighty women murdered in Seattle, around twenty-five in Portland, ten in the Oakland–San Francisco area, another sixteen in Los Angeles and nine in San Diego. That's just the West Coast. There's the usual racism [and economic classism] because most of the women who are murdered are black street prostitutes. The police and society don't seem to care; they feel that since these women are prostitutes, they deserve whatever they get. . . . Rather than go after the murderers, the state spends millions of dollars trying to round up prostitutes and does nothing against those who violate their rights."[28] And of course, prostitutes are not capable of being raped. How can sex be forced if "she would spread her legs for anyone for the going price"? Indeed, due to her behavior, dress, and dealings in things sexual, a prostitute is viewed as the ultimate "woman who was asking for it." Rape of prostitutes cannot occur.

Given how destructive the current paradigm of the prostitute is to prostitutes and to women as a class, any prostitution policy that is acceptable to feminists must either alter this construction or eradicate it altogether.

5

The Practice of Heterosexuality and Heterosexual Prostitution

The Current Practice of Heterosexuality

"The hallmark of sexuality is its complexity: its multiple meanings, sensations, and connections."[1] Indeed, the current practice of heterosexuality, like its construction, involves myriad factors that are often outright contradictions, embodying what Carole Vance terms "pleasure and danger." Because I cannot do justice to this topic in the limited scope of this discussion, I focus on a gendered perspective of those features most salient to prostitution.

As we are unrelentingly and inescapably told in current culture, heterosexual activity contains positive elements even under current patriarchal practice. Undeniably, part of the appeal of heterosexual encounters for many women is their ability to produce truly pleasurable physical sensation. Among the visceral experiences available to human beings, sexual arousal and orgasm are, at least for many, among the most intense sources of pure physical gratification. Even if only 30 percent of women experience orgasm through intercourse,[2] many are able to orgasm through other forms of heterosexual activity that, though viewed as "perversions" in earlier periods, are now often acceptable. Indeed, discussion of cunnilingus has become frequent in mass media. For whatever reasons, whether intrinsic or constructed or both, sexual pleasure is often more intense and satisfying when experienced with another. This fact, while perhaps obvious, is often lost or dismissed in the harsher feminist analyses. When one is lucky and the moment and one's partner are "right," the sheer physical ecstasy that a heterosexual individual can experience in a heterosexual encounter is both overpowering and ineffable.[3] Heterosexual activity is also a source of adventure, excitement, and "basking in the infantile and non-rational."[4] It allows us to connect with our most basic, visceral, sensual nature in a manner rarely available in other contexts.

Under prevailing U.S. practice, heterosexual activity is viewed as one of the few, perhaps the primary, legitimate sources of emotional connection and intimacy. Although a relatively recent and not a global development, the current U.S. expectation is that one's most intense emotional bonding will occur within a heterosexually coupled relationship and that all other relationships, save perhaps that of parent to child, will be subsidiary and subordinate. Such connections are currently privileged so that uncoupled heterosexuals are seen as "missing something" and "just waiting for the right person to come along." Indeed, for this reason many, especially radical, feminists contend that heterosexual activity is, at least for heterosexual women, compulsory. "By male design, the relationships that ground our social sense of self and self-worth are a package deal—with love, security, emotional support, and sex all going together."[5] "All animal needs for love and warmth are channeled into genital sex: people must never touch others of the same sex, and may touch those of the opposite sex only when preparing for a genital encounter. Isolation from others makes people starved for physical affection; and if the only kind they can get is genital sex, that's soon all they crave."[6]

Current U.S. heterosexual activity also constitutes the favored basis for shared living arrangements. The vast majority of human activities in this country are organized around heterosexual couples and their possible offspring, who constitute the primary unit for the pooling of resources and of cooperative life, including the having and raising of children. This was not always the case. In earlier centuries the extended family performed this function, and earlier in the twentieth century married heterosexual couples did. But in recent decades, non–legally sanctioned heterosexual coupling has been accepted for this role as well. Living within heterosexually coupled relationships is also currently a legally, socially, and economically privileged arrangement.[7] Thus another advantage of current heterosexual activity is that it affords access to a culturally privileged status.

Heterosexual intercourse remains the most common source of pregnancy, an outcome whose value depends significantly on the situation and desires of the woman or couple. As the vast amount of money and time currently spent on in vitro fertilization and other fertility techniques suggests, for many pregnancy is a most desirable goal. Conversely, and as birth control, abortion, and adoption statistics demonstrate, for most

women, at numerous times in their lives, pregnancy constitutes significant personal, social, psychological, or economic hardship and harm.

Current heterosexual activity as culturally constructed is, however,
also the source of many negative outcomes. Heterosexual acts constitute a weapon of patriarchy in a host of ways. Rape, forcible incest,
child molestation, and other forms of sexual assault are painfully commonplace. Because these acts are inaccurately depicted as "stranger"
crimes, they effectively terrorize women, keeping us in at night while
avoiding isolated areas by day, encouraging us to take along male partners for protection, and so forth. The stigmatized designation of
"whore," ubiquitous in contemporary heterosexual practice, still has
tremendous negative impact on the lives of many women, "justifying"
extraordinary degrees of emotional, economic, physical, sexual, and political abuse, including rape, assault, even murder. And despite the so-
called sexual revolution, "women's fear of reprisal and punishment for
sexual activity has not abated."[8] For many women, sexuality and sexual desires are to be suppressed, for fear of uncontrollable and easily
aroused male lust. Women are forced to become "the moral custodians
of male behavior."[9]

A woman's value as a potential heterosexual partner is based on prevailing standards of "sexual attractiveness," which few currently can
achieve without significant, expensive, and sometimes dangerous technological interventions. Because sexual attractiveness is a core criterion
for assessing a woman's value in general, this unrealistic standard becomes a source of torment for many—its significance attested to by the
number of cosmetic surgical procedures, manipulations of food intake
(including not only diets but also anorexia and bulimia), exercise regimens, and other techniques that U.S. women undergo annually.[10] The
culture of sexual attractiveness is competitive, pitting woman against
woman and undermining the female solidarity critical to ending patriarchal oppression.

Heterosexual activity is also a common source of sexually transmitted
diseases, some of which, such as genital herpes, are incurable, while others, such as AIDS, still prove fatal. Condoms may prevent some STDs,
but in many instances[11] they do not. And as studies regularly demonstrate, women are far more likely than men to be infected with an STD
through intercourse.

For our purposes, it is also critical to understand the role of law in
heterosexual practice. As Dworkin notes:

Not only does the law . . . create gender, female inferiority and an ecology of male power; it itself is the guideline, the signpost, for sex outside the law. It says where, how, when, in what ways to be lawless. Sex exists on both sides of the law but the law itself creates the sides. . . . The legal and the illegal fuck create the legal and the illegal woman; but the law controls what is created, how, in what circumstances, under what conditions—the kind and quality of subordination each is subjected to; the inferior status of each; the role of intercourse in the subordination of each.[12]

Heterosexual activity is, therefore, not truly private, falling within the sphere of state regulation. Privacy is respected only when it relates to how men use their property, that is, "their" women and children.[13] Because the current gender distribution of power is in the state's interest (or at least in the interest of the state's own power distribution), the law protects prevailing power relationships by prescribing behavior that heightens gender polarity and proscribing behavior that lessens it. Everything from laws mandating differences in dress to those allowing only vaginal, as opposed to oral or anal, penetration effectively reinforce the status quo, including sexism and heterosexism.

Sexual norms are constructed by social as well as legal constriction. While there appears to be relatively widespread acceptance of some behaviors formerly viewed as perverse—for example, oral sex—others, such as sadomasochism or dominance and bondage, continue to be assigned an outlaw status. Among feminists, the acceptability of such activity is highly contested, with considerable disagreement over whether such behavior can be truly consensual in the current context and whether acceptance of these various practices supports patriarchal domination or undermines it.[14]

The Current Practice of Prostitution

A. Legal Status

Although the law is silent on many activities, many others fall under some form of legal control; acts may be legalized, criminalized, or decriminalized. Criminalization makes the act or practice illegal and open to legal sanctions. Legalization permits behavior when it complies with specified regulations. Decriminalization reinstates legal silence on activities that were formerly criminalized or legalized. A decriminalized behavior is one that is permissible and unregulated, save for regulations that apply to all businesses, such as fair hiring practices and sales taxes.

To understand how the legal system actually works, however, one needs to know considerably more than what formal legislation exists. One must also understand what philosophers call "the law in action," or the nature of legal enforcement. Whether legal machinery will be brought to bear against an action is at least as much a reflection of police policy, and by implication public policy, as is "the law on the books." In any criminal justice system, decisions have to be made about which laws will be most vigorously enforced. All jurisdictions have laws that are never or rarely enforced because the labor force required to do so is not allocated or because arrests under these laws would be viewed with disfavor and would be unlikely to be pursued by an overworked criminal justice system. Acts that are technically illegal but for which legal proscriptions are rarely enforced are generally described as "tolerated." For example, in most jurisdictions private poker parties are technically illegal, but rarely are such laws enforced. Understanding not just formal laws but actual patterns of enforcement is fundamental to understanding the nature of existing prostitution practice. I have argued elsewhere that policies of police tolerance are necessary from a purely pragmatic organizational standpoint, constituting one type of discretionary decision required for the efficient running of any bureaucracy.[15] At the same time, it is crucial to recognize that patterns of police tolerance in the United States in general, and certainly in regard to prostitution, have consistently demonstrated the sexism, heterosexism, racism, and economic classism that infect the larger society.

An additional complication to policy analysis is that historically, legally, and conceptually a distinction has been drawn between prostitution and prostitution facilitation, including pimping, pandering, and brothel keeping. Unquestionably, prostitute facilitators or agents are a primary source of abuse of prostitutes. Often, however, a prostitute or, more problematically, a group of prostitutes may act as their own (collective) agents. The state legally separates the prostitute and facilitation functions even when both are performed by the same individual(s), sanctioning them separately.

B. Research Context

It is impossible to present a clear, accurate, and unbiased overview of the practice of prostitution—either in the United States or globally. Its illegality, both historical and current, requires that those involved systematically keep secret all information about the practice. This is particularly true in countries such as the United States, where the society shows little acceptance of police tolerance of the activity, particularly if the prostituting is public or committed by the nonwhite, the nonheterosexual, or the poor. Indeed, even the number of women involved in prostitution is unclear—I have seen figures ranging from 1 percent to 12 percent of U.S. women estimated to have been prostitutes at some time in their lives.[16]

The unfortunate result is that researchers end up focusing solely on the most visible forms of prostitution, especially streetwalking. Independent of the issue of its illegality, prostitution is so deeply stigmatized that those who participate rarely come forward, and those who do are often activists who are not representative of the larger group. Even academics who work on related subjects have traditionally avoided research on prostitution. As Ester Kosovski maintains:

> The prejudice that exists toward prostitutes and prostitution . . . may be one of the reasons why only recently have researchers addressed these issues [in Brazil], and why there are no official statistics.[17]

U.S. experience certainly demonstrates this phenomenon. When I visited the University of Nevada–Reno in 1994, I was able to locate only one faculty member, Dr. Ellen Pillard, who was actively researching and publishing on the topic. Since this is the only research institution in the United States within an hour's drive of a legal brothel, the lack of local scholarly attention was revealing.

Additionally, U.S. scholars who research prostitution often begin with a fixed viewpoint, a perspective that appears to influence their methodology as well as the focus of their inquiries. The research of some European feminists, for example, has been strongly influenced by prostitutes' rights organizations and advocates. Not surprisingly, the work of these feminists often focuses on the diversity of prostitution practices and on the capacity of women to flourish under some of them. By contrast, U.S.

feminists are often strongly influenced by the perspectives of prostitution victim or survivor advocates and thus tend to focus on the more abusive and exploitative aspects of the practice, especially on street prostitution. But while streetwalking is the most visible form of prostitution, it is not now, nor has it ever been, the most common. U.S. studies estimate that streetwalking accounts for only 10 to 20 percent of all prostitution.[18] Brothel prostitution has historically been the most dominant form and remains so in parts of Asia. In the past fifty years, many Western societies have seen the rise of alternative forms, for example, massage parlors, escort services, and call girls. Yet the overwhelming majority of U.S. research remains focused on streetwalking, though it is recognized to be, in quality as well as quantity, unrepresentative of prostitution as a whole. "This group is most powerless, most vulnerable, and most visible not only to legal authorities, but also to researchers."[19] The vulnerability and powerlessness of street prostitutes result in unrepresentatively high levels of exploitation and abuse.

In the current situation, the policy researcher is confronted with one of two options: to focus on studies of street prostitution in the United States and generalize from these or to include research on other forms of prostitution from foreign studies. The latter strategy is problematic because of the danger of assuming cross-cultural similarity. However, to focus solely on what is recognized as a less common and unrepresentative form is at least equally if not more suspect.

I have therefore opted to use existing U.S. data on prostitution as well as studies from other countries, particularly the Netherlands, accounting as much as possible for cultural differences.[20] The policy I advocate may, however, require adjustment as more information on U.S. prostitution becomes available. I have also used qualitative research gathered from a multitude of interviews, both in the United States and abroad,[21] which reflects the findings of social scientists that there is nothing simple or consistent about the practice. Prostitution involves a broad range of organizations and activities, some of which are highly exploitative, abusive, and damaging, and some of which are not; some of which involve enslavement, and some of which provide relative empowerment. All of these, however, to a greater or lesser degree and like virtually all other activities, are consistently infected by global sexism, heterosexism, racism, economic classism, and so forth. My concern in this section is to give the reader a sense of how broad and diverse the practice is, in terms both of its forms and organizations and of their consequences.

C. Motivation for Prostitution (or "What's a Nice Girl Like You . . . ?")

Probably the most common question asked about prostitution is why a woman would be a prostitute. It should surprise no one that the main motivation for prostitution is money. In study after study, the top reason prostitutes give for entering the profession is financial.[22] In P.H. Gebhard's study, 90 percent of the women interviewed said money was their primary reason for prostituting.[23] Although a recent increase in female prostitution in the West, has been linked to the feminization of poverty and to changes in women's view of gender-appropriate behavior, American women do not generally enter prostitution to escape dire poverty. Severe poverty does appear to motivate women in Asia,[24] but the same does not follow in the United States where women are more likely to enter prostitution to supplement their income or simply to have a higher income overall.[25] Given the relatively limited and lower-paying positions currently available to women, especially to poorly educated or unskilled female laborers, the question is "not . . . why so many women become prostitutes, but why so few of them do."[26] In my interviews, prostitute women consistently cited money as their major motivation—whether to raise a stake to protect a child, provide financial security for retirement, pay college expenses, or simply provide sufficient income for travel. But women also indicate that they are motivated by a desire for "independence, excitement, and the dislike of routine work,"[27] while some are drawn to prostitution because they enjoy the sex.[28]

Although direct coercion is commonly assumed to be a major reason for prostitution, most studies suggest it is not, in general, a significant factor. Only from 4 percent to 13.3 percent of prostitutes report direct force by pimps or other facilitators as their reason for entering prostitution, although the percentage varies greatly with the form of prostitution. Force is obviously a significant motivation for trafficked prostitutes.

D. Motivation for Customers

What functions does prostitution serve for its customers? What is the individual client looking for when he purchases prostitution services? I use "he" because women rarely purchase heterosexual sexual services outright,[29] reflecting traditional gender roles. Whether through marriage, prostitution, or other practices, it is heterosexual access to women rather than to men that has historically been treated as a market commodity. Indeed, in all my research on prostitution I have discovered only two instances of true heterosexual prostitution organized for female clients. The first is an extremely new phenomenon: U.S. women are apparently beginning to contact out-call massage services for pure heterosexual prostitution purposes. The second, a far more established service, involves sex tourism for wealthy German women in Kenya. Unquestionably the predominance of men as clients of prostitution services is due in part to the significant disparity in power currently associated with the prostitute-client relationship. In the Kenyan case, it appears that racism, colonialism, and economic classism are sufficient to trump sexism.

Men traditionally do not seek prostitutes because they lack alternative sexual outlets. Indeed, most clients are married. Sometimes they are motivated by more or less "purely" sexual interests. They cite the desire for "a pleasant hour's relaxation"; sexual variety; easy, anonymous sex without obligation; "fascination"; "curiosity and adventure"; "a diversion"; and "things you can't do at home." At other times the reasons are more clearly emotional: the men "are looking for more comfort, contact and a 'nice chat' [rather] than for 'pure sex', they are seeking 'friendship.'"[30]

The clients' desires seem to involve a conflicting conglomeration of interests and values, many of which, though not all, play out current gender roles and expectations. While prostitution may satisfy the illusion of the *Playboy* ideal ("We're just two adults who enjoy fucking"), it also sometimes provides the illusion of intimacy. It is significant that many brothels obscure the fact that the woman is receiving payment for services; often fees are remitted to managers rather than directly to prostitutes. A prostitute encounter often provides a "safe haven" for the male client where he feels accepted and valued,[31] sometimes as a person but also sometimes as a "sexual stud." Some men revel in their contact with the traditional "bad girl" and in performing forbidden ("dirty") acts, while other, especially younger men are concerned to prove their "overwhelming" sexual power. Some clients come to affirm the patriarchal construction of women as lower, adoring, available, desiring subordination, and so forth. For them, prostitution can provide available, "willing" victims for sexual, emotional, verbal, and physical abuse. In contrast are clients who establish sometimes lengthy friendships with particular prostitutes.

In the United States, all these motivations are shaped by a capitalist and patriarchal structure that, generally places the greatest power in the hands of the purchaser of sexual services. Given the current organization of prostitution, male clients are largely able to determine the nature of a prostitution encounter, a fact that certainly shapes client desire.

E. Global Prostitution Practice

Contrary to the assumptions of many U.S. citizens, ours is one of the few developed nations to criminalize prostitution. In most Western industrialized countries, prostitution is decriminalized.[32] Indeed, the United Nations endorses decriminalization. Since the so-called sexual revolution of the 1960s, three significant changes have occurred in the global prostitution industry. First, the commercial sex industry has experienced significant economic growth, including the development of successful new forms of prostitution—for example, "eros centers," "sex therapy" centers and escort services. Second, and of central importance, globalization has precipitated a rise in transnational prostitution through sex holidays (sex tourism) and trafficking in women.

Sex tourism constitutes a site where the economic desperation of usually rural women from underdeveloped, overexploited countries meets the desire of men from more affluent nations who "imagine certain women, usually women of color, to be more available and submissive than the women in their own countries."[33] With the extensive cooperation of local governments, resorts and networks in larger cities have established large and lucrative sex-tourist markets.[34] In countries such as Thailand, the Philippines, and South Korea,[35] although prostitution may be illegal, the police and government officials not only tolerate but often encourage the practice, viewing it as core to their economic survival.[36] While the women often work under extremely poor conditions, they are willing to participate because they may earn up to six times more in prostitution than in other industries.[37] Once they have entered prostitution, social and economic pressures make it difficult for them to leave. Sex tourism also involves the prostitution of young men and children, whose fates are particularly grim. But as Cynthia Enloe notes, "Sex tourism is not an anomaly; it is one strand of the gendered tourism industry"[38] in which women and their labor are systematically exploited.

It is important to recognize the role the United States has played in the globalization of prostitution, especially the role of the U.S. military in laying the seeds for the trafficking and sex tourism now prevalent in

Southeast Asia. "The sheer presence of thousands of American service-men in military bases and their 'Rest and Recreation' activities in Asia, particularly during the Vietnam War, have fundamentally reorganized women for the sex industry."[39] Whereas there were twenty-thousand prostitutes in Thailand in 1957, there were four hundred thousand by 1964, after the United States had established seven bases in Thailand during the Vietnam War.[40] U.S. military bases have consistently been cited as being responsible for creating or exacerbating conditions that promote prostitution. Large, organized prostitution industries are commonplace surrounding American bases, both in the United States and abroad.[41] In 1987 the Aquino government in the Philippines estimated between six thousand and nine thousand prostitutes were registered and licensed in Olongapo, outside Subic Bay Naval Base, while independent researchers estimated that as many as twenty-thousand prostitutes, including unlicensed workers, lived in the city. It was estimated that another five thousand women would come to Olongapo when an American aircraft carrier docked. A rising number of children, often the offspring of American military personnel and Filipina prostitutes, have been sold into pedophilic prostitution rings.[42]

The U.S. military is more than tacitly responsible for promoting prostitution. Given its apparent belief that safeguarding the morale and physical health of soldiers requires sexual access to local women, it often is explicitly involved in the regulation and control of native prostitutes. In South Korea, for example, the U.S. military requires prostitute women carry venereal disease (VD) cards if they work at clubs frequented by GIs. At Camp Casey there, the military publishes a VD guide to inform GIs about which bars to patronize and which to avoid. It also requires and issues health exams and licenses for prostitutes, despite the fact that prostitution is illegal in Korea.[43] In the Philippines, the U.S. government published flyers with pictures of HIV-positive prostitutes, though it failed to inform the prostitutes themselves of their HIV-positive status; nor did the government consider that most of these women had contracted HIV through contact with U.S. GIs.[44] Historically, when military bases have been abandoned, the surrounding military sex industry has simply been converted by procurers into sex tourism.

Since the 1970s, trafficking in women has escalated into a major international crisis; massive numbers of women have been transported across international borders for prostitution. The vast majority are being trafficked; they are deceived, subjected to "threats, extortion or brutal force and violence."[45] In 1991 it was estimated that 30 million women had been sold worldwide since the mid-1970s.[46] Not surprisingly, little is known statistically about the experiences of these women, nor about the experiences of other, migrant, nontrafficked women prostitutes, though anecdotal evidence consistently confirms that the fates of the former are generally bleak. Many women are, however, trafficked for purposes other than prostitution, ranging from "mail-order" brides to domestic laborers. A good deal more is said on this topic below.

Third, we have seen the emergence of a global sex-workers' rights movement, fighting to keep brothels open, exposing sex industry corruption, and attempting to undermine the stigma of sex work.[47] They have already had some success in influencing UN policy and affecting the perspectives of international policy researchers.

F. U.S. Prostitution Practice

Perhaps surprisingly, prostitution as a specific act was not illegal in the United States until 1917, when the first law banning it was adopted in Massachusetts.[48] During the early quarter of this century, the "purity crusaders" succeeded in obtaining criminal sanctions against prostitution across the country. Today, prostitution is illegal, though often tolerated, throughout the country except in thirteen Nevada counties that have legalized brothel prostitution.

According to one study, nearly half a million prostitutes worked in the United States in the few years prior to 1986.[49] A 1979 study estimated there were 292,000 full-time U.S. prostitutes but that marginal prostitution "at least equals, and probably substantially exceeds" full-time prostitution.[50] In 1988, Diane French estimated that 1.3 million U.S. women worked as prostitutes, while a 1993 study estimated that 5 million U.S. women between the ages of sixteen and sixty-four have engaged in some form of sex work.[51] Ninety-nine thousand people were arrested in the United States for prostitution and prostitution-related charges in 1996. New York City saw 9,746 arrests for prostitution in 1990 and 6,371 in 1995, but in 2000 there were 9,344 arrests despite the fact that, according to New York Police Department spokesperson Detective Walter Burnes, "Prostitution as a profession has kind of pushed its way out of New York City."[52] "In 1985, police in the nation's sixteen largest cities made as many arrests for prostitution as for all violent crimes combined."[53]

Despite these figures, in reality U.S. law enforcement, like that globally, tolerates most prostitution while reflecting the existing politics of power. In the United States "the aim of legislation and enforcement strategies is mostly symbolic. The goal is to control prostitution, not to eliminate it."[54] The likelihood and degree of tolerance varies among states, cities, communities, and neighborhoods and depends on a host of factors, ranging from visibility of the activity to whether it is an election year. Prostitution is usually tolerated in large urban areas unless the community mobilizes against it. Predictably, enforcement of existing laws against prostitution reflects gender discrimination; it is applied relatively infrequently against male customers, despite the fact that both sides of the transaction are prohibited in most jurisdictions. Of those arrested for prostitution, approximately 70 percent are women; male customers constitute only about 10 percent of prostitution-related arrests.[55]

Enforcement in the United States further reflects the global bias against visibility. Prostitution is tolerated unless "we have to look at it." Although it is estimated that only 10 to 15 percent of U.S. prostitutes are streetwalkers, streetwalking is the source of 85 to 90 percent of prostitute arrests. (Enforcement of laws barring streetwalking has increased here while lessening in Europe.) Because streetwalking generally involves significantly poorer and more disenfranchised women, the result of this selective enforcement is that poor and undereducated women with few employment options are more likely to be arrested than those who are financially better off.[56] Control of streetwalking in the United States has involved not only creating more laws but also utilizing vague ordinances such as anti-loitering regulations, which "allow the authorities to arrest either 'any person' or 'any known person' . . . if they repeatedly attempt to engage passersby in conversation or beckon to them. . . . They do not require that any specific behavior be observed, only that gestures or utterances be noted." Similarly, ordinances against "mashing" criminalize "accosting, insulting, or following a person of the opposite sex."[57] Such vague laws are certain to be enforced in a discriminatory manner, not only against women who are actually engaged in prostituting but also against known prostitutes who are not working,[58] former prostitutes, or for that matter any women deemed to be "suspicious."

Patterns of legal tolerance of prostitution strongly reflect U.S. racism. According to Eleanor Miller, Kim Romenesko, and Lisa Wondolkowski, although women of color constitute approximately 40 percent of streetwalkers, they constitute 55 percent of those arrested for streetwalking

and 85 percent of those incarcerated.[59] The effect of these vague ordinances and the bias in enforcement is evidenced by the chilling case of
Yvonne Elizabeth Dotson, "a 48-year-old African American nurse who
also holds a Master's in Public Health from the University of California,
Berkeley" who, on February 23, 1993," while waiting *inside* the . . . Re-
gency Garage to pick up her car . . . was arrested by two San Francisco
officers on suspicion of engaging in prostitution." After the police informed her they would not accept bail at the station, "she was . . . re-
handcuffed, transported in the police van to the Hall of Justice where
she was booked, fingerprinted, and photographed, and finally
released."[60] Such instances underline that "the sexual and civil rights of
any woman [and especially any black woman] are only as secure as the
rights of any whore."[61]

In addition to the problem of biased and arbitrary enforcement is the
issue of police assault. Prostitute rights activist Norma Jean Almodovar
stated, "I would like to address the issue of violence towards prostitutes,
much of which comes from the police. I speak from experience both in a
police department and as a prostitute. Policemen force prostitutes to
have sex with them before arrest."[62] Indeed, rape of prostitutes by the
police is regularly reported, but actions against those accused is almost
never forthcoming.

Individual prostitutes generally do not limit their activity to one form of
prostitution, commonly participating in two or more venues during the
same time period. Although I have been unable to locate any similar figures for the United States, a 1990 study in Denmark found that 70 percent of prostitution occurred in massage parlors or brothels, 15 percent
with streetwalkers, 12 percent with bar prostitutes, and 3 percent with
escorts. Given the amount of U.S. advertising devoted to escort services
(the Internet, yellow pages, and "throwaway" newspapers are filled with
their ads, even in relatively small towns), I suspect that escorts are a
larger part of the industry here.

Streetwalking consistently appears to be the most risky form of prostitution. The life of a U.S. streetwalker, like that of streetwalkers globally, tends to be decidedly harsh; she/he begins from a position of comparative vulnerability and goes on to face a far higher likelihood of arrest and incarceration relative to prostitutes working in brothels, escort
services, sadism-and-masochism (S&M) clubs, massage parlors, hotels,
bars, or homes. Both her relative vulnerability and the social ostracism

expressed by more frequent incidents of arrest and incarceration put the streetwalker at greater risk for customer abuse. Mimi Silbert and Ayala Pines's study revealed that of two hundred streetwalkers in the Bay Area, 70 percent reported rape by customers or that clients "went beyond the work contract," 66 percent said they had been "beaten many times by customers," and an equal number reported being "beaten regularly by their pimps."[63] Streetwalkers are at significant risk for customer abuse for a variety of reasons. In general, they tend to be a more "desperate" population than those in other types of prostitution. Many are terribly poor, usually with dependents, or drug addicted, or both. They experience significantly higher rate of illness, especially from HIV/AIDS. The stigma of "dirt" attaches most strongly to these women because of their economic, racial (they are disproportionately women of color), and sexual (a large number are gay and transgendered)[64] makeup, as well as because of their visibility and the relatively small fees they charge. The virtual anonymity of the customer, lessening the likelihood of his being caught or punished if he is abusive, significantly increases risk. Additionally, the tendency for streetwalkers to provide services in isolated locations, particularly cars, where kidnapping and assaults will go unnoticed, increases vulnerability.[65] Figures on violence against streetwalkers are comparable to those on violence against homeless women since both populations "live on the street." This vulnerability, in turn, makes street-level prostitutes more likely to become involved with potentially abusive pimps.

A common organization of prostitution, particularly in larger cities and resort areas, is "bell-desk" or hotel prostitution. Hotel bell captains act as prostitute facilitators for guests, generally in exchange for 40 percent of a prostitute's fees. This process depends on an organized network involving at least tacit acceptance and sometimes active participation by security guards and hotel management. "Bell girls" have a relatively high status in prostitution, exceeded only by self-employed "call girls" and prostitutes on call to services with a select clientele. Bell captains maintain a list of twenty to seventy prostitutes whom they contact at guests' request. The captain then attempts to determine if the guest is a policeman or "could be potentially threatening." If he is cleared, the captain then contacts the women in order of the captain's "favorites," so there is significant pressure on the women to ingratiate themselves to him. Standard fees in Las Vegas in 1984 were $100 per hour or per male ejaculation—whichever came first.

Bell-desk prostitution greatly increases client security. While fees for "freelancers" and bell girls is similar, "there is the sharply reduced risk of being robbed or possibly blackmailed" when using bell-girl services.[66] Similarly, prostitutes benefit by this organization. In addition to the relative lack of anonymity of the client, whose identity is known by the bell captain, additional security measures are often instituted. In some hotels a prostitute is required to call the bell captain when she arrives in the room and when she is about to leave; he will meet her at a predetermined location in the hotel. This serves to protect the prostitute significantly, although the purpose of the procedure is to ensure that the captain receives his "fair cut." Relative to other forms of prostitution, bell-desk prostitutes also can increase the volume of their business because they don't have to waste time hustling in bars or on the street. If the prostitute is assaulted or arrested, however, she is expected to "take it on the chin," that is, not to report or make a fuss about an assault and never to implicate the bell captain in the event of her arrest. Currying favor with bell captains requires obedience to a variety of rules and may require providing free sexual services. It is also accepted that a bell captain may "beat the hell out of" a woman if he believes she is cheating him out of his cut. Because the hotels and local economies benefit from bell-desk prostitution if it is "controlled and discreet," it is a highly tolerated practice.

Escort services have become ubiquitous in contemporary American culture. Their organization varies widely, but in general, agencies advertise openly to provide escorts, or "private dancers," understood as a thinly veiled reference to prostitutes. Women are sent to a variety of private settings, a process that creates various levels of risk. When escort services allow client anonymity, worker vulnerability to assaults is increased. If, however, the service requires client identification, the woman is at less risk for violence. In New York City, one escort service manager I interviewed reported that her agency requires identification, including phone numbers and credit card numbers, when clients call in. The information is verified before a woman is sent out, and she is required to call in when she arrives, to reverify the information, and again when she leaves. The customer is informed beforehand of these procedures.[67] This agency, however, was rather expensive, with a minimum fee of several hundred dollars. The manager maintained that her agency had never had a problem with escorts being assaulted or abused[68] but indicated that many agencies, particularly less-expensive ones, had no security measures in place, sending women out with no information beyond an address. This appears to have been the case for Carmen Cash, who worked for an escort service in San Diego in 1994–95. Although the base rate for nude dancing was $175 an hour, and Cash charged an additional $325 to $1000 for intercourse, the agency appears to have provided no security measures. She reports being "scared almost all the time."[69] The independent call girl is likely to fare far better: "As an independent call girl working out of her own home, [Laura] Anderson can make as much as $250 per one-hour session, reject a customer for any reason without risking management displeasure, and come and go as she pleases. 'I have much more control this way.'"[70]

"Massage parlors" have also become commonplace, existing openly on the streets, in strip malls, and in mobile homes throughout the country. The term is often used synonymously with "brothels," although the former are distinguished by the fact that they constitute "fronts" that operate publicly by providing legal "therapeutic" massages. Both massage parlors and brothels involve wide ranges of organization. Charges vary dependent on anticipated clientele, as do working conditions. In East St. Louis, one of the parlors prosecuted in a sweep charged a basic fee of $30 to $40 per thirty minutes, but "the amount of the additional tip . . . would determine how sensual the massage was."[71] Generally, clients were charged $60 for manual stimulation, $100 for oral sex, and $150 for intercourse, with the massage parlor supplying condoms. Some massage parlors and brothels are centers for trafficked women. In the recent past, significant numbers of Korean women have reportedly been trafficked into U.S. massage parlors and many nontrafficked Korean women work there as well. According to Corpus Christi police Captain Luther Kim, there is a network of transient Korean prostitutes who know each other and staff massage parlors nationally.[72] In 1994, in a sweep of massage parlors in Nassau County, Long Island, of the 163 people arrested at thirty-one locations, 90 percent of the women were Korean nationals; most were divorced from American GIs, and otherwise unemployed, with an average age in their early forties. Because divorced women are stigmatized in Korea, these women remained here and returned to their former profession.[73]

At some parlors and brothels, women earn high fees. A sex worker at the Fantasy Club in East St. Louis reported earning between $300and $600 per day,[74] while Kim estimated that one woman, who complained that business was slow, had brought in $9,000 in the two-week period Kim worked undercover at a Corpus Christi parlor. The masseuse-prostitute kept half these untaxed fees, with the other half going to the parlor owner.[75] Security measures also run the gamut. Carol Leigh reported being "raped, at knifepoint, 16 years ago while she was working in a massage parlor, . . . where, despite the seedy neighborhood, the owner refused to hire a security guard for fear of alienating customers."[76] Conversely, "Iris" reported working in a parlor where clients were checked for weapons and entry and egress were controlled by large bouncers.[77] Some expensive "dance clubs" with private rooms for lap dances are equipped with cameras or peepholes for security.

Illegal brothels and massage parlors are often the source of considerable profits for owners. One East St. Louis owner of three brothels was estimated to have grossed about $5.5 million between 1989 and 1997.[78] Among the working conditions the women face are a variety of rules. Many massage parlors and brothels require that women line up when a customer enters so that he may have "his pick." At the East St. Louis facility, women were fined $25 for being late for a shift, $100 for missing a shift, and $300 for fighting. One hundred percent of room rental charges went to the owner, who required sex workers to have medical checkups, including STD tests, and banned a variety of dress.[79]

G. Legalized Prostitution

Brothel prostitution in certain jurisdictions in Nevada is the sole form of noncriminal prostitution in the United States, yet little is known by the general public about its actual functioning. For this reason, and because the majority of *non*feminist American public sentiment appears to favor legalization, I explain in detail how the practice is organized and regulated—information that constitutes compelling evidence against legalization.

Although much of the information that follows was gathered from traditional printed sources and documentary films,[80] much was also gained through observations and interviews that took place in Nevada in July 1994.[81] During that time, over a two-week period, I visited three Nevada brothels: the Mustang I and II (now closed by the Internal Revenue Service) and the Kit Kat Ranch. The conditions described here specifically apply to these brothels, although they are indicative of the larger practice.[82]

I initially attempted to access the brothels directly but was consistently informed that women were permitted entrance only under the auspices of

George Flint, president of the Nevada Brothel Owners Association.[83] Although I had hoped for a less controlled observation, once I contacted Mr. Flint, my reception—unlike that of some feminist authors[84]—was universally gracious. Because of the tenuous political position of legalized prostitution in Nevada, brothel owners appear to understand the value of good public relations. As the following discussion should make apparent, however, the problematic nature of the practice for women is evident, despite all efforts to "put a good face on it."

According to Flint, in Storey, Nye, and Lyon counties, 90 percent of legal brothel prostitutes are not Nevada residents. In 1994 only 250 women worked in legal brothels at any one time; the majority of prostitutes in Nevada work illegally in Reno and Las Vegas.[85] Despite the loss of potential profits, only women are permitted to perform sex work in legal brothels. When I asked Flint about male prostitutes, he maintained that the idea had been rejected as "unworkable." I suspect that brothel owners fear the political fallout surrounding the employment of gay or transgendered prostitutes.

I cannot sufficiently underscore the intensity of the impact of the physical environment of legalized Nevada brothels. They are both shocking and richly symbolic. Two of the three I visited, as is also the case at the infamous Chicken Ranch outside Las Vegas, were actually several mobile homes strung together. They, like *all* brothels according to Flint, are surrounded by high fences, some electrified, with barbed wire or spikes on top. Entrance and egress are controlled; you must be buzzed in and out. The Mustangs also had what appeared to be an unused lookout tower, reminiscent of a prison or fort. At one point Flint said (joked?) that the gates were installed to keep out "jealous wives."[86] The fences, of course, are about far more than that. They constitute a significant source of control of everyone connected to the brothel: "jealous wives," staff, clients, and sex workers. One of the workers I interviewed indicated that, historically, prostitutes had to bribe floor maids to leave before the end of their shifts.

Like many western states, Nevada traditionally tolerated prostitution. Before 1911, the state had no law specifically dealing with prostitution, prosecuting some acts under nuisance-abatement statutes. In 1911 and 1913, however, Nevada adopted laws that made streetwalking, pimping, pandering, and locating brothels near schools and churches illegal.[87] The law changed in a peculiarly indirect manner when, in 1971, the Nevada legislature accepted an amendment to a statute governing dance halls, escort services, and gambling games and devices that stated, "The license board shall not license anyone to operate a house of ill fame or repute for the purpose of prostitution in a county of 250,000 or more."[88] In 1978 the Nevada Supreme Court upheld that statute, ruling that it allowed for, albeit tacitly, the licensing of brothels in sixteen of Nevada's seventeen counties.[89] As a result, legalized prostitution has been established in seven counties (Nye, Esmeralda, Churchill, Lyon, Mineral, Eureka, and Storey) and in municipalities in five counties (Elko, Humboldt, Lander, Pershing, and White Pine).

There is some variety in the specifics of the ordinances, but Nye County's is reasonably representative of many. It establishes a board to license and regulate brothels while specifying permissible locations and limiting them to one in each of four communities. It requires all prostitutes be registered, undergo weekly medical exams, and have a valid police card (also required of casino and state employees), for which they are fingerprinted and undergo a police background check.[90] It also sets a minimum age for prostitutes—bizarrely, you must be eighteen years old to prostitute in a state whose minimum drinking age is twenty-one.

According to then sheriff Robert Delcarlo, in 1994 the Storey County licenses required to operate a brothel cost $35,000 per year. Work permits were required for *all* brothel employees, including runners, maids, and security.

Delcarlo maintained that policing of brothels with regard to age and immigration status of prostitutes, medical examinations, and so forth was handled by the state health department, not the police department, and that photos and fingerprints of prostitutes and other employees were kept on file by the health department for their inspections. But even after a tenacious search, I could locate no one at the health department who would claim responsibility for or knowledge of these supposed inspections.

In a 1983 article, Ellen Pillard noted with surprise that legal authorities in more than one jurisdiction explicitly acknowledged enforcing "the law in action" or "regulation by custom" in the governance of legal Nevada brothels. These included such rules as that all prostitutes must live in a licensed brothel and, when they have their one of every four weeks off, they must leave town, and that prostitutes' children cannot live in the community. The City of Winnemuca requires that prostitutes be inside the brothels by 5 P.M., and if a prostitute owns a car, it must be "registered with the police and its use is very limited." In some jurisdictions, prostitutes may not own cars at all. In Ely, written copies of the rules are handed to prostitutes when they register. These specify that a prostitute can go to movies but not to bars; indeed, she can go to restaurants with bars only if they have a separate side entrance, and then she may not be accompanied by a male escort or "she will not be allowed to return to this city or county."[91] Regulation of legal prostitution in Nevada effectively eliminates some of a woman's most basic presumed constitutional rights.

The brothels themselves enforce numerous unwritten regulations.[92] In general, women contract for from five-day to three-week (7 days a week) shifts. At the Mustangs, prostitutes were required to work twelve or fourteen hours a day and were not permitted to leave the premises at any time during their three-week shifts. At the Kit Kat Ranch, women worked anywhere from three to fourteen hours per day. The brothel is open twenty-four hours a day, seven days a week, with the preponderance of work occurring between 11 A.M. and 1 A.M. Brothel prostitutes are considered to be self-employed and thus receive no benefits. Each woman pays room and board[93] during her shift (in 1994, $15 a day), as well as for linens. She is also expected to "tip" each of the three shift managers $2 to $3 a day. Since they are not permitted to leave the property for the entirety of their sometimes three-week tours, the prostitutes have to pay runners to perform all errands, from purchasing toiletries to dropping off mail, at a charge of $10 per errand. They are also required to have and pay for weekly medical exams, at $25 per exam.

Each room is equipped with a "panic button" to alert security. Each room also has an audio bugging system, although the prostitutes I interviewed believed this was more to monitor their behavior, especially their monetary arrangements with clients, than a safety precaution. In various interviews I was told that historically, and even occasionally now, women have been "roughed up" by management to "keep them in line." Flint said that prostitutes' suitcases are searched each time they arrive for their shifts in order to prevent drugs from being brought onto the premises. Clients, however, are not searched. Prostitutes are required to negotiate the price and ground rules of each transaction and are responsible for making sure the men pay up front.

To my surprise, whenever I raised the issue of abuse with prostitutes, they consistently cited first financial abuse by brothel owners. The house takes 50 percent off the top of all income generated through prostitution fees, as well as 100 percent of profits from its bar and souvenir items.

Brothels, especially those near Reno and Las Vegas, encourage tourist trade by paying cab drivers to bring them business. Whenever a client arrives by taxi, cabbies receive 20 percent off the top of the entire bill, no matter how long the client stays or how expensive the services, even if the client was not actually referred by the driver, indeed, even if the client is a "regular." Half this fee comes directly off the prostitute's income. Delcarlo estimated that, on average, after all fees and service charges were deducted, prostitutes cleared $1,000 of every $5,000 paid for their services. If the estimates of Flint and "Pepper," one of the Mustang prostitutes, were correct, the average full-time sex worker at the Mustang cleared $40,000 before taxes in 1994.[94] An interesting side note underlining the brothel owners' concern about public image was Flint's response, three years later, to public criticism of Nevada brothels "for taking a high percentage of the women's earnings."[95] The *Las Vegas Sun* quoted Flint as saying, "The earnings are generally split 50–50."[96] Given the tacked-on charges, however, it is clear, as Flint explicitly acknowledged in our 1994 interview, that the actual split is closer to twenty-eighty.

Staff and management consistently view prostitutes with suspicion. They are presumed to be dishonest and eager to cheat the brothels of their "legitimate" cut. For example, the justification I encountered that was usually given for not permitting a prostitute to leave the premises during the entirety of her shift was concern that she would service clients outside and unbeknownst to the brothel. What was consistently ignored was that this risk is run by *all* service industries. Repair garages, hair salons, nursing or maid service agencies all run the risk that employees may "steal a customer" and provide additional services without paying the business its fee. I found the moral distrust—indeed, moral contempt—of prostitutes by brothel management to be a particularly pervasive and oppressive feature of the practice.

One of the more disturbing customs of Nevada legal brothel practice, which is shared with many illegal venues, is the lineup. Prostitutes are required literally to line up and pose whenever a new customer enters, thus displaying "his options." This presentation of women as merchandise is not only symbolically problematic but, I was told, emotionally demoralizing. One of the women I interviewed not only described her emotional struggle with this practice but also explained that brothel owners sometimes used the lineup as a form of punishment or abuse. She related one instance, early in the establishment of the Mustang I, when then-owner

Ms. Sally Conforti required all prostitutes to line up naked for the entirety of a shift. Although it had occurred many years before our interview, the woman was still visibly angry and upset by the incident. Worse, it is evident that the lineup is not justified by business needs. Not only do some legal brothels dispense with this "custom," but, according to Flint, 80 percent of clients decline selecting a woman from them, preferring to sit at the bar and interact with the women before choosing.

To understand the overall experience of the working conditions at these legalized brothels, it is important to understand that brothel prostitutes may not refuse a customer because he is "dirty, fat, ugly, smelly," and so forth. Indeed, according to Alberta Nelson, R.N., who was responsible for the medical exams at the Mustangs, prostitutes were permitted to refuse to service clients only if the clients were African Americans—"because of the size of their penises." (Yes, she actually said this!) In addition to racism, legalized brothel prostitution reflects the sexism and ageism of the larger society. "Pepper," who was fifty-nine, complained of her difficulty in competing with young women in a culture that rejects older women's sexuality.

My impression was that the overarching focus of brothel management was the satisfaction of its customers. Little interest was shown in the well-being of the workers. Rooms do have panic buttons and bugs that may increase prostitutes' safety. But, in general, customers are not viewed as a source of physical danger. Women are unlikely to suffer severe bodily assaults by customers simply because the physical logistics of these brothels make it difficult for an assaulter to flee. Some concern for medical harm is evidenced in the house rules: Not only are condoms required for intercourse and fellatio, but kissing and insertion of fingers in the vagina are against house rules; both are considered a possible source of illness, and the latter a source of possible injury. Some brothels also require Saran Wrap for cunnilingus, to prevent the spread of STDs. At least one woman told me, however, that such restrictions, especially the requirement of condoms, were regularly disregarded for an additional fee and that brothel management made no serious effort to prevent this.

In all my interviews, prostitutes appeared more concerned with possible assaults or abuse by facilitators than by customers. When pressed, however, the women I interviewed acknowledged that they occasionally encountered customers who were overly rough but that they shared techniques to prevent such instances or to deal with them if they arose.[97] Overall, with women in all forms and legal statuses of prostitution except for streetwalking, I consistently found that concern about customer assault was significantly less than I had expected. Sadly, however, those in prostitution appear even more likely than the society as a whole to blame the victim for rape. I was regularly told that if ("in the rare event") a customer raped a prostitute, it was because she was not sufficiently "professional"; otherwise, "this would never happen." As someone who has counseled rape victims for ten years, I found this attitude particularly disheartening.

During my observations in the brothels, I was struck by how uncomfortable, if not downright embarrassed, clients often appeared. Rather than the bravado I had anticipated, most were surprisingly meek and overtly polite and respectful. The only obvious exception was when young men entered in groups. Then, as in the case of window prostitution in Amsterdam, the men displayed "fraternity behavior," including high-fiving when one of them went off with a woman. In those cases, hiring prostitutes appears to be fundamentally an exercise in male bonding. Apparently, the awkwardness commonly experienced by clients continues even after the men go to the bedrooms. Two of the women I interviewed reported that they regularly begin with massages to ease the feeling of "being a stranger," both for the client's comfort and their own. According to the manager of the Kit Kat Ranch, "Some of the men come in here just to talk and get a massage," while some customers never hire prostitutes but come in only to drink and "sightsee."

Of the working prostitutes I interviewed, all indicated that they were motivated by money. Although working brothel prostitutes ranged in age from eighteen to at least fifty-nine, those I was permitted to interview were generally from the older end of the scale. Gena, a forty-five-year-old former secretary, had been prostituting for six months so she could afford to relocate her son, who was in trouble with the police. She saw it as her "last chance to make some real money" but said that the only way she could handle the job was not to think of what she was doing as prostitution. Pepper, who at fifty-nine had been working as a prostitute for eight years, said she "burned out" as a social worker for the state and turned to prostitution to enable herself to purchase a home and a motor home and to begin a business. She was providing for her retirement in a way her government pension would never allow. These stories were typical of the different women I interviewed. Most were looking to establish a stake for some long-term goal or to cover immediate expenses.

I was particularly lucky to have the opportunity to interview "Bridgit," who, at the age of seventy, managed the Kit Kat Ranch. She said she "was turned out at fourteen" and had consistently been involved with prostitution for fifty-six years. She was able to detail significant changes in brothel prostitution during this period. Although prostitutes were still expected to work fourteen-hour days, seven days a week at the Kit Kat, they were no longer required to work three weeks in a row. Fifteen to twenty years ago, prostitutes were expected to service twenty to twenty-five customers per day; now they are expected to service "only" five to six. According to Bridgit, previously "the girls were able to do anything," but today, with AIDS and other STDs, prostitutes' options are limited. Changes in sexual beliefs have also had significant effects on client-prostitute relations—now men are often concerned that the woman have or appears to have an orgasm.

Bridgit reported that the number of women willing to work for the brothels has narrowed considerably since the 1960s and 1970s. (Flint also indicated that legal brothels were experiencing some difficulty in locating sex workers.) She maintained that changes in work opportunities for women in general, as well as the increase in hazards through AIDS and other STDs, explained the relative lack of prostitute workers. Prostitutes and others, however, suggested that the lower numbers are the result of the severe financial exploitation and rigid, dehumanizing rules the brothels impose. Since most Nevada prostitutes prefer to work outside the legal system, even in riskier venues, the latter explanation appears far more compelling. I have great concern that the difficulty legal brothels have finding prostitute workers significantly increases the risk of trafficking. Given the physical logistics of the security conditions that exist in these brothels, it would be virtually impossible for the government to monitor who is actually employed there. Even in instances of surprise inspections, the brothels can control the entry of inspectors long enough to hide illegal (trafficked, underage, and unregistered) women. Given the financial exploitation and dehumanizing work conditions of legal brothels, perhaps the really puzzling question is why women choose to work for them at all. In general, women appear to do so because they fear the legal and apparent increased physical risks of illegal venues. I did not speak to a single prostitute worker who was genuinely satisfied with the legal brothel system.

It is clear that the legalized brothel system in Nevada not only does not "normalize" prostitution but actively enforces official and unofficial regulations that disempower and further stigmatize prostitutes. As Pillard accurately and succinctly states, it is a policy of "accepting prostitution, rejecting prostitutes."[98] "Gaming" (i.e., gambling) openly and ubiquitously permeates the Nevada culture and environment, with slot machines in supermarkets and airports, but legal brothels are isolated and hidden by law. While state statute forbids them from locating in Las Vegas's Clark County,[99] they are banned from Reno by Washoe County ordinance. Most brothels are literally "in the middle of nowhere" in rural areas. In 1994 three brothels were only nine miles from Reno, in a neighboring county, but they were clustered in an isolated area not visible from the highway or any other structure. In Lyon County, small, discreet signs on Highway 51 indicate the location of three brothels at the end of Kit Kat Road, zoned for brothels and salvage yards only. Because the stigma that attaches to prostitution is both intense and global, enforced registration, including photos and fingerprinting, particularly in the computer age, is a far more effective system for exposure than any scarlet letter could be. Further, the existing policy is one that makes "upward mobility" or even autonomy within the system highly unlikely. According to Sheriff Delcarlo, who helped create the 1994 Storey County policy, the brothel license fee of $35,000 a year was intended effectively to prevent individual women from owning small or self-employing brothels. It is clear that legalization is not to be confused with acceptance or normalization.

H. Prostitution as Current Practice—The Netherlands

As I indicated at the outset, I want to contrast American with Dutch prostitution law in part because the Netherlands "is known as one of the least repressive countries for prostitution," whereas the United States has "the most repressive approach towards prostitution of all western industrial democracies."[100] Contrary to the belief of many Americans, this is not because the Dutch have a lower moral standard. In fact, the Dutch are, in many respects, a morally "strict" society, heavily influenced by Calvinist traditions in the north and Catholic ones in the south. They have a higher rate of teenage virginity than the United States, and prostitution still suffers significant social stigmata.[101] Nor are differences in approach attributable to a "homogeneity" in the Dutch population, as is sometimes alleged. The Netherlands, although quite small, is in fact extremely diverse, particularly in Amsterdam and the Hague as well as in smaller cities. And, as Jan Visser notes, this diversity has required that all governments be built on coalitions, demanding a populace capable of adaptation and compromise.[102] Additionally, the Dutch economy is deeply dependent on global trade, forcing the Dutch to recognize and accommodate differences in values and norms. The differences in the American and Dutch positions appear to me more a product of an intense Dutch pragmatism[103] and exceedingly different approaches to governance. Unlike the United States, the Dutch are loath to criminalize behaviors *purely* on the basis of morality or legal paternalism. Additionally, the Dutch criminal justice system appears to function effectively with a striking degree of police "tolerance." The Dutch regularly pass laws that legislators intend to be enforced only when some associated crime is being committed or a public nuisance created. Police tolerance is not the decision of individual police officers but constitutes an official policy. "In the Dutch legal system the Ministry of Justice can declare that public prosecution will refrain from prosecuting in certain fields."[104]

Dutch prostitution policy cautiously and insistently reflects the participation of diverse groups, often with conflicting interests and goals, including politicians; civil servants; prostitutes; those in criminal justice, medicine, and social work; the Red Thread prostitute union; brothel owners; the general public, especially those in locations most affected by prostitution; and the Mr. A. de Graaf Foundation. The de Graaf, originally established by private trust but now subsidized in large part by the Dutch Ministry of Public Health, embodies the Dutch approach to policy by attempting to diminish problems associated with prostitution through research and education. "We support the general aims of the government to normalise the relations in prostitution and to accept prostitution as a profession."[105]

Acts of prostitution between consenting adults are decriminalized in the Netherlands, as in almost all Western European nations.[106] Prostitution exists in one-third of Dutch municipalities, particularly in larger cities and along the German and Belgian borders; twelve cities contain window prostitution, where two thousand prostitutes work daily, while ten cities permit streetwalking (with 320 women estimated to streetwalk daily.) Nationally, between six hundred and seven hundred apartments and sex clubs (closed brothels) employ thirty-five hundred to four thousand prostitutes each day. No figures on home workers or escort services were available, nor were data on legal alien status; however, "in some regions, foreign illegal women [i.e., undocumented non–European Union members] were a majority."[107] The de Graaf estimates that there are twenty-thousand "professional prostitutes" currently in the Netherlands. Their income varies significantly, though fees have not increased in twenty years. The de Graaf maintains that prostitute income is generally exaggerated; once one accounts for hours spent waiting for clients, most average 30 guilders an hour (U.S. $12.52/hour), with call girls averaging 61 guilders an hour ($25.46/hour) and home workers, 81 guilders an hour ($33.80/hour). However, the latter two groups do not work full time, so their annual income approximates that of window and brothel workers.

Like other nations, the Dutch distinguish between prostitution and facilitation. Traditionally, Dutch law made it illegal to engage in "a profession or habit of causing or encouraging indecent acts by others"[108] or "living off the earnings of a prostitute."[109] But Dutch tolerance resulted in the acceptance of brothels, sex clubs, escort services, and, in specified locations, street and window prostitution,[110] as long as no associated crimes or public disorder resulted. On October 1, 2000, this policy of tolerance was formalized: The Dutch legalized "organizing the [consensual] prostitution of an adult female or male person." Article 250a of the Dutch Penal Code made only forced prostitution, prostituting a minor, and trafficking illegal. The maximum sentence for those crimes was increased to six years, and brothels and sex clubs were required to be licensed and to meet standardized occupational health and safety conditions. Legislators justified these changes based on the need to control and contain the industry, to combat forced or underage prostitution and prostitution-related crime, to improve the lot of prostitutes, and to lower the number of illegal immigrants.

Specifics of policies are left up to local municipalities, but the national government has "prepared a number of blueprints and suggestions [on] how to organise this legalisation on a community and regional level,"[111] including for licensing, criminal justice enforcement, and aid for victims of trafficking. Amsterdam, which has imposed licensing restrictions since 1996, has already seen several brothels closed because they were unable to meet restrictions on worker immigration status. This law also provides police with the newly acquired power to ask prostitutes for identification papers (e.g., passports or driver's licenses) in order to determine age, nationality and immigration status. By law, if the individual is working legally, the police are barred from recording names. Currently, the police appear reluctant to make use of this potential source of abuse of power. Those within the prostitute rights sector, however, fear this is simply due to police concern with negative press coverage. They worry that the long-term effects of this policy may drive underground prostitutes who seek anonymity. In 1997, in response to the horrors of sex tourism involving children, the Dutch passed a law that allows for the possibility of prosecuting, in the Netherlands, a Dutch citizen for having sex with a minor in another country.

According to my 1995 interview with policewomen Hordine Verhees, head of the Amsterdam prostitution and vice unit, and Andrea Rietberger, head of the unit dealing with Amsterdam streetwalkers, there were at the time ten thousand prostitutes in Amsterdam, the Netherlands' largest city. Amsterdam then had 65 heterosexual brothels (clubs), eleven gay brothels, 430 windows in three locations, seven peep shows (women behind windows masturbating), six live-sex theaters, one hundred home workers (women who prostitute from their homes), sixty-five escort offices, three S&M clubs, twenty massage parlors, and three hundred to four hundred streetwalkers. While the law required that prostitutes be eighteen, uncoerced, and legal residents, the policewomen estimated that 70 percent of window and 30 percent of club prostitutes were illegal immigrants. They believed thirteen to fifteen prostitutes had been killed between 1985 and 1995.[112]

The recent Dutch response to streetwalking has been creative and relatively successful, particularly at lessening prostitute risks of assault. As of 1998, safe parks had been established in six Dutch municipalities. These are areas where a man can drive in, survey the available prostitutes, select one, and proceed to a car stall with the person he has hired. The stalls are separated by metal barriers high enough to provide privacy but adjacent to one another so that cries for help are likely to be heard. They are constructed so that it is hard to back out of them—giving the prostitute additional opportunity to get help if the client attempts to kidnap her (or him). Stalls are equipped with wastebaskets for condom disposal. Parks are open from 9 P.M. to 6 A.M., 365 days a year. It is estimated that eighty prostitutes per day use the Amsterdam park and about twenty per day use the parks in smaller cities. Police are posted at the entrance to these "parks" to further discourage kidnapping and abuse but are barred from collecting names, license plate numbers, or other identifying information.

All Dutch parks have "living rooms" or shelters associated with them. In 1995, these were run by private foundations: the Stichting HAJ in

Amsterdam and the HAP Foundation in Utrecht. (The former is a prostitution-saving organization fighting to abolish prostitution, the latter more neutral.) According to Hilda Blank of the Stichting HAJ, the year before the parks opened witnessed three known cases of streetwalkers killed by clients, and every night a minimum of one rape, often violent, was reported to the organization. In the six months after they opened, there were no known murders or assaults requiring hospitalization connected to the Amsterdam park. Some rapes occurred in the stalls, but all had resulted in arrests. According to the HAP Foundation, although there were some relatively less violent rapes and assaults, only one kidnaping and severe assault took place in the first eighteen months at the Utrecht park. Although both instances are far from exemplary, they appear to have significantly decreased the violence streetwalkers are otherwise subject to.

The living rooms provide invaluable resources for streetwalkers, including a place where they can take a break, escape the weather, have a cup of coffee, eat and talk with colleagues and staff, and obtain condoms. Some provide a hot shower; others offer referrals to social agencies, negotiations with the police, AIDS prevention education campaigns for clients, as well as detailed public information. Social workers and doctors are generally available at least twice weekly for consultations, but STD testing is *never* required. Some living rooms advise prostitutes who are drug addicts on safe use of needles and condoms. Amsterdam even provides a makeup specialist to help women with their self-image. Collegial conversations include discussions of safety issues, while in Amsterdam there is a bulletin board where prostitutes post warnings about dangerous and difficult clients, including a description of the man and his car.

The establishment of the parks was motivated by the belief that complete repression of streetwalking is counterproductive. Streetwalking often involves drug addiction, including underage addicts. Arresting streetwalkers undermines the government's ability to extend health and social services to them—trust is lost, and it becomes harder to locate them. Sweeps encourage streetwalkers to engage in high-risk behavior— the streetwalker has less time to assess a client and is more likely to get into a car with more than one man. "It is well documented that in periods of frequent police raids, the women [were] more [often] robbed, raped and assaulted."[113] Repression of streetwalking also caused dissension and dissatisfaction within police departments. Uniformed officers were frustrated by the uselessness of such arrests (streetwalking arrests merely result in revolving-door policies),[114] and conflicted with the work of plainclothes officers in the vice squad, who were concerned with maintaining good relations with the women since their primary function was to solve rape and assault cases. The Dutch, however, like most communities, were unwilling fully to decriminalize streetwalking because of concern about public order and nuisance. "Residents kept complaining that their privacy was being invaded and that they could not sleep at night because of the cars queuing in front of their canal mansions."[115] But as Visser notes, it is difficult to assess nuisance objectively; streetwalking is problematic mainly due to noise from cars and shouting people and additional street litter. It is clear, however, that "the source . . . [from] which it derives makes the difference; that [source] brings about feelings of psychological emotional and moral nuisance that cannot be simply reasoned away."[116] Community concerns that prostitution and related crimes will spread, that property values will be lowered, and that those living in streetwalking areas will be viewed with contempt cannot simply be dismissed. "Residents often claim that they have the right to live without activities that society condemns as immoral in front of their homes."[117] The ever-pragmatic Dutch therefore settled on these "safe parks" as the best current solution.

The success of these parks is largely dependent on community reaction, especially to their location. According to Visser, Dutch tolerance depends upon the maintenance of public order.[118] In Amsterdam, in response to public outcry, the park was located at the very edge of the city in a warehouse area. It is difficult to reach by public transportation and so isolated that coming or going by bus would be quite dangerous after dark without police oversight. Indeed, in 1998 the park was used primarily by Latin American transsexual prostitutes, but "the place is so remote from the inner city, that only a few of the drug using prostitutes— for which the zone was intended—do go and work there. Many prefer to stay in the centre where the drugs are and take into account the risk of being arrested."[119] As the Dutch have learned, locating parks more centrally requires a significant educational and political campaign. Indeed, a lengthy attempt to locate a park in Herleen, a provincial city in the Catholic south, has failed due to public protest. (Residents of the impacted area occupied the park for months during hours when it was intended for streetwalkers.) Conversely, in the Hague, where the park was located in "a minor industrial area" due to the political weight and astuteness of the mayor, the park has been a significant success. The parking boxes, which are decorated with small trees, by day are used by employees from the small factories in the area. But because the park is sufficiently central to the city (near one of the main railway stations), it is also used by the target population at night. The mayor established a forum to handle complaints from residents and users, which has aided significantly in lessening community concerns about the project. It is clear, however, that those involved in Dutch prostitution policy development see these parks as "works in progress" that will, through education, ultimately enable the development of more centrally located parks.

On the other end of the Dutch prostitution spectrum is the member of a small cooperative brothel. One of my interviews was with Petra, a college-educated Dutch woman in her late twenties or early thirties. Along with two other prostitutes, Petra had rented an apartment and hired a "motherly" and highly efficient older Dutch woman to act as a secretary-receptionist. (It was she who scheduled my appointment with Petra.) Petra was totally self-employed and paid taxes on her earnings. She clearly considered prostituting a profession and was extremely professional in her approach. All Petra's clients came as referrals. The receptionist arranged client appointments so that the apartment was never used by more than one prostitute at the same time, largely to avoid the appearance of a brothel. The receptionist also met the clients at the door, making her presence in the apartment obvious in order to discourage any untoward behavior. She clearly constituted a potential witness to any abuse while still maintaining a friendly atmosphere.

Petra is unquestionably a prostitutes' rights advocate, defending her decision to prostitute and indicating significant job satisfaction. Prostitution, she reported, allowed her to earn more than would be possible in a "straight" job. The independence and income she obtained through prostituting enabled her to travel extensively while she was still young. She said that outside the profession, sex was of no interest to her; she apparently had no libidinal drive. As will become clear, this factor, along with her education and organizational and business skills, contributed to Petra's ability to flourish as a prostitute. After our interview, and totally on her own initiative, she made a follow-up call to me to be certain we had covered all the issues I wanted to discuss.

The relative autonomy and high income women such as Petra find through prostitution must not be dismissed. Although she is not the norm among Dutch prostitutes, she is also not an anomaly. As the Dutch studies described below indicate, many women find real satisfaction and independence in prostituting. But the ability to do so appears to depend significantly on both the abilities of the woman and the organizational structure under which she prostitutes. Small, cooperative brothels seem to be one of the more successful arrangements for women's well-being and autonomy.

During the 1990s in the Netherlands, a variety of social scientists began to generate research that differed dramatically from the information previously available about the prostitution industry and prostitutes' lives. The first such work to be translated into English, and the only one I know of to date, is Ine Vanwesenbeeck's *Prostitutes' Well-Being and Risk*. In this groundbreaking work, the experiences and psychological states of prostitutes working in all forms of prostitution were analyzed.

The subjects of Vanwesenbeck's two studies described in the book were women working in Dutch prostitution. The population was preponderantly Dutch but included immigrant prostitutes, especially from Germany and Latin America. Therefore, the results cannot be assumed to be representative of U.S. prostitutes' experience. Two differences of particular significance between the Dutch and American experience of prostitution are that acts of prostitution have been decriminalized since early in the twentieth century in the Netherlands and the Dutch public stance on prostitution is significantly less stigmatizing. (However, as Vanwesenbeeck notes, "Public discourse contrasts with the widespread ambivalent or even negative private opinions and behavior.")[120] For these reasons, one should assume that the experiences of prostitutes in the Netherlands is, overall, more positive than that of U.S. prostitutes.[121]

Vanwesenbeeck's study of well-being describes broadly "how someone fares."[122] "Well-being" involves the ability to adapt to "(ever changing) environmental demands and the ability to manage 'stressful life events'."[123] It is a product of the individual's personality, the context in which the individual functions, and the interaction of these factors and reflects subjective as well as objective assessments, that is, the way an individual perceives his or her situation as well as objective criteria. The study includes the context-related factors of stigmatization, financial need, migration, working conditions, and demographics, including age and education. Personality factors considered include previous stressful life events, especially childhood trauma and adult victimization, and "health locus of control"—broadly, the degree to which individuals perceive themselves to be in control of their own situation and able to solve problems, as opposed to perceiving their experiences as controlled by external agents. Prostitutes' coping behaviors are also an important factor in Vanwesenbeeck's analysis.

Under the umbrella of well-being, Vanwesenbeeck considered psychosomatic complaints; work-related physical complaints; emotional well-being, for example, depression, anxiousness, and aggression directed outward and inward; social problems; social insecurity; and job satisfaction. The studies cover issues of "protective behavior" involving, for example, condom usage, coping behaviors, and drug usage, as well as sexual and physical violence on and off the job and throughout the life of the subjects.

As opposed to earlier research that focused solely on streetwalkers, the two studies in this work included subjects involved in other forms of prostitution. The Dutch National Center for the Fight Against AIDS estimates the percentage of prostitutes engaged in the different types of prostitution to be as follows: streetwalking, 10 percent; window prostitution, 30 percent; clubs and brothels, 30 percent; escort services, 15 percent; and home workers, 15 percent. Vanwesenbeeck attempted to reflect these percentages in her two studies.[124]

The results support Vanwesenbeeck's contention that "when it comes to well-being, 'the' prostitute does not exist. . . . Where well-being, job satisfaction, and risk management are concerned, at least three totally different groups of prostitutes work in prostitution in The Netherlands."[125] Approximately one-quarter of the women studied suffer severely—even more "than the average of the control group of heavily traumatized non-prostitute women." Approximately half of the women studied are certainly doing far better than normally presumed—"only slightly less well than the average non-prostitute." And, surprisingly, more than one-quarter are faring "quite well," that is, "even better than the average non-prostitute."[126]

The differences in how women fare appear to depend on five factors: childhood experiences, economic situation, working conditions, survival strategies, and interaction with clients. Overall, women who were sexually abused as children are more likely to be "physically or sexually victimized by private partners as adults, including being forced into prostitution." Prostitute childhood sexual trauma survivors fare far worse physically and emotionally, suffering more psychosomatic complaints and far greater "social insecurity" ("low self-esteem, anxieties, fears, and depression"). They are prone to greater risk taking—especially "relatively often and non-selectively having work sex without a condom." Vanwesenbeeck maintains, "Having been traumatized in private life before entering prostitution determines to a large extent how one fares once one works in prostitution, and accounts strongly for differences between prostitutes." Indeed, child sexual abuse is a stronger determinant of psychosomatic complaints than are "victimizing experiences" once in the profession. This revelation, however, simply mirrors the results of Dutch studies of nonprostitute women: that is, a childhood sexual abuse survivor is likely to fare relatively badly, whether the women is a prostitute or not.

The economic situation of a prostitute, like that of childhood experience, demonstrates a clear correlation between vulnerability and "faring badly" within prostitution. Women in the studies were "relatively low educated women with little opportunity for economical gain."[127] Far fewer were married than the general population of women in their age group (21 percent versus 71 percent, although 68 percent had "a steady male partner"). They had a slightly higher rate of child custodial responsibility (50 percent versus 43 percent among women in the general population under age thirty-eight) while having significantly greater economic responsibility for their households (66 percent of prostitutes versus 4 percent of women generally are the main contributors to household income, among women with male partners.)[128] Those in the most dire economic need were either responsible for large household expenses or were drug dependent. "Our data show that increasing economic need is related to lower levels of well-being and job satisfaction as well as to working more often without a condom."[129] At highest risk were those women who would never prostitute but for great economic necessity. "Abuse by a private partner" was often the source of this extreme economic need. Many women prostituted after fleeing an abusive partner on whom they were economically dependent or because drug addiction is more common with "histories of traumatization." "Grinding economic need, often in combination with experiences of abuse and partner violence," clearly correlates to faring poorly in prostitution. Almost all prostitute women in dire financial need had been victimized in their private lives.[130]

Contrary to the propensity to paint prostitutes with one broad brush, the evidence demonstrates that prostitute well-being depends significantly on working conditions. Streetwalkers and window prostitutes fare relatively poorly. Although "the frequency of drug use and abuse among prostitutes is generally overstated,"[131] street prostitutes are unquestionably the most likely to use drugs. (It is important to note that of the women who used drugs, especially heroin, two-thirds started using before entering prostitution.)[132] Additionally, those with "a relatively high number of clients," or those who "have a faster working routine," or who are paid less per client (generally, streetwalkers and window prostitutes) fare relatively badly. Women working in "unorganized" forms of prostitution ("in window, streets and, to a lesser extent, at home") felt less at ease on the job than those working in organized settings (clubs and brothels). Vanwesenbeeck attributes this to the "less stable social network and frame of reference" as well as to the lack of protection and support in "unorganized" prostitution. The isolation of street and window prostitution makes women particularly vulnerable to physical and sexual assault and harassment, which are associated with "more severe psychosomatic complaints and social insecurity and lower job satisfaction." The stress of the situation is exacerbated by the fact that rape and assault of prostitutes are dismissed or denied by the larger society and often blamed on the prostitute.[133]

Why, then, would women "choose" to work in these unorganized forms of prostitution? The answer once again is that these are generally the most vulnerable populations, women who "have been victimized in their private lives," are in greater economic need, are migrants, or are drug addicted. They tolerate lower fees, more customers, and greater danger because they are "more willing to settle for anything they can get, although perhaps reluctantly. For these survivors, the negative effect of bad working conditions seems to be in line with the negative effect of their burdened life-histories."[134] However, brothel and club prostitution are certainly not ideal. Indeed, as in Nevada, prostitutes in the Netherlands repeatedly complained of economic exploitation by and dehumanizing regulations of brothel owners. Significantly, Vanwesenbeeck concludes, "It is our strong impression that if safer independent working sites were available, many women would prefer these."[135]

Vanwesenbeeck's research deals extensively with prostitutes' "survival strategies" and coping mechanisms. She accepts R. L. Silver and C. B. Wortman's definition of "coping responses" as "everything a person does, feels or thinks in reaction to a negative, stressful or victimizing condition or event."[136] Responses are divided into two categories: "problem-focused reactions" and "emotion-focused reactions." The former "refer to a manipulation of the stressful situation and/or attempts to change external problematic conditions" (e.g., "direct intervention, purposeful action" gathering relevant information, seeking help), while the latter involve "internal manipulation of one's own feelings or cognition in order to be able to bear the emotional distress which is the result of the stressful situation or event" (e.g., "seeking diversion, wishful thinking, self-blame, tension reduction, identification with the aggressor, dissociation, denial and redefining the problem").[137] Although problem-focused reactions are not always successful (they "are especially harmful and frustrating when change is altogether impossible"),[138] overall they appear to be a more effective long-term strategy than emotion-focused reactions. While emotion-focused reactions are effective in the short run, "they may be associated with psychosomatic and psycho-social problems in the long run." They lessen immediate emotional impact but interfere with the development of problem-solving behavior that might ultimately ameliorate the situation. In addition, they generate unhealthy behavior such as smoking and drug abuse.

The coping reaction employed depends on individual personality differences as well as the nature and severity of the situation. Emotion-focused reactions are more likely the greater the anxiety and tension, the more insurmountable and hopeless the problem appears, and when coping resources such as status and control are less available. The fewer protective resources (such as social support) available, the more likely people are to turn to emotional manipulation and distancing. As is commonly recognized, prostitutes often use internal survival strategies, manipulating their emotions through denial, dissociation, and palliative reasoning. "There was a remarkably high reporting of dissociative experiences such as depersonalization ('feeling as if I'm not in my own body' or 'as if I'm not myself')."[139]

Reliance on emotion-focused strategies generally is associated with faring worse, experiencing less job satisfaction, and greater risk taking. Vanwesenbeeck argues that a number of factors account for the prevalence of emotion-focused reactions, especially dissociation. First, the very nature of the work appears to make these reactions necessary:[140]

> It seems as if a certain dissociative "proficiency" is called for to be able to work professionally or at all. Although this also holds true for other professions like service occupations, house work, police work, working as a surgeon, or stressful occupations in general, it holds pre-eminently

true for prostitution. Not only is the work of an extremely intrusive character, calling for the "switching off" of certain kinds of awareness and consciousness, but it is also "emotion work." . . . Prostitution is a kind of labour where one has to act in a way that is known to be false or that actually transforms one's feelings. Prostitution work is to a certain extent built up from fake behavior and untrue emotions on the part of prostitutes; they *play* the whore, they are *on the game*. In this context, it is extremely likely that problem feelings of all kinds are being split off, denied and dissociated.[141]

However, the likelihood of emotion-focused reactions in prostitution is also tied to a variety of related socially constructed features, specifically the secrecy and stigma attached to the work; the lack of alternative coping resources, especially status and control; and the lack of supportive social structures and services. But here again, there is great variety in the experiences of individual prostitutes. Prostitutes who are particularly vulnerable are also most likely to turn to emotion-focused reactions as coping mechanisms. Women with histories of violent victimization, particularly of childhood sexual trauma, who work in the more vulnerable forms of prostitution (i.e., windows and streets), experience the greatest amount of dissociation and denial. Vanwesenbeeck maintains, "The more prevalent use of internal coping strategies and the connected high prevalence of victimizing experiences, in fact, explain to a large extent why prostitutes as a group fare less well than other women."[142] Younger women are also more likely to dissociate than older ones, but Vanwesenbeeck notes that this mirrors the differential in the larger population and may also be the result of a "sample-effect."

Finally, differences in how prostitutes interact with clients are significant to their well-being and job satisfaction. Those who are or feel helpless in those interactions are most likely to fare poorly, to take risks, to work in "dangerous sites" (windows and streets), and thus to be confronted with troublesome and recalcitrant customers with whom they often "engage in fight scenarios." Of this group of risk-taking prostitutes Vanwesenbeeck maintains:

Their interaction with [their clients] is characterized by extreme powerlessness and a lack of grip on the situation they find themselves in. . . . We tend to see this lack of control over clients as another manifestation of the lack of grip they have on their own lives; we consider this to be the consequence of learned helplessness as a result of their extremely burdened life histories and an ongoing decreasing capacity to shape their lives according to their own wishes.[143]

Thus, contrary to common conceptions, the experiences of prostitutes cannot be generalized into one coherent and consistent picture. The vast majority of women prostitutes fare "slightly worse" than the average nonprostitute woman. For approximately 25 percent of prostitutes, the experience ranges from bad to nightmarish. But the vast majority of this group represent a population that was especially vulnerable prior to their entry into prostitution. These are women who are most likely to have suffered childhood or adult nonprostitute violence and sexual assault, to be poor, to be unmarried while having a greater-than-average economic burden, to be immigrants, to be drug dependent, or to utilize weak survival strategies. They are, in effect, the ready-made victims of exploitation and abuse. Not surprisingly, they generally become involved in the most abusive and unprotected forms of prostitution, especially streetwalking and window prostitution, where they must deal with a relatively high number of clients, spend less time with each, and receive less pay per client. Conversely, approximately 25 percent fare better than the average woman. These women work in an organized setting where they are less likely to experience violence on the job. They are self-employed, able to determine their own working conditions, and thus able to serve fewer clients but earn more per customer. They are not migrants, are well educated, a bit older, and have a level of professionalism that makes them unlikely to work without condoms. Petra's organized "home work," really a small cooperative brothel, unquestionably appeared to me to constitute the best arrangement for prostitutes; self-employment provides the woman with relative autonomy, safety, and an extraordinary degree of independence, while the more relaxed atmosphere of the brothel allows less risk-taking behavior. It is clear, however, that to establish such an arrangement, prostitutes must "have their act together." They must have some economic resources and organizational skills and not be desperate in any sense.

The importance of the social science data cannot be underestimated or dismissed by those analyzing prostitution policy. These data, along with the voices of some of the prostitutes I interviewed, forced me to give up the essentialist anti-prostitution position I held when I began this project. The lesson here is one that should be familiar to feminists. In the early days of second-wave feminism, women spoke of "women's experience," failing to understand that what we described were the experiences of white, middle-class, American (or Western European), noncolonized women. It took a good deal of struggle for the movement and related academic literature to understand the reality of multicultural experience. Until now, many feminists who have done an extraordinary service by uncovering the severe abuse that occurs in the most exploitative forms of prostitution have refused to hear the voices of diverse experiences. They have refused to admit that for some prostitutes the experience is not one of violence or abuse; they have refused to understand that a woman's background, including race, class, and individual life history, will impact significantly on her experience in prostitution. It is my sincere hope that the studies currently coming out of the Netherlands will force a reconsideration of what are, essentially, absolutist positions on prostitution. It is time to call an end to the "prostitution war" as well as to the "sex war." This diverse picture of prostitution clearly calls for a policy that is sensitive to and distinguishes among the experiences of those in the industry. While the experiences of those in the better-faring 75 percent (whose experiences are only slightly worse or better than the average non-prostitute) call for improved working conditions, the experiences of those in the worse-faring 25 percent call for special legal and social protections, both for those already in prostitution and for those in the vulnerable populations described, to ensure that they have genuine alternative.

Finally, any discussion of prostitution as current practice is decidedly incomplete unless it speaks to the issue of stigmatization. Although Vanwesenbeeck's studies do not test specifically for this factor, she devotes a significant amount of space to discussing how stigmatization impacts on the well-being of prostitutes. To say that prostitutes suffer from social stigmatization is to state the glaringly obvious. Prostitutes in effect embody female stigmatization. They are "the other of the other." The stigma of prostituting is, under patriarchy, inescapable, casting a shadow that remains throughout a woman's lifetime. The stigma not only impacts on attitudes (of others and oneself) but also is associated with various objective mechanisms of discrimination and disfranchisement. Vanwesenbeeck maintains that "people are more likely to isolate the stigmatized, to stereotype them and think that they are 'all alike,' to be aggressive and punish them, to differentiate strongly between 'them' and 'us,' to feel uncomfortable in their presence, to be extremely curious [about them], to interpret all behavior in terms of the deviant character-istic and to generalize and attribute negative characteristics to them."[144] Gayle Rubin notes that the sexually stigmatized are presumed mentally ill, disreputable, and criminal.[145] Both Rubin and Vanwesenbeeck list various objective discriminatory mechanisms that impact on the sexually stigmatized in general and prostitutes in particular: they are socially and physically restricted and suffer economic sanctions and a significant loss of institutional support (including police, courts, hospitals, coroners, and banks). At the same time, stigmatized individuals often experience feelings of guilt and shame and are likely to isolate themselves socially. Any feminist looking at this description should recognize it as familiar to women in general. But while women are clearly stigmatized under patri-archy, the prostitute is *the* stigmatized woman, the stigmatized of the stigmatized. She becomes a special target for physical and sexual assault and for "the presumptuous and aggressive behavior of men," who are "more likely to claim all sorts of sexual rights" against her. While stigmatization generally leads to ambivalent feelings (and thus to more extreme behavior against the stigmatized), it is worse for the prostitute, who is "both the idol and scape-goat of sex, worshiped as well as de-spised." Ambivalence is core to violence against women in general, but "prostitutes are subject to it in the extreme." While prostitutes are more likely to be victimized by physical and sexual violence, however, they are likely to receive the least institutional support when they are victimized. Vanwesenbeeck cites one Dutch study in which vice-squad police identi-fied rape of streetwalkers walking alone at night as "the least serious of all rapes."[146]

Similarly, lack of institutional support and concern is ubiquitous in the United States. Attacks on and murders of prostitutes in this country appear to raise little interest in or concern by the police.[147] Often high-profile cases of serial murderers appear to be taken seriously only when at least one of the victims is a nonprostitute.[148] Press coverage mirrors police attitudes. When prostitutes are the victims of violent crimes, they are often identified in the media only as prostitutes (along with their age)—their names are not even mentioned or are provided only at the end of the article. It is enough that we know that a murder victim was a prostitute; she requires no further identity. Where "blaming the victim" in physical and sexual assaults of women is painfully commonplace, it is far more common when the woman is a prostitute. In my interviews with prostitutes, brothel owners, and a variety of support personnel, when I asked about physical and sexual violence, including rape, of prostitutes, I was nearly universally informed that this happened only when a woman was not a professional, not doing her job, not competent. When I asked about abuse of prostitutes in brothels, one Nevada police official informed me that he had heard that prostitutes did get "slapped around from time to time to keep them in line when the brothels first opened, but you had to expect that—after all, they're prostitutes" (said with a chuckle).

At the same time, it is crucial to understand that globally, nonprostitute women who fail to obey patriarchal requirements of female sexual purity face similar fates. Whether adult or child, too great an involvement or interest in sexuality by a female is dangerous. As Meda Chesney-Lind notes, the perception of a woman as "unfeminine" (which includes sexually available) is liable, in the United States, to lead to greater jail time. Christine Alder holds that "the concern with girls' sexuality and independence . . . remain central to justifications for the use of coercive practices, including the juvenile justice system, with young women."[149] Alder goes on to argue that "the ways in which girls' peers, parents, teachers and juvenile justice personnel, police girls' behavior [is] through sexual reputation. Girls can earn a reputation as a 'slut' or a 'slag,' based not necessarily on whether or not she is 'doing it,' but on broad ranging criteria of acceptable feminine behavior concerning such matters as her clothes, makeup, who she spends time with, her hairstyle, and her speech."[150] It is no accident that the vast majority of girls deemed "behaviorally disordered" by the U.S. state and school systems are so designated due to sexual behavior.

Insistence on female sexual purity is used to justify the social and legal denial of a woman's most basic rights globally, whether the issue is "honor" killings in fundamentalist Muslim communities or female genital mutilation in Africa. In India, where widowhood is sufficient to establish sexual impurity, 33 million Hindu widows constitute "one of the darkest blots on the nation's conscience." To be a Hindu widow in the 1990s, at least a poor one, is still to suffer "social death." Many end up alone, without family, often without proper shelter, desperately poor, outcasts in their native villages. "For the younger widows—some barely teen-agers, . . . there is the additional threat of being forced into sex with landlords, rickshaw drivers, policemen, even Hindu holy men. . . . This, too, has historically been part of the widows' lot. The tradition of their being forced to have sex with other men in their husbands' families, or to sell sex was once so widespread that the Hindi word 'randi,' or widow, became a synonym for prostitute. . . . Murders of widows are much more common."[151] Thus the mechanism of stigmatizing prostitutes is only a piece of the larger patriarchal mechanism of stigmatizing women who do or are perceived to "step over the line" of female sexual purity.

Conversely, as in the case of "delinquent" girls who "act out" sexually, some women are drawn to prostitution because of its stigma, viewing their work as a form of rebellion and an expression of their legitimate anger in the existing context. Indeed, several of the prostitutes I interviewed, especially prostitute rights spokeswomen, view prostitution as a source of empowerment. They get to "thumb their noses" at societal attempts to enforce the madonna role while earning significant fees for doing so. For these women, prostitution is a feminist strategy of resistance.

I. Illegal Immigration and Trafficking in Women

Two of the most difficult problems that must be seriously addressed by any prostitution policy at this moment in history are illegal immigration and trafficking in women and children. Where both have always required some consideration, globalization in the context of vast disparities of wealth and opportunities has only fueled these problems. Immigration has never been a straightforward matter for known prostitutes—they have often been and remain unable to visit, let alone relocate to, many countries. As noted earlier in this chapter, trafficking in women now constitutes a global crisis—predominantly from underdeveloped nations (of color), although with the fall of the Soviet Union a significant increase in women being trafficked from Eastern Europe has occurred. In trafficking, people from poorer nations are traditionally purchased or enticed by false promises, only to be made virtual slaves in other countries.

Although trafficking is of central importance to any prostitution policy, it has often been discussed and dealt with in ways that are both highly problematic and politically charged. To avoid a common tendency to equate trafficking with *any* migration of prostitutes or to conceive "trafficking" so narrowly that one eliminates vast numbers of non-prostituted persons from the category, I use the definition in "The Human Rights Standards for the Treatment of Trafficked Persons, January 1999"—coauthored by the Global Alliance Against Trafficking in Women (GAATW, headquartered in Thailand), the Foundation against Trafficking in Women (STV, Stichting Tegen Vrouwenhandel, in the Netherlands), and the International Human Rights Law Group (from the United States)—as "forced labor where people are lured or deceived into forms of contemporary slavery." Similarly, the definition of trafficking accepted by the 1994 International Conference on Traffic in Persons, in Utrecht, the Netherlands (November 15–19), maintains that "the element that defines traffic is force and not the nature of the labor to be performed."[152] I use this definition not only for the purpose of clarity but also because I am concerned not to undermine the seriousness, the horror, of those women, children, and men who are truly victimized by trafficking. Nothing, apart from promotion of a political agenda directed at the abolition of all prostitution, is served by equating a woman's uncoerced decision to migrate and prostitute (into a position where she receives the agreed-upon wages and working conditions) with the plight of a woman who has been coerced or tricked into migrating and finds herself a prisoner, often physically or by threat, within some form of coerced labor.[153] Under the concept of trafficking I also include those women who migrate, intending to work as prostitutes, but who are then coerced into accepting working conditions other than those they agreed to.

It is also critical to understand that women, children, and men may be coerced into virtual slavery for nonprostitute labor, most commonly as mail-order brides, domestic workers, "entertainers," and sweatshop workers as well as construction workers, security guards, agricultural workers, beggars, and other occupations. Often such labor involves sexual abuse, although it need not do so. Alison Murray notes the death and abuse of trafficked women workers in sweatshops both here and in Asia, while Kathleen Barry describes the trafficking of women as wives and domestic workers and the commonality of their abuse. Barry also cites a study, developed by the Philippine Embassy in Singapore, that reported assault, maltreatment, molestation, torture, and harassment of domestic workers. Furthermore, the mail-order bride industry not only constitutes a form of trafficking but also is often a source of forced prostitution. Even when people are legal immigrants, they are considered trafficked if they are subject to significant abuse due to their resident status, as, for example, in the case of the mail-order bride, who can be deported at the whim of her spouse.[154] It is sufficient to constitute trafficking if the individual is a foreign national being forced to provide labor and/or sexual services due to violence, the threat of violence, deception, or blackmail in a country other than his or her country of residence and as a result of legal status as a (non)resident. Often traffickers use "malafide marriage and employment agencies, so-called artist visas, phoney marriages or direct kidnapping" to bring the individuals into a country where they then "take away the women's documents, threaten and abuse the women and take most, if not all of their earnings."[155]

Is trafficking as large a problem as is often maintained? This is altogether unclear. It has been estimated that since 1987, between one and two thousand women per year are trafficked through the Netherlands alone (HAP interview). Murray, however, maintains that the worldwide numbers reported are highly inflated and that the figures provided by legitimate agencies, such as the Norwegian government and Asia Watch, are not "referenced, nor do they explain what research has been done, if any."[156] Still, if the true scale is not apparent, what is clear is that trafficking does occur; that women, children, and men caught in trafficking are horribly vulnerable and often subject to unspeakable conditions; and that trafficking in persons, including for prostitution, has occurred and continues to occur in the United States. This concern becomes ever more urgent. There are now more women than men involved in mass migration; the majority are employed as foreign domestic workers, also "in situations which often involve debts, exploitation and sexual abuse."[157] Further, as Murray notes of Australia, even when the prostitute is not trafficked, "because the sex industry is not fully decriminalized and sex workers cannot obtain work visas freely, some of the terms and conditions of contracts are exploitative and working conditions may be poor. Australia's own racist policies contribute to exploitation. . . . Police and immigration activity depresses business and means that workers have to hide their activities. This makes it harder for them to be contacted by support organizations providing information, condoms and HIV/AIDS information."[158] How much worse is the case in the United States, where, although we may share the same history of racist policies, in all but Nevada prostitution and much sex work is fully criminalized. This illegality ensures that prostitutes cannot appeal to authorities to escape exploitation or abuse. And because clients are likely to see illegal immigrants as helpless victims, they are more likely to abuse them.

J. The United States and Trafficking in Persons

In 1997, "Maria," an eighteen-year-old Mexican woman, was told by an acquaintance in Veracruz that she could make significantly more money for herself, her daughter, and her family by being smuggled into the United States to work in a restaurant or bar. Once over the border in Florida, she was ordered to work in a brothel to pay off a $2,200 smuggling debt. In her testimony before the U.S. Senate Foreign Relations Committee, she stated:

> I was given tight clothes to wear and was told what I must do. There would be armed men selling tickets to customers in the trailer. Tickets were condoms. Each ticket would be sold for $22 to $25 each. The client would then point at the girl he wanted and the girl would take him to one of the bedrooms. At the end of the night, I turned in the condom wrappers. Each wrapper represented a supposed deduction to my smuggling fee. We tried to keep our own records, but the Bosses would destroy them. We were never sure what we owed. . . . There were up to four girls kept at each brothel. We were constantly guarded and abused. If any one refused to be with a customer, we were beaten. If we adamantly refused, the Bosses would show us a lesson by raping us brutally. They told us if we refused again it would be even worse the next time. We were transported every fifteen days to another trailer in a nearby city. This was to give the customers a variety of girls and so we never knew where we were in case we tried to escape. I could not believe this was happening to me. . . . We worked six days a week and twelve-hour days. We mostly had to serve 32–35 clients a day. . . . If we became pregnant we were forced to have abortions. The cost of the abortion would then be added to our smuggling debt. . . . I was enslaved for several months, other women were enslaved for up to a year. Our enslavement finally ended when the INS, FBI and local law enforcement raided the brothels and rescued us. We weren't sure what was happening on the day of the raids. Our captors had told us over and over never to tell the police of our conditions. They told us that if we told we would find ourselves in prison for the rest of our lives. They told us that the INS would rape us and kill us. . . . After the INS and FBI freed us from the brothels we were put in a detention center for many months. Our captors were correct. We thought we would be imprisoned for the rest of our lives.

Later, our attorneys were able to get us released to a women's domestic violence center where we received comprehensive medical attention, including gynecological exams, and mental health counseling.[159]

Preliminary data suggest that of the seven hundred thousand people trafficked globally each year, about fifty-thousand are brought to the United States.[160] People are trafficked for all varieties of labor, including migrant agricultural and factory work, domestic service, and prostitution. In 1995, three years after the U.S. Labor Commission had been informed of the literal enslavement of Thai workers, state, local, and federal authorities raided a garment sweatshop in El Monte, California, where seventy-two male and female Thai nationals had been imprisoned for up to seven years. The workers, who had survived torturous conditions, were then turned over to the Immigration and Naturalization Service (INS), which led them in shackles to detention camps. It took the local Asian community some time to get their bail reduced (to $500 apiece) and free them. The INS provided no services appropriate to their needs during their detention. The sweatshop owners, however, were successfully prosecuted for violations of involuntary servitude, conspiracy, and immigration laws.[161]

In 1997 authorities uncovered a smuggling syndicate that had enslaved dozens of hearing-impaired Mexican nationals who were forced to peddle trinkets on the streets of Los Angeles, New York, and Chicago. They were coerced through beatings, physical restraint, and torture. "Eighteen defendants . . . pled guilty to slavery conspiracy charges as well as immigration, money laundering and obstruction of justice offenses."[162] In 1998 federal authorities uncovered the prostitution trafficking ring in which Maria and other Mexican women and girls (some as young as fourteen) "were lured into the United States and forced to work as prostitutes and sexual slaves in brothels in Florida and the Carolinas."[163] The U.S. Labor Department continues to intervene in instances of trafficking in the Commonwealth of the Northern Mariana Islands (CNMI), whose citizens have the full rights of any U.S. citizen save for voting in federal elections. There, trafficking may involve up to forty-thousand workers employed in construction, security, sex work, domestic work, gardening, clerking, and work in garment factories. (Garments produced in the commonwealth carry a "Made in the U.S.A." label.) Workers are generally brought from Bangladesh, Sri Lanka, the People's Republic of China (PRC), and the Philippines. The

CNMI has a thriving sex-tourism industry, primarily for Japanese businessmen, which uses workers trafficked most often from the Philippines, PRC, Russia, and South Asia. Most of these workers appear to have been deceived, believing they would become waitresses only to be turned out as prostitutes or as "consummation hostesses." The latter constitutes a kind of modern B-girl, working in nightclubs, encouraging male clients to drink and buy them drinks. However, these women are often required to leave the clubs with the clients, and rapes of the hostesses, which are legally tolerated, are common. In some instances the hostesses are required to perform sexual acts in booths in the clubs. Women acquiesce to being prostitutes or consummation hostesses through extreme coercion; their passports are confiscated, and they often face threats of bodily harm to themselves or their families back home. Because they earn less than minimum wage (they work a fifty-hour week and their wages range from $150 to $750 a month), they cannot earn enough for airfare to escape the commonwealth. Although the U.S. government has successfully prosecuted three individuals in the CNMI for trafficking women from China and forcing them to prostitute in a karaoke bar–brothel, the general attitude of those involved in trafficking in CNMI has been relaxed due to the "lavishly funded campaign to dissuade the U.S. Congress from acting."[164]

While the Global Survival Network has documented trafficking in women from the former Soviet Union to the United States for sexual slavery, American GIs abroad are also responsible for significant trafficking of women particularly from Asia into the United States. In 1994, Hyun Sook Kim reported that servicemen commonly bought "temporary wives" in Korea, as well as marrying Korean women (approximately three thousand annually), many of whom were then abandoned (along with the children produced by these marriages). Korean women thus became vulnerable to traffickers who would arrange sham marriages with GIs, who were paid up to $10,000 to bring a woman to the United States to work in a massage parlor. Even legal marriages between Korean women and American GIs are a significant source of trafficking. Since up to 80 percent of these marriages end in divorce, Korean women find themselves in the United States alone, broke, and often with limited English. Their only option is to (re)enter prostitution (or become homeless—a growing phenomenon). In 1989, 99 percent of Korean prostitutes working in the United States had migrated by marrying an American GI stationed in South Korea.[165]

Hence any public policy on prostitution, including any U.S. public policy, must address the problem of trafficking. Trafficked persons, like illegal immigrants in general, are always vulnerable to coercion, blackmail, and the like simply because they face deportation, often to home countries where their lives will be economically desperate at the least. But in the case of trafficking, what is distinctive is the reality of virtual enslavement, usually facilitated by organized syndicates. In addition, when returned to their country of origin, many of these workers, especially prostitute workers, are subject to extensive social stigmatization and legal sanctions; thus threats and blackmail are more than usually effective in keeping these women enslaved. In light of clear evidence that trafficking and immigrant-worker exploitation was occurring in the United States, in 1998 then attorney general Janet Reno created the Worker Exploitation Task Force to investigate and coordinate U.S. anti-trafficking activity. The United States is also involved in drafting United Nations anti-trafficking policy, although, as I discuss below, our position has been highly problematic.

6

The "Ideal" Character of Heterosex/Intercourse and Prostitution

Ideal Heterosex/Intercourse

Much of the stigma that attaches to objects and activities in a culture reflect that culture's social construction of power. This is critical to understanding a feminist reconstruction of heterosexual activity. What, from a feminist perspective, would an ideal of heterosexuality and heterosexual activity be? What would heterosexuality and heterosexual activity look like in a nonsexist world? My first instinct is to say that I haven't a clue. Heterosexual activity and its representations are so deeply shaped and limited by patriarchy that it is impossible for me, as an individual whose views are inextricably constructed by my cultural context, to envision what nonsexist heterosexuality would look like in any detail. But I can, in fact, envision such an ideal in a decidedly broad outline, particularly in terms of those qualities that currently construct heterosexual acts but would surely be absent or altered in a nonpatriarchal context.

During my 1993 discussion of his recently completed report on trafficking between Belgium and the Netherlands, the Dutch criminologist Cyrille Fijnaut said with great certainty, "You'll never normalize prostitution." Given what I knew of Fijnaut's work, as well as my knowledge of the Dutch government position which he has influenced, this comment surprised me. I thought about it for some time and finally came to believe that Fijnaut was partially correct. We will never normalize prostitution unless we normalize sex and sexual activity. And we will never normalize sex and sexual activity unless we normalize women. Unless women are normalized, gender and sexual identities will remain a source of oppression. In a nonsexist world, sexuality, genitalia, and sexual acts would be normalized. Any act that does not cause harm to another would be viewed as not just acceptable but unworthy of any special notice. Although I am unable to agree that sexuality and reproduction are *the* source of women's oppression (as many radical feminists traditionally have contended), I am certain that sexuality and reproduction constitute one of the most important sources and focuses of women's oppression. From heterosexism to rape, from the madonna/whore dichotomy to the cultural rejection of "illegitimate" children, women have been made to pay for our sexuality and reproductive functions by the cultural valuation of these as sacred or profane. Because sexual acts and reproduction are currently bifurcated into either stigmatized or mystified behavior, they are made abnormal, morally value-tiered and definers of moral character. This abnormalization is central to the subordination of women.

A social stigma emerges in response to some feature(s) in the nature of certain objects or behaviors that are seen as problematic in the context of specific cultures. Sometimes those features are relevant to the welfare of the culture, sometimes not. I firmly believe that part of the stigma that attaches to acts of sexuality is related to the historical biological consequences that may follow from various sexual activities. Because heterosexual intercourse can, intrinsically, be the source of spreading diseases or of unplanned and unwanted pregnancies, it is not surprising that many cultures have stigmatized it and other sexual behavior that may encourage intercourse.[1] But these concerns, which are sometimes appealed to in order to justify the continued stigmatization of heterosexual activity, no longer need be significant, at least not in Western industrialized nations. Because we have the technological means to vastly lower the rate of unplanned and unwanted pregnancies and STDs, they cannot be the basis for justifying the continued stigmatization of sexual acts.[2]

But much of the stigma that attaches to objects and activities reflects that particular culture's social construction of power. It is in the interest of patriarchy to continue the stigmatization of sexual behavior because it is an excellent device for maintaining sexism, in an inextricable web with racism, colonialism, economic classism, heterosexism, and other "isms." It is women's bodies, sexual activity, and sexual roles that are stigmatized in heterosexuality; "boys will be boys" while sexual and reproductive access to women can be controlled by maintaining the madonna/whore dichotomy. Men can continue to "own" women sexually and ensure that "their" women are producing only "their" biologically related children. This continued stigmatization is of particular value in "first world" countries, where the relevant protective technology is readily available and women's roles as mothers and nurturers have become less defining. Stigmatization is, in our current context, the main source of control of women's sexual activity. Therefore, feminists' long-range goals for sexual activity in an "ideal" world in which gender and sexuality are not the basis for allocating power must require that sexual acts no longer be stigmatized. This realization is behind many feminist attempts to normalize ranges and varieties of sexual identities and activity. Nearly all feminist texts on sexuality recognize the narrow range of nonstigmatized sexual behaviors available to women and sexual stigmatization as one of the great dangers, the significant price to be paid, by women who engage in any but heterosexual, "partnered," "nice" sex.[3] The drive to de-stigmatize sexuality also underlies the movement to de-stigmatize women's bodies, to treat them as the embodiment of neither filth nor holiness but as simply biological entities. This commitment is exhibited in feminist works as diverse as *Our Bodies, Ourselves* (Boston Women's Health Book Collective, 1973) and *The Vagina Monologues* (Eve Ensler, 1998).

While the abnormalization of sexual activity and women's bodies has been achieved in part through stigmatization, an equally important aspect of maintaining sexuality as abnormal has been the mystification of sexuality—imbuing it with characteristics that make sexual acts incredibly significant in one's overall life history. Modern U.S. culture constructs sexuality as the most important or sole source of the highest level of pleasure and spiritual experience that human beings can hope to achieve. We are encouraged to believe that sexual orgasm, the current goal of heterosexual activity, is (one of?) the greatest sensual pleasure available to human beings, and that the best kind and source of the "wedding of two souls" is achieved in (hetero)sexual activity.

I am convinced that in a nonsexist context, sex would no longer be mystified anymore than it would be stigmatized. There would be no privileging of any sexual activity other than that belonging to the broad description of "not causing harm to others." This seems to be resisted by many feminists who, though they want to eliminate the sexual stigma, maintain that certain reproductive functions and sexual behaviors are or should be, in some sense, sacred. The problem is that by privileging some behaviors and relationships, one will, albeit inadvertently, disprivilege others. The sacred and the profane are, after all, corollaries. Maintaining that sexual acts between those who are in love or who have deep intimate connections are, in whatever sense, "the best or most desirable" necessarily sets up a hierarchy such that other behaviors are judged and assigned their value on the basis of that standard. By exchanging "acts of sexually intimate spiritual and emotional communion" or "connectedness" for the traditional patriarchal standard of "marital, procreatively motivated intercourse," one simply exchanges justifications for distinguishing the madonna from the whore.[4] Not only does the glorification of specific sexual behaviors encourage the bifurcation of women, it also misrepresents women's lived experiences. Unquestionably, some of the more memorable and cherished sexual experiences I have had have involved the expression of love and connection with a "committed" sexual partner. But others have involved experiences that were simply extremely sexually pleasurable or that gave me greater knowledge and awareness of my sexual self.

Conversely, I have enjoyed some of my most intense and important emotional and spiritual connections with others with whom I was not sexually involved, sometimes through the sharing of sensual pleasures (a superb meal, a nonsexual massage, or dancing). Indeed, both historical and current evidence indicates that the genuine "spiritual connection" people experience with each other often (perhaps more often than not) occurs in nonsexual relationships. Here it may be objected that this is because, as constructed, heterosexual activity is inseparably a battleground of heterosexism and misogyny. But I can see no reason to assume that without heterosexism, heterosexuality could plausibly be accorded this mystified status. Given the degree to which sensual pleasure is the response of each individual to a stimulus as experienced within a political, social, and cultural context, I can see no prima facie reason to presume its vaulted status on a hierarchy of sensual pleasures or its status as the basis for emotional intimacy. In a nonsexist ideal world, there would be no more reason to wed sexual acts with "communion" or "true intimacy" than there is to wed any particular nonsexual acts with these spiritual and emotional relationships. In what follows, I couch the discussion in terms of the concept of intimacy, since this is the terminology that appears most common to feminist discussions of the spiritual and emotional aspects of heterosexuality, as well as being core to the positions of many U.S. feminists with regard to prostitution policy. Feminists often argue that sex for sale is intrinsically objectionable because it is wrong to sell intimacy, and intercourse is (ideally and "properly") intimacy.[5]

Because the term intimacy is used in a variety of ways and is sometimes simply intended to mean sexual contact (e.g., "Were you intimate with him?"), I stipulate a definition. By "intimacy," I intend the feeling that one is safe with and accepted by (and usually "emotionally bonded" to) another individual. The safety the individual experiences is largely connected to issues of self-disclosure or exposure; there is a relationship between two or more individuals such that at least one of them is comfortable about disclosing or exposing what he or she views as (some) private or personal information or aspect of the self that makes the individual vulnerable in a variety of ways. "True intimacy" includes a willingness to be physically, emotionally, and/or socially vulnerable. Intimate relationships may involve a comfort with disclosure or exposure of, for example, physical weakness, physical desire, or what is constructed as physical oddity. They may also involve emotional vulnerability—the disclosure of information that individuals view as highly personal and fear will precipitate emotional rejection by the other individual or be used against them. Or intimate relationships may involve social vulnerability—exposure of behavior that may cause rejection in the larger society. Finally, it is important to note that intimacy need not be reciprocally shared by both individuals in the relationship. Many individuals who see mental health counselors would maintain that they have an intimate bond with their counselors, feeling safe and comfortable about disclosing information that they would otherwise never disclose. Yet most realize that while the relationship is intimate for them, it is not reciprocally intimate for their counselors.

The first issue that must be clarified is whether sexual acts are intrinsically intimate or whether this notion is part of their social construction. As I suggested in Chapter 3, heterosexual acts are clearly not intrinsically intimate, given the commonality of nonintimate heterosexual acts. Further, the assumption that heterosexual acts and intimacy are somehow necessarily connected is altogether ahistorical and acultural.[6] Therefore, tying heterosexual acts and intercourse to intimacy must be a characteristic that is socially constructed.

But then we need to ask, are sexual acts ideally intimate? In an ideal world, without sexism, heterosexism, racism, economic classism, and such, would it be desirable that acts of sexuality be shared (always or mainly) in the context of an intimate relationship or as an act of intimacy? Would sexual activity be one "in which the 'I love you' is made flesh"?[7] It seems apparent to me that the answer is no; for since, in such a world, sexual activity would make one no more vulnerable than would most other behaviors, the perception of vulnerability that is a necessary component to intimacy would be lacking. Physical vulnerability incurred through sexual activity already need not be greater than that connected with many other activities. The risk of harm through unwanted pregnancy can be virtually eliminated, (and certainly its negative moral value would be) and the risk of disease transmission can already be lowered significantly. Furthermore, physical risk need not, even ideally, require any level of intimacy. I am at real risk of catching a disease from my massage therapist, hair cutter, or gynecologist, and indeed, unlike in the instance of sexual behavior, I have few, if any, means available to lessen my risks. But I do not feel that I would, ideally, prefer to have an intimate relationship with any of these professionals. What of women's physical vulnerability due to the size and strength differential between the "average" man and the "average" woman? Not only has technology significantly lessened the importance of this difference through weapons such as pepper sprays and, especially, guns, which "even the playing field," but also it has become acceptable for women to develop greater physical strength and self-defense skills. Far more important, were sex not a weapon of patriarchy, women would have no more concern about the "physical advantage" men "in general" have over women in sexual acts than we do in any situation in which we might find ourselves alone with a man (including when he provides a service in our home, meets us for a one-on-one conference in an office, or accompanies us on a drive). And as already noted, the belief that sexual acts should be performed "privately" is itself the product of the stigmatization of sexual activity, and thus, in a nonsexist culture, sexual behavior would probably be no more private than any other normalized behavior.

If sex were not a weapon, and if sexual desirability were not one of the defining characteristics of a woman's value, then a woman's emotional vulnerability would be no greater within sexual activity than within nonsexual activity. Because social vulnerability involves fear of exposure for participating in stigmatized or devalued acts or experiencing stigmatized desires, if sexual behavior were not stigmatized, there would be no social vulnerability connected with it (as long as it did not involve harm to others.)

There does not appear to be any reason to believe that, ideally, sexual behavior should involve intimacy any more than should nonsexual behavior, or that sexual activity should be accorded some vaulted, mystified status. This belief is part of patriarchal ideology, which still insists that women be "selective" when the fear of pregnancy, diseases and death, and absolute dependence on male protectors no longer exists. It is what keeps us "faithful" or at least sexually less active. The claim that sex is or should be intimate is the good girl's, the madonna's, view and is as effective as stigma in controlling women's sexuality and sexual behavior. Given these arguments, the clear feminist agenda for sexual activity should include the sustained effort to normalize (large ranges of) sexuality and sexual activity. This normalization would involve elimination of both stigma and mystification while requiring only that sexual activity be consensual, mutually respectful, and demonstrate a genuine concern for the well-being and pleasure of others.[8] Finally, the very question "What would heterosexuality and heterosexual activity look like in a non-sexist world?" would be incoherent since it is based on a category "heterosexual" which presumes the indefensible bifurcations of physiology, gender, and sexual orientation and identity.

Ideal of Prostitution

On the assumption that in a nonsexist ideal world, labor will still be exchanged for material gain,[9] given the discussion above it follows that the ideal of prostitution will be whatever will facilitate and instantiate the goals of normalizing sexuality and sexual activity. This will require the normalization of prostitution. If the vagina is de-stigmatized, so, too, will access to it be. If sexual activity and sexual access are de-stigmatized, so, too, will the sale of sexual access and sexual services be. Why would we need to eliminate paid sexual services rather than de-stigmatizing them? If we allow psychologists, massage therapists, and other professionals to charge fees for providing personal services, why should sexual services not be similarly available for a fee?

Some feminists argue that in a nonsexist world there would be no prostitution, no reason to purchase sexual services. They maintain that prostitution is simply another sexual weapon of patriarchy, one that "institutionalizes the concept that it is a man's monetary right, if not his divine right, to gain access to the female body and that sex is a female service that should not be denied the civilized male."[10] In effect, many argue that what is paid for within the prostitution contract is the right to play out the role of gendered subordinator. But this ignores some nonsexist reasons why men, even currently, purchase prostitution services. Sometimes they do not have an appropriate person in their lives to provide the outlet, and sometimes the professional is able to provide sexual services in a way that is superior to that provided by nonprofessionals. Broadly, these are the same reasons people hire psychologists, massage therapists, hair cutters, and so forth. For example, we hire psychologists because sometimes we do not have a person we trust sufficiently to speak our innermost selves to, at least without opening ourselves to expectations and connections that we do not desire. By contrast, even when we have someone in our lives who will counsel us emotionally, that person may not be as skilled as a professional; and that skill is sometimes of great importance. And sometimes it is the very anonymity and disconnection from the rest of our lives provided by the psychotherapist that has a particular value. These functions would similarly be served by prostitutes in a non-sexist world. There would still be good reason for prostitution, although its nature would be almost unrecognizably transformed.

Most obviously, prostitution would provide large ranges of sexual services for nearly all sexual orientations and for clients of all sexes and genders.[11] The same labor protections would be in place within prostitution as outside it. No additional protections would be required.[12] Prostitution would be de-stigmatized and de-mystified, consensual, mutually respectful, and would demonstrate concern for the well-being of the participants and the pleasure of the client.[13]

7

Evolving a Policy—Legal Status

Principles and Strategies for Evaluating Legal Policies

Given the previous discussion, what prostitution policy makes the greatest sense? This chapter is concerned with the question of what we ought to do legally about prostitution.

Before entering into a specific evaluation of legal options for dealing with prostitution, however, it is critical once again to visit some more general methodological matters. In the first part of this chapter, I offer a necessarily brief overview of political principles and strategies that inform my evaluation of both the three possible legal treatments of prostitution and possible extralegal supports. However, this section may not be of interest to readers who are concerned solely with the question of prostitution policy, rather than with policy analysis. For these individuals, it is sufficient to skip over the discussion of the more theoretical issues in this section.

Until now I have been engaged in describing what I hope and intend is not just a feminist analysis and vision of prostitution but a radically feminist one that is sensitive to the need for major revamping of some of the most basic organizations and structures of contemporary human life and society. In moving to the question of public policy, however, it is essential to be equally sensitive to one's actual political context if one's efforts are to yield real change. Because, unfortunately, I see no sign of a gender revolution anywhere on the horizon, I have come to believe that it is critical to distinguish between one's vision and one's strategy for establishing it. I therefore advocate for three distinct strategies to further a feminist public policy agenda that, because they are a response to the current U.S. legal and political context, are not radical. They suggest methods to improve women's lives within a system that includes a variety of highly problematic presumptions, including the values of classical liberalism, social contractarianism, individualistic rights, and the public/private distinction. Space limitations unfortunately allow me to address these strategies only briefly, but they are key to understanding my proposal for a U.S. prostitution policy.

A. "Liberty-Limiting" Principles

Historically, in mainstream philosophy, political science, and the law, there has been much disagreement about what sorts of reasons justify state intervention in individual liberties. Political theorists have argued that the state is justified in limiting individual rights, liberties, or activities on the basis of quite disparate justifications.[1] Joel Feinberg provides a useful description of the kinds of justifications generally offered:

1. The Harm Principle—"to prevent harm to persons other than the actor" (or to society's institutions).
2. The Offense Principle—"to prevent hurt or offense (as opposed to injury or harm) to others."
3. Legal paternalism—"to prevent harm to the very person it prohibits from acting, as opposed to 'others.'"
4. Legal moralism—"to prevent inherently immoral conduct whether or not such conduct is harmful or offensive to anyone."[2]

There is no general agreement about which, if any, of these principles actually justifies limiting individual liberties. A few political philosophers hold that none of them is adequate, but most believe that the Harm Principle and a very limited version of the Offense Principle are justifiable, whereas legal moralism and legal paternalism are far more controversial. Often specific legal-political positions appeal to more than one kind of justification; for example, anti-abortion stances often appeal to claims that abortion harms others (the fetus), encourages immorality (immoral sexual behavior), and requires paternalistic protection (because aborting will cause the woman serious regret in the long run).

J. S. Mill, the classic liberal, held that "the only purpose for which power can be rightfully exercised over any member of a civilized community, against his [sic] will, is to prevent harm to others."[3] As a matter of political strategy, I am convinced that feminists need to adopt a neo-Millian stance. Coherence requires acceptance of a limited Offense Principle that confines materials and behaviors that are the source of serious offense to almost all members of a community to private (e.g., bookstores and movie theaters) rather than public (e.g., subway posters) venues.[4] This seems a reasonable addition to Mill's view; few are willing to live in a society where they may be unwittingly confronted with large billboards explicitly depicting acts of human defecation on their way to the office. An additional alteration of Mill's position, significant to all concerned with the rights of the subordinated/oppressed, requires that "harm to others" extend beyond "harm to individuals and/or institutions" to include "harm to subordinated classes." This alteration recognizes that the creation of negative images of subordinated groups may result in both social and individual harm. Thus, for example, feminist proponents of government censorship of (nonpublic) pornography base their arguments on the claim that pornography causes harm to women as a class and thus, ultimately, to individual women as members of that class. Controversy then resides in the factual question of whether or not pornography actually causes such harm.

As a general rule, however, I am convinced that it is strategically critical for feminist public policy analysts to reject appeals to either legal paternalism or legal moralism, given the current context. Legal paternalism necessarily assumes that those creating and enforcing the laws of the state are better able to understand and evaluate what is in (any) individual's interest than is that individual her or himself. This has historically worked rather consistently against women, "justifying" many so-called protectionist laws that have, in fact, simply constrained and oppressed women.[5] From laws excluding women from some forms of employment (e.g., bartending) to laws "protecting" women from jury duty, we have seen legal paternalism act to disfranchise women rather than promote our welfare. Given that the current distribution of power continues to reward patriarchy and those who defend it, giving the state the power to decide and legally enforce what it presumes is in "women's best interest" is nothing less than political suicide.

Similarly, legal moralism has traditionally undermined women; "public morality" or what is "required by decency" has been nothing less than the rules that secure and perpetuate patriarchal organizations of power, including laws against birth control and homosexuality or homosexual acts, laws that disproportionately control women's dress and deportment, and a host of laws and policies enforcing "the sanctity of marriage" or "family values," such as historical divorce laws.

Therefore, although there may be exceptions to this approach, as an overall stance feminists should distrust appeals to legal paternalism or legal moralism, requiring an extreme degree of justification to override a presumption against them.[6]

B. Bodily Autonomy/Bodily Integrity

Mirroring my concerns above is my discomfort with appeals to "bodily autonomy/integrity." In legal and moral discussions the terms bodily autonomy and bodily integrity are used interchangeably, but this confuses two distinct concepts—with drastically different political implications.[7] One can understand "bodily autonomy" as involving what Diana Meyers calls a "negative conception," that is, a right that defines restraints on governments or others. It is the presumed right persons have to determine what happens in and to their bodies, the right of bodily self-regulation, of bodily self-governance, without undue interference by others.[8] Often collapsed into this is the distinct idea of what I prefer to designate the "right of bodily integrity," a presumed standard governing the treatment of human bodies. This standard recognizes that a special status, a level of respect, must be accorded to persons' bodies and explains the typical contemporary reaction to such vastly different phenomena as the sale of human kidneys, necrophilia, and eating the bodies of human beings who have died of natural causes. Understood in this way, the "right to bodily autonomy" speaks to the question of who should decide the fate of individual bodies, while "the right of bodily integrity" asserts a general standard to be applied by anyone making a decision about a human body. Clearly, although these rights usually intersect and overlap, they may also sometimes conflict.

Governmental interference with bodily autonomy has historically been harmful to women and other subordinated groups. Such interference has included diverse policies: state intervention in reproductive choice (e.g., anti-abortion laws, attempts to coerce the use of Norplant in some populations, instances of forced surgeries to protect the fetus at the cost of the mother's health or life), anti-miscegenation laws, forced lobotomies for the mentally ill, and anti-homosexual legislation, among others. Sometimes encroachment on bodily autonomy takes the form of failing to provide information necessary for "informed consent," as when the government allowed testing and sale of birth control pills without requiring disclosure of side effects, and as in the now infamous "Tuskegee experiment," in which four hundred men, all poor African Americans, were told they would receive free treatment for syphilis from the Public Health Service and instead became unwitting subjects for the four-year government-sanctioned "Tuskegee Study of Untreated Syphilis in the Negro Male," never receiving treatment.

Appeals to bodily integrity often constitute a justification for legal paternalism or legal moralism by enforcing a presumed "communal" standard. If, as I maintain, it is exceptionally dangerous for women and other subordinated groups to allow a government to decide what is morally required or in our best interest when harm to others is not at issue, this danger also applies to many appeals to bodily integrity. Most laws restricting sexual and gender activity, from anti-sodomy laws to those regarding appropriate dress, have been at least partially "justified" by appeal to this standard.

Given both historical use and meaning, therefore, as a matter of contemporary political strategy, feminists should hold a presumptive value hostile to any government interference with bodily autonomy while being decidedly suspicious of appeals to bodily integrity.

C. Standard of Secondary Discrimination

I have argued at length elsewhere[9] for adoption of a standard of secondary discrimination that would legally bar policies or practices not themselves explicitly discriminatory but whose application unfairly disadvantages a race, gender, ethnic, or economic class because they are dependent on or derivative of current or historical practices, laws, or policies that were explicitly or intentionally discriminatory. On this standard, a contractor cannot adopt a policy of hiring only union electricians if the local union refuses membership to African Americans. Even if the contractor did not intend to discriminate, she or he is still guilty of secondary discrimination. Application of this standard often bars de facto discrimination when "intentional" discrimination cannot be proven and is thus critical for feminist policy analysis.

The application of a Millian liberal strategy, avoiding legislation based solely on legal moralism or legal paternalism, and of the standard of secondary discrimination and right to bodily autonomy but not to bodily integrity should be apparent in the discussion that follows.

Which Legal Arrangement?

In what follows, I am concerned to demonstrate that the history of the criminal justice system and regulatory systems directed at prostitution makes it apparent that continued criminalization or legalization will serve only to further gender discrimination, along with racial and economic class discrimination.

As noted in Chapter 1, the available legal options to address prostitution include continuing to criminalize it, as we currently do in forty-nine states; legalizing it, as in the case of Nevada; or decriminalizing it, as is done in most Western European nations. In this discussion, it is critical to distinguish between acts of prostitution and acts that facilitate prostitution. The latter category includes the activities of organizations, individuals, and businesses that profit from the labor of prostitutes, for example, brothels, escort services, pimps, and massage parlors. Furthermore, although prostitution is currently governed by state, county, or city ordinances, this discussion is framed in terms of a federal policy. This is because I believe that interjurisdictional inconsistencies are problematic in a variety of respects and especially in encouraging interstate trafficking in women. However, given existing precedents and constitutional protection of state's rights, it is most likely that policies will continue to be legislated on a local level. But as in many other instances, the federal government can "encourage" the adoption of specific prostitution policies, similar to the case of speed limits where federal support for highway construction was tied to accepting a lower maximum speed.

A. Criminalizing Prostitution

In criminalizing prostitution, two justifications are most often cited. First is the belief that by criminalizing prostitution one can eliminate or at least decrease it. The desire to abolish prostitution is generally motivated by humanitarian or moralistic concerns. As my discussion of current practice should make clear, prostitution often results in significant harm to prostitutes. But it can also be argued that prostitution causes harm to clients. Though men are less likely than women to contract STDs, especially AIDS, through heterosexual activity and intercourse, they are clearly at risk. And since the use of condoms does not prevent the spread of many diseases (in part because condoms are known to break), having sex with someone who is as sexually active as a successful prostitute obviously increases the risk of infection. This, in turn, places other sexual partners of the client at greater risk. Additionally, there is clear evidence that some clients become dependent on (or "addicted to") sex with prostitutes. Many clients also experience religious, moral, or economic guilt.

Finally, areas of a city where (visible) prostitution is practiced often suffer. Wherever streetwalking or window prostitution is prevalent, more "family-oriented" businesses often do not survive. These visible forms of prostitution often increase other criminal activity in the neighborhood and decrease the overall "appearance" and maintenance of the impacted area.

The second justification for criminalizing prostitution is the view that it is immoral and that society must use the law to take a public stance on its immorality, even if criminalization is not practically successful in lessening the practice. This position can be motivated by two rather discordant concerns. The traditional (conservative) position arises usually from religious or traditional patriarchal moral convictions. Christianity, Judaism, and Islam, among others, maintain that prostitution constitutes moral sin. For those who accept legal moralism, criminalizing prostitution is not only permissible but morally obligatory. Indeed, prostitution is often cited as the paradigmatic example justifying legal moralism.[10] In contrast, support for criminalization justified by purely moral concerns may emerge from a feminist perspective. Although the vast majority of feminists reject criminalization, one can hold that failure to make prostitution illegal communicates societal acceptance of the treatment women suffer as prostitutes and the view that women are merely sexual objects who can be purchased.

The most compelling response to the argument that prostitution should be criminalized in order to decrease or eliminate it is that criminalization has never, to date, done so.[11] Indeed, rates of prostitution are relatively unaffected by the adoption of differing policies.[12] The failure of criminalization is effectively demonstrated by the fact that although prostitution is illegal throughout forty-nine states, the practice in the United States appears to be on the rise, just as it is globally. It is clear that criminalization is not working here.

Further, criminalization clearly harms prostitutes. Arresting prostitutes often serves only to heighten their isolation and estrangement, not only from friends, family, and the community but also from the very social services they may need in order to access alternative means of income. This, in turn, leads to lower self-esteem, which often increases drug and alcohol usage and thus requires an increase in prostitution activity to support these habits. Criminalization also strengthens the prostitutes' dependence on pimps, who will post bail, arrange child care, and obtain legal counsel when they do get arrested. Criminal enforcement may force prostitutes to move to other cities—leaving them even more isolated and hence, again, more likely to turn to a pimp. Furthermore, there is excellent evidence that prostitutes who are incarcerated often connect with pimps through their contact with other prostitutes while in jail. Not only does the arrest of prostitutes permanently and officially stigmatize them, it also often results in the loss of child custody, deportation, and housing and other forms of discrimination. Criminalization makes prostitute organizing, whether for political rights, occupational safety, or protection from corrupt police or exploitative bosses or dangerous working conditions, extremely difficult. It constitutes "an institutionalized attempt to isolate and silence whores."[13]

Criminalization has a negative impact on both prostitutes' and clients' health because the more nefarious and marginalized a behavior, the more likely it is to be transacted hastily, particularly where urban renewal has forced streetwalkers out of cheap hotels and into cars or other, more public places, thereby discouraging the use of condoms and other time-consuming safety measures. Fear of legal repercussions makes prostitutes less likely to access medical treatment for job-related illnesses. Thus, contrary to the claim that criminalization will lessen the spread of STDs, it may contribute to their increase, especially among street prostitutes. Fear of exposure further discourages prostitutes from seeking medical treatment for job-related assaults and from reporting these to the police, thereby allowing assailants to victimize prostitutes at will. Most important, by driving prostitution underground, criminalization makes it nearly impossible to obtain information on prostitute abuse and trafficking. One is unlikely to report trafficking and abusive practices if one fears arrest while doing so.[14]

Nor is criminalization justified to prevent either sexual addiction or the moral guilt of clients. Because criminalization does not lessen prostitution, neither of these concerns is positively impacted by such a policy. In addition, similar concerns about addiction or guilt are not seen as sufficient to justify criminalization of sexually explicit material, alcohol, or many products that can be chemically abused (e.g., White Out, gasoline, magic markers, and, for that matter, chocolate and coffee), even though addiction or moral guilt may be experienced by those who use or abuse them. Responsibility for addictive behavior or moral guilt is, in general, ascribed to those adults who can actually control the behavior or guilt feelings; that is, it lies with the adult client and not the provider. In the case of prostitution, this even more obviously should be the case since, on the whole, it is client demand that fuels prostitution.

Although most forms of prostitution do not seem to affect the neighborhoods in which they are located, illegal streetwalking sometimes causes significant harm to the surrounding neighborhood. Enforcement has historically been directed toward "containing" streetwalking—that is, moving it out of "public view," usually into poorer, more marginalized neighborhoods (and out again when neighborhoods are gentrified). Such containment serves only to further marginalize the neighborhood, resulting in increases in the crimes that often accompany illegal streetwalking and a lowering of the quality of life of nonprostitute women, who may be mistaken for prostitutes and hence harassed or solicited. Criminalization simply is not an effective way of protecting communities from nonprostitute criminal activity or a general "lowering" of neighborhood quality of life, but as I argue in Chapter 9, there are a variety of creative solutions that can do so.

Given the history of the criminal justice system, continued criminalization will almost certainly only perpetuate further gender discrimination, along with racial and economic class discrimination. Although a general presumption is that the criminal justice system is "chivalrous" in its treatment of women (including in harshness of sentencing), whatever chivalry may exist depends on the perception of the woman's "sexual character." Research discloses that the criminal justice system not only is significantly influenced by the madonna/whore bifurcation of women but effectively reinforces and perpetuates the dichotomy. "Women once cast in the role of 'whore' were never the beneficiaries of . . . [chivalrous] orientation";[15] rather, once tainted, women receive a generally harsh response to relatively trivial female crimes. Historically, females have received far more severe treatment for "immoral conduct" than males. Indeed, "girls charged with status offenses have often been more harshly treated than their male or female counterparts charged with crimes."[16] Criminalization thus serves only to encourage continued gender, racial, and economic class bias by the criminal justice system.

If criminalization harms prostitutes and clients, it unquestionably also harms the community at large. The economic costs alone are substantial. In 1985, the sixteen largest cities in the United States spent an average of $7.5 million enforcing anti-prostitution policy. "Half of them spent more on prostitution control than on education or public welfare, and five spent more than on health services and hospitals."[17] Add to this the loss of tax revenue for unclaimable prostitute income and the economic loss to communities is truly staggering.

What of the argument that criminalization gives the "right message" by communicating and reflecting appropriate values? If this view arises from a desire to enforce traditional religious values, then we must consider this country's presumed separation of church and state. This "separation" is highly complex, even in sexual matters, being adhered to in some instances (e.g., adultery) but not others (e.g. sodomy). While this inconsistency is highly problematic, it requires a far longer discussion than can be offered here. Hence, while I would emphatically argue that all sexual activity between consenting adults that does not cause harm to others should be beyond the reach of the law, minimally consistency requires that for-profit sexual acts be treated in the same way as not-for-profit sex, unless an argument can be provided to explain the difference in their moral status (one that does not simply reiterate the madonna/whore dichotomy). But, more important, supporters of legal moralism explicitly hold that the moral values that should be codified into law must reflect a genuine community sentiment. Criminalization of prostitution does not, in fact, reflect the preponderant perspective.[18] Nor, as I have indicated above, does legal moralism represent a perspective that feminists can safely adopt.

Most important, the values and standards that criminalization communicates support the continued stigmatization of the prostitute, negatively affecting prostitute and nonprostitute women alike. Criminalization codifies the taint of sex and the bifurcation of women. As Chesney-Lind argues, "We often . . . overlook the important role of the concept of criminal as 'outsider' in the maintenance of the existing social order. Clearly, harsh public punishment of a few 'fallen' women as witches and whores has always been integral to enforcement of the boundaries of the 'good' woman's place in patriarchal society. Anyone seriously interested in examining women's crime or the subjugation of women, then, must carefully consider the role of the contemporary criminal justice system in the maintenance of modern patriarchy."[19] Feminists must oppose criminalization as part of an agenda to eliminate laws that function as a source of patriarchal control and ideology.

Finally, criminalization clearly violates prostitutes' right to bodily autonomy.[20] And although, as discussed earlier, this right is not absolute, unless it can be established that criminalization lessens harm, outlawing prostitution does not fall into the category of legitimate exceptions.

B. Legalizing Prostitution

There are, in general, four reasons given for favoring legalized prostitution: to protect public sensibilities, to protect public health, to protect public safety, and to protect women (and men) in the business. These are supposed to be achievable by restricting the locations of prostitution and by required medical testing.[21] A Nye County, Nevada, ordinance explicitly justifies legalization by holding that

> the legalization of prostitution under strict medical and police supervision, control and enforcement will operate to substantially reduce the incidence of venereal and other contagious diseases and the crime rate within Nye County, and as such is necessary for the preservation of the public health, safety, and welfare of the citizens and residents. (Nye County Ordinance no.83)

Legalization is viewed as a middle ground between the uncompromising position of criminalization and the "anything goes" perception of decriminalization.

With regard to health concerns, at the time the Nye ordinance was enacted, no empirical evidence existed to support the claims therein. Rather, this policy, as with similar legislation, stems from the traditional conceptual construction of the prostitute as diseased and dirty. Historically, such policies can be traced to fears, such as those expressed in Alexander John Baptiste Parent-Duchatelet's *De la prostitution dans la ville de Paris* (1836), that working-class women will leave prostitution and "blend back" into the working class, where they will spread their "filth" to unwitting, "good" working-class men; or to the fear addressed by the British Contagious Disease Acts, which were concerned to protect military men from a similar fate. But the assumption that prostitution is a significant source of venereal diseases is actually belied by the available evidence. In the Netherlands, where such studies are possible, it has been found that only 10 percent of the national STD rate is attributable to prostitutes or their clients, while, according to a New York Times article, "over the last decade, there have been several reports of . . . women who had contracted AIDS from husbands infected by prostitutes, but scientists now believe that female-to-male transmission is relatively rare."[22] Recent studies of Nevada brothel prostitutes required to undergo such tests do indicate a lower rate of HIV compared to those prostituting illegally in Nevada. However, the difference between the groups appears to be attributable to required condom use rather than to testing. Nor is there any evidence of a lower STD rate in Nye County overall. In reality, medical exams simply force prostitutes who are infected to work in an illegal venue, where they are often more likely to infect their clients due to the related difficulties of practicing "safe" sex.[23] Required testing of prostitutes may actually increase the danger of STD transmission. In Nevada as in other jurisdictions, there is a common tendency for many men to offer prostitutes bribes not to use condoms.[24] Regulations requiring medical testing of prostitutes are only likely to increase this tendency because they lead to the false expectation that the prostitute is disease-free. It is quite possible that a prostitute has been exposed to an STD since her most recent test, particularly since three months must pass between the time of exposure to HIV and detection by currently affordable testing methods.[25] There is therefore no clear value in such tests but significant danger in encouraging clients to believe that prostitutes are disease-free.

More important, such a policy is both illogical and guilty of gender discrimination. If these policies were justified by a desire to "reduce the incidence of venereal and other contagious diseases and [were] necessary for the preservation of the public health," then why should it be only prostitutes who are required to undergo medical tests? Such policies are concerned only to protect the male customer from STDs, not the female prostitute. What about her risk? Logically, if one's concern is with preserving the public health, then it is more important to protect prostitutes than their customers from disease, since a prostitute is likely to have sexual contact with more partners than are her clients. There should therefore be more effort made to keep her from contracting these diseases. If we choose to adopt a system of medical screening, then logically male clients should also be required to participate, particularly for those STDs that can be diagnosed immediately. Even when testing does not provide an immediate diagnosis, a system of preregistering and pretesting of clients, with an appropriate "waiting period," could, in theory, be instituted. I am not advocating for such policies. Not only is it obvious that male customers will never submit to these, but I oppose enforced medical testing altogether. It is, however, important to understand that the desire for mandatory medical testing of prostitutes arises from the conceptual construction of the prostitute as diseased, conjoined with the (unconscious) acceptance of a larger gender hierarchy; for logic dictates that if one is genuinely concerned with public health, it is more important to administer STD tests to customers than to prostitutes.

Finally, such approaches are demonstrably less successful than are less stigmatizing and limiting ones. Despite the open and international character of prostitution in the Netherlands, the Dutch have the lowest spread of HIV in the world—though they have no required testing of any populations! They have chosen to deal with venereal diseases with an aggressive and explicit public education campaign run by the Dutch Ministry of Health. When I arrived in Amsterdam on my most recent visit, I immediately noticed a large poster outside the railroad station with a frontal view of a woman, wearing only underpants, facing a naked man (back shot) and holding up a condom. She was saying, "I'll take something off if you put something on." There were lengthy, explicit public promotions for condom use on MTV, and women dressed in condom-box costumes sold condoms on beaches. Innumerable educational pamphlets were actively distributed to working prostitutes, including the comic book *Work and Health*, which not only discussed STDs, particularly HIV, but explained, with cartoon pictures, how to apply condoms with one's mouth without the client detecting it. In the middle of the pamphlet was a quiz containing photographs of male genitalia infected with syphilis, gonorrhea, herpes, and chlamydia to enable prostitutes to spot these diseases once they become visually detectable. Prostitutes are encouraged to do visual examinations of clients' genitalia whenever possible. Most impressive, this comic book is published in seven languages, including Arabic. The Dutch recognition that prostitution policies must address the diversity of the country's prostitute population is further evidenced by their willingness to financially support relevant studies—for example, Hans Roerink's 1990 paper "Orientation on Possibilities of Care/Treatment and Aids Prevention for Drug Addicts of Turkish and Moroccan Origin in the Netherlands," funded by the Dutch Ministries of Welfare, Health, and Cultural Affairs, which discusses strategies for combating the spread of HIV, especially among North African homosexual prostitutes. This approach is apparently successful; it is estimated that 80 percent of all Dutch prostitutes use condoms regularly. If our concern is genuinely one of public health, education rather than required testing appears to be the most effective approach.

As to the expectation that "the legalization of prostitution . . . will operate to substantially reduce . . . the crime rate . . . and as such is necessary for the preservation of the public . . . safety, and welfare of the citizens and residents," this, too, is not supported by the evidence. According to the Canadian Fraser Committee report, the then–West German system, which zoned prostitution activity and required registration, health cards, and medical exams for prostitutes, was hardly a success. The number of sex clubs and juvenile prostitutes increased; more prostitutes were unregistered than registered; and street prostitution remained as high as before the institution of these measures. Most West German prostitutes still had pimps. In Boston, which attempted to develop a red-light district where prostitution was tolerated, zoning also proved to be a failure. According to their Bureau of Municipal Research report, existing nonsex businesses in the zoned area moved out, further stigmatizing prostitution activity; "sexual services became more blatant, which changed attitudes about the area: and crime increased while enforcement decreased. The Area became rundown and unsafe."[26]

A pattern of noncompliance to prostitute registration appears to be global. In Peru, Singapore, and Uruguay as well as Germany, despite legal requirements fewer than 50 percent of working prostitutes are registered; in Indonesia, the figure is fewer than 30 percent, while only an estimated 10 percent of Greek prostitutes are registered (the same percentage as for Nevada). An unknown but clearly small percentage of prostitutes in Geneva, Switzerland; Mombasa, Kenya; Chiapas, Mexico; and Guatemala are registered, and even in Austria, where registration entitles prostitutes to participate in the government health plan, only 50 percent are registered. This is partly the case because many prostitutes are temporary and work only when necessary. But, more important, few women are willing to open themselves to this bureaucratic stigmatization.[27]

Although Nevada law may not be representative of all U.S. policies that would be developed if prostitution were legalized, it indicates the approach that is likely to be taken. As long as we are under a patriarchal governance, and particularly given both our puritanical heritage and our propensity for absolutes, there is good reason to believe that whatever laws the various states and municipalities might enact, they would likely be at least as repressive as Nevada's. Nevada prides itself, after all, on rejecting legislation driven purely by concerns about sin, as is evidenced by their longtime legal stances on gambling and divorce as well as prostitution. Yet even here, the treatment of prostitutes under legalization is horrific; women are stripped of some of their most fundamental rights, dignity and humanity.

How can such laws be possible in twenty-first-century America? They are defensible only if one accepts the current representation of "the prostitute." Exchange "prostitute" for any other worker and the insanity of such laws is overpowering. It is because living, embodied prostitutes continue to be reduced to mere paradigms and metaphors, to disembodied stereotypes, to one-dimensional objects without individual identity, that such laws appear reasonable. As long as hegemonic "wisdom" holds that a prostitute's life and reality can be understood totally through "the prostitute" construct, such laws will be attractive. The legal brothel prostitute is a "willing prostitute," and as such, she is the prostitute victimizer—a diseased criminal, heartless, greedy, altogether untrustworthy, a dishonest seducer who would do anything for money. And that is all she is—pure prostitute, pure paradigm. She cannot be trusted with the freedoms of honest people. If she is not circumscribed in these ways, if she has a car, if she can leave the brothel, if she goes to a bar, she is, according to this construction, likely to service customers outside the brothel, where she can cheat brothel management of their "cut." Although the same possibility exists with almost any other service provider be it garage mechanics, hair stylists, tax preparers, or even lawyers, there is no presumption that they will cheat their employers. But they're not prostitutes. Nevada law isolates prostitutes from the community because they are "an embarrassment," sexual deviants and symbols of the disintegration of the society. "Decent" people do not want to be confronted with prostitutes. The prostitute must be watched and monitored, and thus the codified stigmatization of registering, fingerprinting, and photographing her is a necessity; for it is ultimately she, and not the brothels, who must be controlled.

The Nevada regulations result not only in a system that reinforces the stigmatization of prostitutes and denies them their most basic rights, but it also creates a working environment and conditions that are so unattractive that legal brothels are hard pressed to find women who will work in them. It is for good reason that prostitutes in general prefer to work in illegal venues. Nevada's policies altogether disfranchise prostitutes as citizens and rights holders, violate them as workers and persons, and promote dangerous client expectations, all in order to control the "victimizing" prostitute. Nowhere is the importance of conceptual constructs to the construction of policy more evident. Systems of legalization not only promote such representations of prostitutes but carry along, on this tide of misogynistic control, a correlating contempt for nonprostitute women. In Nevada, various unwritten rules circumscribe the behavior of non-prostitute women. As Pillard notes:

> One of the most curious unwritten rules is that [in Winnemucca] no non-establishment female can visit any of the brothels or even drive through the area. [Winnemucca] police chief [Lee] Jones told me in an interview that this rule was enforced to protect customers of these broth-els. Apparently there is some concern that an angry wife could drive through the Line [a public road] looking for her husband's car.[28]

Like criminalization, legalization embodies and perpetuates the continued stigmatization of the prostitute and sexual activity and maintains the correlative subordinate status of nonprostitute women. It violates bodily autonomy and actively worsens the quality of life of prostitutes, making most of them criminals for noncompliance, and it promotes the spread of STDs through unrealistic expectations. It does, however, effectively achieve its purpose: the control of the prostitute body.

C. Decriminalizing Prostitution

It's the controls.
—Carol Leigh (a.k.a Scarlett Harlot)[29]

Although most feminists favor decriminalization of prostitution, our reasons for doing so often conflict. Certainly, there are key reasons for favoring decriminalization on which feminists agree, but the issues on which we disagree significantly affect our perspectives on an overall policy. I begin by considering justifications for decriminalization that most feminists would accept and end the discussion with a serious examination of our disagreements.

Under global systems of patriarchy, women's economic options are relatively limited. For poor women (disproportionately women of color from underdeveloped nations or lesbians),[30] prostitution is one of the few, and sometimes the only, sources of livable wages. For middle-class women, prostitution may present the only opportunity to earn "real" money. It is therefore inevitable that many women will end up working as prostitutes at some point in their lives. Unquestionably, all feminists must strongly advocate programs that will significantly expand women's economic opportunities and improve women's wages. Additionally, because many women prostitute to support their drug addictions, it is critical that feminists insist on expanded state-funded drug treatment centers—particularly ones directed at female populations, including pregnant women, for whom few programs currently exist. Feminists also agree that prostitution must be made safer and more humane for those who do enter it.

Both criminalization and legalization have proven to be empirical failures, demonstrably harming prostitute women and the community at large. Decriminalization combined with appropriate social services significantly improves the lot of prostitutes and the larger community. Prostitutes do not have to face possible criminal sanctions, nor are they limited to working in abusive state approved brothels or streetwalking zones. Decriminalization facilitates the development of state-funded social services directed at improving the lives of prostitutes, an impossibility for most such services under criminalization. And since, under legalization, the vast majority of prostitutes remain outside legal venues, few working prostitutes would be able to access these services under that strategy. By removing the codified taint of illegal or legally stigmatized practices, decriminalization also significantly increases the likelihood that state-funded social services will have a different tenor: Instead of services dominated by a desire to control prostitutes, we are, for example, more likely to develop nonpunitive, nonjudgmental shelters for women wanting to leave prostitution. Furthermore, as the European experience demonstrates, the harm women suffer due to legalizing or criminalizing prostitution is not justified by the potential harm to society from STDs. Indeed, the opposite appears to be true—with appropriate public educational campaigns, the rate of sexually transmitted diseases can be most effectively lowered under a decriminalized system. In fact, the United States has been able to keep the spread of HIV relatively constant in the population at large by just such an aggressive educational campaign.

Given the harm all women experience due to the madonna/whore dichotomy, and particularly the harm caused to those stigmatized as prostitute-whore (which, as I have argued, may include any woman), it is clear that a feminist prostitution policy must aim to destroy this bifurcation and particularly the debilitating construct of the prostitute-whore. In terms of "what a policy means," no approach is as effective as decriminalization in undermining this paradigm. Criminalization clearly defines the prostitute as outlaw, as stigmatized other. Legalization effectively does the same by insisting that prostitutes be controlled in a way distinct from other workers. It consistently reaffirms the construct of the prostitute as untrustworthy, diseased, and engaged in commercial sin. It "tolerates prostitution but not prostitutes." Decriminalization, while failing to single-handedly remove the cultural stigma of "the prostitute," is the only legal approach that does not codify it. And when conjoined with adequate support services and strict controls on prostitute facilitators, decriminalization can communicate an official stance that recognizes the moral value, rights, and diversity of prostitutes while reflecting the need to protect them from the abuse that has been a traditional part of the industry.

Both criminalization and legalization of prostitution constitute forms of secondary discrimination; decriminalization does not. As already noted, many women have few real economic alternatives to prostituting, given prevailing systems of patriarchy, racism, capitalism, and so forth. Women in the United States and globally continue to earn significantly less than men while having greater responsibility for child care and elder care, among other tasks. Some of the discrimination women suffer in the workplace is or was caused by explicitly discriminatory laws and policies. Conversely, the sexual double standard is also caused, in part, by prevailing or historical policies and laws discriminating against women and, in turn, generates the circumstances that give market value to sexual access to women by men, but rarely the reverse. As a result, "there are virtually no other occupations available to unskilled or low skilled women offering an income which compares to prostitution."[31] For these reasons, it is almost exclusively women (and, given heterosexism, gay men and transgender or transsexual individuals) who enter prostitution, and thus it is overwhelmingly this population who are subject to the legal sanctions connected with criminalization and legalization. But this constitutes a clear form of secondary discrimination. In effect, by prior and existing policies,[32] the state supports the devaluation of women's nonsexual labor and then arrests women or places women under invasive and egregious controls if they engage in sexual labor.

While criminalization and legalization are often justified by appeals to legal moralism and legal paternalism ("protecting" prostitutes and their clients from themselves), decriminalization does neither. Additionally, discussions of the acceptability of prostitution often juxtapose the right of bodily autonomy against the "conflicting" right to bodily integrity.

Thus some hold that although the individual who opts to prostitute is exercising her or his right to bodily autonomy, she or he is violating her or his right to bodily integrity because sale of sexual access violates the value of the human body, cheapening it by making it an object of barter. But, as I have argued above, for feminists or for anyone involved in civil rights movements, it is clearly preferable to give the individual the greatest degree of bodily autonomy possible while severely limiting the persuasiveness of appeals to an abstract standard of bodily integrity in the determination of public policy. As such, even if prostitution could genuinely be said to violate bodily integrity (which is a highly controversial claim), it is far from apparent that this is as salient as the violation of bodily autonomy embodied in criminalized or legalized prostitution laws.

8

The Feminist Debate

Much of this book is a plea for rejecting absolutes. Because I contend that prostitution is not an absolute, is not an either/or but a "both and then some," my analysis of what is wrong with prostitution currently and what should be done about it reflects my commitment to recognizing its deep diversity and contradictions. For this reason, my analysis differs significantly from prevailing American feminist approaches.

The traditional opposing positions on prostitution not surprisingly tend to mirror the opposing positions in the feminist "sex wars." In the United States, these perspectives are mainly represented by, on the one hand, the radical and socialist feminist perspectives, which yield the prevailing American feminist position today, and, on the other hand, the feminist sex radical and liberal feminist approaches. In England, socialist feminists provide a third view, more purely focused on capitalism as the source of prostitution.[1] My analysis is intended to bridge the gaps among these positions, adopting those aspects of each that I find compelling while rejecting others. Normally, philosophers are trained to avoid such an approach, believing that if two or more positions begin with contradictory axioms or presumptions, then the claims that follow from them are also likely to be contradictory. But this is not an appropriate strategy in the case of policy development and particularly *in re* policies governing practices as diverse and contradictory as prostitution.

In this discussion, I engage in more formal philosophical debate than I have previously in this work. This involves careful analysis and critique of specific texts that are representative of positions with which I disagree.[2]

Critique of the Prevailing American Feminist View

My position is in many respects antithetical to the currently established and prevailing American feminist position[3] on prostitution, both because of differences in our treatment of anti-abolitionist advocacy perspectives described in Chapter 1 and because I argue for the restructuring and normalization of prostitution whereas the prevailing American feminist position maintains that in a normalized world, one in which *women* were normalized, prostitution would not exist. The prevailing American feminist perspective defends decriminalization solely because it is viewed as the least of all evils. Advocates of this perspective believe that prostitution is more damaging to the individual and to the class of women overall than are other forms of labor or heterosexual activity, that "prostitution is inherently gendered, a component and manifestation of the patriarchal institution of heterosexuality," and "serve[s] to perpetuate women's social subordination"[4] in a more damaging manner than other practices and professions in which women engage. "We cannot examine the labour performed by prostitutes as something separate from the industry of prostitution. And while it is important to work to increase protection against dangers faced by women who do that labour, that is not the same thing as working to protect their jobs."[5]

I will begin by focusing on Carol Pateman's *The Sexual Contract*, both because her view of private sexual contracts, including marriage and other heterosexual noncommercial liaisons, is significant to my overall position and because hers is a particularly strong and developed version of the prevailing U.S. feminist position. Pateman insightfully and compellingly argues that the traditional conception of the "social contract"[6] presupposes and accompanies a sexual contract. Through historical analysis, Pateman demonstrates that the original social contractarians (e.g., Locke, Hobbes, and Rousseau) did not conceive women to be members to the contract. While they explicitly argued against the justification of father/son patriarchy, they either implicitly or explicitly defended male/female patriarchy and depended on a (implicit) sexual contract. Pateman maintains, "The original pact is a sexual as well as a social contract: it is sexual in the sense of patriarchal—that is, the contract establishes men's political right over women—and also sexual in the sense of establishing orderly access by men to women's bodies. The original contract creates . . . 'the law of male sex-right.'"[7]

Although Pateman spends the majority of the book considering the marriage contract, she devotes one chapter to prostitution as exemplifying how the sexual contract currently structures the public sphere. While she believes that, in general, "the employment contract gives the employer right of command over the use of the worker's labor, that is to say over the self, person and body of the worker,"[8] she finds something more gravely wrong with prostitution than with being either a wife or a worker under capitalism. Hence Pateman spends a considerable amount of time attempting to distinguish prostitution from other forms of labor.[9] Ultimately, Pateman's answer to why prostitution is worse than other slave wage labor appears to be that commonly found in many feminist analyses, that is, that prostitution is not the sale of services but the sale of the person herself. "Prostitution differs from wage slavery. No form of labour power can be separated from the body, but only through the prostitution contract does the buyer obtain unilateral right of direct sexual use of a woman's body."[10] But as should by now be apparent, in the less-abusive forms of prostitution, as in the less-abusive forms of marriage and consensual noncommercial sex, no *unilateral* right of direct sexual use of a woman's body exists. Nor, as I have indicated, do prostitutes literally "sell their bodies."

Pateman acknowledges that "there are also other professions in which bodies are up for sale and in which employers have an intrinsic interest in their workers' bodies . . . the bodies of professional sportsmen and sportswomen are also available to be contracted out."[11] However, on Pateman's view, there is a critical difference between these professions: "Owners of baseball teams have command over the use of their players' bodies, but the bodies are not directly used *sexually* by those who have contracted for them."[12] But why, on Pateman's view, is *sexual* use worse? She argues that although identity is not subsumed in sexuality, it is

> inseparable from the sexual construction of the self. [Because] sexual mastery is the major means through which men affirm their manhood . . . in relations between the sexes, unequivocal affirmation is obtained by engaging in "the sex act." Womanhood, too is confirmed in sexual activity, and when a prostitute contracts out use of her body she is thus selling *herself* in a very real sense.

Shannon Bell quite correctly objects that "at the center of Pateman's sexual contract is a silent value judgment on commercial sexuality and certain sexual activities."[13] Bell maintains that Pateman's analysis unwittingly assumes the traditional bifurcation of women because, if Pateman is correct, the woman who marries or contracts noncommercially to some sexual activity, access, or arrangement is also selling (or "giving away") *herself* in just as real a sense as is the prostitute.

Feminists consistently argue that sexuality, including sexual history, orientation, and activity, *should* be no more defining of individual identity than are many other characteristics of the self, and that under patriarchy the sexual identity of the self is both overemphasized and deeply perverse and perverted to maintain male privilege. Indeed, many radical feminist works can be understood as analyses of the perversion of the sexual construction of the self under patriarchy and of the deeply problematic nature of viewing oneself as solely or primarily sexual. It thus seems problematic, at the least, for Pateman to maintain, because "womanhood, too is [under patriarchy] confirmed in sexual activity," that "when a prostitute contracts out use of her body she is thus selling *herself* in a very real sense." Patriarchy certainly maintains this is so, but as feminists, shouldn't we resist such self-definitions, values, and beliefs? While I do not believe either that any *individual* is capable of changing patriarchal constructions or that any individual can altogether escape them, I do believe that we are obligated to resist them and to encourage and support any mass movement that attempts to do so, because it is only through mass resistance and struggle that structural change is possible.

Prostitutes' rights activists have raised this issue repeatedly, but their voices have generally been ignored by feminist prostitution abolitionists. That the sale of sexual services and access is, under patriarchy, different from the sale of nonsexual services and access is not in contention here. Under patriarchy, women unquestionably pay, in many senses and ways, for selling sexual services; these activities are stigmatized and "othered." But the same is true, if less intensely, for the sale of innumerable nonsexual services under patriarchy, either because the services and providers are even vaguely connected with sex (e.g., massage therapists) or because they violate gender norms (e.g., being a female professor or carpenter or a male nurse or secretary). Such behaviors are also stigmatized, and one certainly pays for violating them. I am stigmatized and "othered" as a female philosophy and Women's Studies professor. (I am "unfeminine," "masculine," "weird," a "dyke," a "man-hater," a "ball-buster.") But no feminist has ever suggested that these judgments or the integral connection between my *intellectual* construction and my identity is reason to believe that in my academic contract I am "selling . . . [*my*]*self* in a very real sense." Pateman and others who offer similar arguments need to make explicit why the sale of *sexual* services and access is different in kind from the sale of other (nonsexual) services and access that are also stigmatized under patriarchy. It is further critical that they make clear how noncommercial sexual arrangements are different in either kind or severity from commercial ones. Without such an explanation, it appears that the difference between the prostitute and the female carpenter or wife, on such accounts, is simply that between the whore and the madonna.

Pateman's analysis incorporates an additional assumption that I find highly problematic and commonplace in many, particularly radical, feminist analyses of prostitution: to wit, that "sexual mastery is *the major* means through which men affirm their manhood." Such a view fails to consider all perspectives, for this is not the case in all cultures or classes or stages of individual lives, either historically or currently. In many societies, manhood has been and is confirmed by producing children (often just sons),[14] by capitalist success, by physical strength and prowess (often a matter of being able to physically subordinate or to kill other human beings), and by being a politically and socially powerful member of the community. Womanhood, by contrast, is affirmed by producing and nurturing children, nurturing and caring for others, accepting subordinate social and political roles, meeting prevailing standards of physical beauty and grace (including using all the debilitating means required to achieve them), and the like. Any feminist analysis, whether of public policy or otherwise, that fails to give considerable weight to patriarchal subordination through other spheres of domination and mastery, those involving nonsexual physical, economic, psychological, and reproductive domination, will necessarily be inadequate.[15] What positions like Pateman's fail to acknowledge is that for many women, economic subordination, for example, is far more crippling and annihilating of the self than is sexual subordination. This is clearly the perspective of many prostitutes.

Peculiarly, Pateman acknowledges:

> Men do not want solely the obedience of women, they want their sentiments. All men, except the most brutish, desire to have, not a forced slave but a willing one, not a slave merely, but a favorite. An employer or a husband can more easily obtain faithful service and acknowledgment of his mastery than a man who enters into the prostitution contract.[16]

Rather bizarrely, however, she appears to see the fact that prostitutes are better able than wives or long-term employees to resist male emotional subordination as insignificant. All she says is that "such distancing creates a problem for men, a problem that can be seen as another variant on the contradiction of mastery and slavery."[17] She never appears to entertain the possibility that this may be a significant advantage of prostitution over marriage or long-term traditional employment, although this is an advantage that prostitutes often point to.

Later, Pateman argues that in other contracts, such as those of civil slaves and wives, obedience is exchanged for lifelong protections (e.g., benefits beyond wages for civil slaves and "the family wage" for wives) that are not available to the prostitute. "The short-term prostitution contract cannot include the protection available in long-term relations."[18] Clearly, in a nation in which more than half of all marriages end in divorce, the notion of "lifelong protection" does not apply; but what is most peculiar about this passage is that, as she indicates earlier in the book, such "protection" is really a mechanism of exploitation of the worker / wife, binding "the subordinate more closely to the contract."[19] Why, then, does Pateman suggest that the lack of such protection is a deficit for the prostitution contract? For the answer to her question "Where is the protection in the prostitution contract?"[20] is straightforward: In the less-abusive forms of prostitution, unlike less-abusive marriages, the protection becomes located in the woman herself. Prostitutes who earn decent fees and are not victimized by facilitators or boyfriends are not economically dependent on men (or capitalist employers) for their "protection." Their wages are *theirs*, not family wages. Because they control their own income, they can purchase their own insurance, pensions, and other job related benefits (I have met prostitutes who did just that.) What should count for Pateman as a lessening of male economic mastery to be weighed against relative sexual mastery somehow becomes transformed into a deficit on this account.

Some of the beliefs that underlie Pateman's account can be found in feminist arguments that view prostitution as unusually problematic for women *as a class*. Kate Millett, for example, maintains, "It is not sex the prostitute is really made to sell: it is degradation. And the buyer, the john is not buying sexuality, but power, power over another human being, the dizzy ambition of being lord of another's will for a stated period of time."[21] What the prostitute is selling, on this view, is the acceptance of patriarchy. The prostitute is paid for not just acceptance of but reveling in her own sexual subjugation, in accord with the patriarchal fantasies of her clients. Millett and other feminists maintain that thus prostitution constitutes a propaganda tool for patriarchy that is a particularly egregious source of perpetuating women's social subordination.

But is prostitution responsible for such harm? Is it a particularly egregious political practice? After looking at a significant variety of prostitution practices, it seems to me that sometimes, though probably not in the majority of instances, it is. As I indicated at the outset, my definition of prostitution is intentionally narrow and relies on the distinction between private and public acts. When a prostitute sexually interacts *privately* with a male client, can her behavior be classified as any more or less a patriarchal propaganda or perpetuating tool than either the private heterosexual interaction that any female may engage in or other forms of paid labor? Other types of sex work are much more genuine propaganda in this regard. Whether one is speaking of films or live sex shows, public depictions of misogynistic sexual behavior and attitudes, particularly in the male viewing contexts in which these often occur, are, I believe, significant contributors to cultural misogyny. (Although here I must add that I am convinced they are not as effective tools of patriarchal propaganda as many—perhaps most—mainstream films, plays, or music videos, which are both ubiquitous and socially acceptable and which generally carry pervasive patriarchal messages. I do not believe that nudity or sexual explicitness, even in misogynistic, violent X-rated films, is any more efficacious in promulgating women's subordination than, for example, the messages in teen coed terrorize-and-slash films. Furthermore, as evidence on gang rape and fraternity mentality suggests, sexually expressed misogyny often occurs in group contexts as part of male bonding. Men appear to egg each other on, encouraging one another into ever more misogynistic behavior.[22])

But in private sex acts, the story appears much more complex. It is, as most feminist sex theorists acknowledge, impossible to interact heterosexually (or homosexually) at this time in history in a nonsexist, nonpatriarchal fashion. Our very conception of and language for sexuality and sexual activity are so deeply tainted by constructs of male domination that we are incapable of altogether stepping out of hegemonic sexist conceptual constructions, no matter how deep our feminist commitments or how hard we try. The best we can hope for is to lessen, through constant self-politicization, the degree to which sexism impacts on us and on our sexual lives. But while acceptance of female sexual subordination occurs to a greater or lesser degree in both paid and unpaid sexual encounters, it may be more likely to occur in prostitution than in unpaid sexual activity. This is in part because some prostitution, particularly streetwalking, draws an especially vulnerable, economically desperate population of workers who are likely to sell services on the buyers' terms—terms that often include female degradation. But it is also the case that, in all service transactions, the buyer generally has greater power over the seller than he (or she) would over someone who is providing the service for free. Any paid service worker, after all, depends on customer satisfaction for return business. And given that male power and female degradation are currently eroticized, it is *likely* that they will be expressed more often in paid sexual exchanges. Given the diversity and complexity of the industry, however, the degree to which this occurs varies widely, and at times the reverse may be the case.[23] Furthermore, under a prostitution policy that gives prostitutes genuine power over their work, it is far less likely that they will acquiesce to such treatment and thus less likely that prostitution will promulgate such values.[24] Finally, but of critical importance, although the *degree* of acceptance of female subordination and degradation *may* be greater in paid than in unpaid sex, it is far from apparent that, overall, prostitution perpetuates patriarchy more than unpaid sex. Because men generally have considerably more unpaid sexual experiences than paid ones, and because women act out patriarchal erotic values and fantasies in all heterosexuality to a greater or lesser degree, it is far from apparent that prostitution is a more egregious contributor to the support of sexist sexuality. Prostitution is an easy target, but empirical evidence would be required to support the claim that it is a greater source of patriarchal propaganda cumulatively than are unpaid sexual acts.

The question that remains is why the degree of acceptance of male power and female degradation in prostitution constitutes greater harm to women as a class than does the acceptance of male power and female degradation in other instances of paid labor. What about secretaries, nurses, or waitresses, for example, who, for a fee, provide traditional female nurturance, often in a context where they are required to accept significant female subordination and degradation? Why are these not equally activities and industries that constitute an opportunity for the expression of male power and the perpetuation of women's subordination? Debra Satz provides perhaps the clearest statements of two somewhat different feminist arguments that maintain prostitution is worse:

There are two significant differences between prostitution and other gender-segregated professions. . . . First, most people believe that prostitution, unlike secretarial work, is especially objectionable. Holding such
moral views of prostitution constant, if prostitution continues to be primarily a female occupation, then the existence of prostitution will disproportionately fuel negative images of women. Second, and relatedly,
the particular image of women in prostitution is more of an image of inferiority than that of a secretary. The image embodies a greater amount
of objectification, of representing the prostitute as an object without a
will of her own. Prostitutes are far more likely to be victims of violence
than are secretaries. . . . If prostitution is wrong . . . it is because the sale
of women's sexual labor may have adverse consequences for achieving a
significant form of equality between men and women.[25]

The first difference Satz cites simply amounts to the claim that because
prostitution is more stigmatized than secretarial work, it reflects more
badly on women as a class than do other gender-segregated occupations.
Surely, this is not an argument that should persuade feminists. Doing feminist work or living according to feminist ideals necessitates performing
activities that most people find objectionable. Significant social stigma attaches to being a single mother rather than a married one, a lesbian rather
than straight, or a feminist rather than a nonfeminist, but it does not follow that being a single mother, a lesbian, or a feminist is wrong because
it may "have adverse consequences for achieving a significant form of
equality." It is these very stigmata that must be undermined if women are
to overcome subordination; and no stigma, including the stigma of being
"woman," will ever be undermined if we insist that women must remain
"good"—that is, must avoid activities, including prostitution, that most
people find objectionable in order to avoid fueling negative images of
women.

What of the argument that the concept of the prostitute is constructed
as inferior to that of the secretary and embodies greater objectification—
an "object without a will of her own"? As discussed in Chapter 4, there
are two competing images of the prostitute: victim and victimizer. The
prostitute victimizer is not constructed as the image of "an object without a will of her own"; quite the reverse: She is a dangerous "subject"
who must be guarded against. Her concerns are purely with her will and
desires, without concern for anyone else's welfare. In contrast, it is far

from apparent that the image of the prostitute victim is more object-like than the image of the overburdened invisible secretary or dutiful nurse, both of whom embody the values of total self-sacrifice, self-effacement, and obedience to their "superiors" (bosses or doctors). The prostitute victim is imaged as sexual object, the secretary, nurse, waitress, wife, or mother as nurturant object. The question remains: Why is one worse for women as a class than the other? And while streetwalkers are more likely than secretaries to be victims of violence, this is far from clear for all forms of prostitution.[26] Secretaries, however, are far more likely to be horribly underpaid.[27]

In speaking with my feminist acquaintance Judy, I tried to explain the perspective of women in prostitution who opted to prostitute rather than working a "straight" job for less pay. She repeated several times that she "just didn't get it." I think this may be the case for many feminists. Given our desire for bodily autonomy and our sense of heterosexuality as a weapon, I understand why it is hard to get it. But I also know that many women do not "get" the choice to be a licensed practical nurse or secretary when this often requires accepting dismissal or contempt in exchange for relatively low wages. Some women experience a greater sense of violation in those situations, particularly because of the financial subordination and the corresponding dependence on men, than in prostitution. The point here is not that women do not experience male sexual mastery in prostitution, for they clearly do. But male mastery, privilege, and domination are unequivocally affirmed in a great many other ways and activities. Not only do all women suffer from sexual mastery when engaging in any form of heterosexual activity (although perhaps to a lesser extent in unpaid sex), but there does not appear to be a compelling reason to presume that sexual mastery is worse than other kinds of mastery. Depending on the perspective of the individual woman, the subordination and degradation in prostitution may be preferable to that experienced in other areas. The economic and emotional independence possible through nonabusive prostitution may, for many women and at different times in their lives, significantly outweigh the possibly greater degree of sexual subordination within prostitution. And the greater economic and emotional independence found in the less-abusive forms of prostitution, as compared to marriage and long-term employment, makes it possible for some prostitutes to have greater control over their sexual use and activity than is often supposed and than is the case for many nonprostitute women.

Analyses like those described above unwittingly reaffirm the bifurcation of women by presuming that the situation of the prostitute is different in kind and involves greater subordination or harm to the class of women than that of the madonna. Given the central role of the madonna/whore dichotomy in the victimization of *all* women, this is an extremely dangerous error. It is incontestable that prostitution contains the unspeakable horrors described by many feminist and nonfeminist analysts. It is unquestionably true that it contains a grotesque parasitism, a world in which one may be reduced to pure object and, ultimately, where one may be forced to accept that vision of oneself. But the same can and has been said of marriage and heterosexuality in general and of innumerable jobs, particularly traditionally female ones. How can any of us, male or female, escape the patriarchal "tapes" on which we were raised, the paradigms that shape the very way we think? But this is not all that is true of these relationships and occupations, anymore than it is all that is true of prostitution. Marriage, heterosexual acts, and the various female employments contain many other elements, some of them extremely rewarding and pleasurable, to a greater or lesser degree. If they did not, women would never willingly choose to engage in them. There is nothing new in this suggestion; feminists have understood for a long time that patriarchy works, in part, by rewarding obedience and acceptance of patriarchy. If marriage or heterosexual acts or these jobs were unremittingly evil and abusive, they would not be so common. But the same is true of prostitution. And in refusing to recognize that not all prostitutes are victims or egregious dupes for patriarchy, we not only dismiss the voices of many women but continue to make prostitutes Other. Prostitutes are, as the statistics demonstrate, not Other; "They" are us. Why, then, do some feminists continue to insist that women cannot fare better (rather than worse) in prostitution than in other occupations, cannot work in prostitution as willingly as some women enter marriage or become secretaries? Why can't these feminists believe that prostitution offers some women a reasonable way of satisfying their goals that they find preferable to the alternatives—without their necessarily being misguided, being victims, or having false consciousness?

It is essential that American feminists attack this stigma instead of perpetuating it. We must refuse to define all acts of prostitution as victimization unless similarly defining all nonprostitute heterosexual acts and female labor as victimizing. We must recognize that all of us are, to a greater or lesser degree, victims of and collaborators with patriarchal heterosexism, and that broad generalizations about prostitution are as inaccurate as those about "women" as a class.

Critique of the Sex Radical Feminist View

Although I find a variety of aspects of the sex radical feminist view valuable, I depart from it and from some prostitute rights activists' views because I do not believe that, save for stigma and illegality, prostitution is simply another form of work. Rather, because, as I have argued at length in Chapter 5, current sexual behavior is constructed within and as a weapon of patriarchy and heterosexism, sex work cannot simply be another form of work in contemporary culture. Prostitutes must contend with the misogyny and degradation that attach to all heterosexual activities, regardless of legality, and thus must be accorded the relevant protections. For that reason, decriminalization by itself is not an appropriate policy response. Policies must include such protective features as government-funded social services and legal controls on prostitute facilitators, in recognition of the harm built into the current construction of sexuality and prostitution.[28]

In addition, while I reject the radical feminist ideal of the abolition of prostitution altogether, I also reject the notion that prostitutes should ideally be viewed as sexual healers or "practitioners of a sacred craft," and "sexual service as a 'nourishing, life-giving force.'"[29] If, as I have argued, feminists must fight to normalize sexuality and sexual activity, it is altogether counterproductive to attempt to mystify the role of the prostitute, since this too undermines normalization.

The position of some sex radical feminists favoring acceptance of "outlaw practices," including "intergenerational" sexual activity between adults and minors and sadomasochism and dominance and bondage practices,[30] requires a protracted discussion that goes well beyond the topic of this investigation. Whether children are capable of having reciprocal and genuinely consensual sex with adults in the current context is both highly complex and controversial. The issue of intergenerational sex with underaged prostitutes is, however, far less problematic. I am very much in agreement with Ann Ferguson's view:

Our society creates conflicting consciousness in teenagers by infantilizing them through economic dependence and authoritarian prison-like schools at the same time as the media and market forces of sexual consumerism encourage them to think of themselves as sexual commodities. Such a situation creates youth who may want to consent to sex with an adult yet do not have the minimum economic independence to give them bargaining power.[31]

Given the lack of economic alternatives, as well as the lack of political, social, and legal protections, currently available to those under eighteen years of age, the claim that a minor is capable of genuine informed consent to prostitution is altogether implausible. (Nor have I seen any argument from the sex liberal camp to suggest otherwise.) More complex is the question of permitting prostitution for underaged clients. Although this issue is somewhat less clear-cut, I believe several factors mitigate against it. The pressure of media and market forces on teenagers to conceive of themselves as "sexual commodities" and consumers, along with enormous peer pressure, especially on males, to be sexually "experienced," makes claims of genuine informed consent highly suspect in a population with relatively low maturity. In addition, studies in the Netherlands suggest that some clients, particularly those exposed to prostitution at a young age, become addicted to sex with prostitutes. Furthermore, given the current gendered and aggressive construction of sexuality and prostitution, it would appear preferable, as in the case of alcohol, pornographic material, and other items, to withhold such access from those deemed emotionally and intellectually too immature to take on the responsibilities associated with adulthood.

Sadomasochism, dominance and bondage are, in my view, even more complex issues for feminists. Many, especially radical, feminists view such practices as eroticizing hierarchical roles of dominance and subordination "so as to perpetuate male dominance."[32] Even gay S&M is held to be "based upon fetishised masculinity and femininity [which] make[s] clear . . . that the traditional heterosexual system is an S/M romance."[33] Conversely, sex radicals hold that "S/M violates a taboo that preserves the mysticism of romantic sex"; that it "is not a form of sexual assault . . . [but] a consensual activity that involves polarized roles and intense sensations"; and that it is not "the result of institutionalized injustice to a greater extent than heterosexual marriage, lesbian bars or gay male bathhouses."[34] However, feminist defenders of S&M and bondage and dominance recognize that "some consensual sadomasochistic sex is plainly unsafe, harmful or unhealthy. Neck clamps can be too tight, time spent in bondage can be too prolonged or unmonitored, penetration can be with sharp or unclean objects."[35] While sex radicals argue that S&M and bondage and dominance are simply alternative sexualities that can legitimately be explored, other feminists argue that such practices simply mirror and promote the eroticization of hierarchical power and violence. While I am exceedingly uncomfortable with the wedding of sex and violence or dominance, (even as theater or erotic fantasy), I am in full agreement with Ferguson's view that "there is no clear proof either way and therefore consensual S/M [and bondage and dominance] should be considered a risky but not a forbidden practice for feminists."[36] Given this view, sadomasochistic and bondage-and-dominance prostitution should be viewed as permissible but as requiring particular monitoring when located within systems of legalized facilitation. Not only would special attention be required to ensure consent, but safe-sex practices would need to be established and enforced.

Critique of the British Feminist Socialist View

Finally, briefly, I depart from the perspective on prostitution of British feminist socialists—a position associated with the English Collective of Prostitutes—in rejecting their view that prostitution is *purely* the outgrowth of poverty.[37] While I agree with their claim that, given the current situation, prostitution is a legitimate choice, I do not, as discussed at length in Chapter 6, believe that it will disappear when women are economically solvent and able to support themselves and their families. Not only do I resist any analysis of human behavior based purely on an economic (or any other absolute) approach, but, given that middle-class women currently enter prostitution and that some enter for reasons that are not purely economic (e.g., enjoying sex or the desire for adventure), I find it likely that some will opt to enter prostitution even when other equally high-paying opportunities exist.

9

Prostitution Solution
Policy Recommendations

Although feminist positions generally favor decriminalization of prostitution, differences in justifying this legal preference lead to different programs and legal support policies. All feminists favor improving the situation of working prostitutes and former prostitutes, as well as ending trafficking in women and children for prostitution. But the specifics of how this should be done differ significantly according to differences in our larger analyses. Similarly, all feminists are or should be concerned with ending the debasing and dangerous construct of "the prostitute." Logically, however, there are two ways to address this problem. One may argue for a policy that would lead to the elimination of this construct altogether or for one that would lead to its radical reconception.

If, as I have contended in Chapter 6, there would be, in a nonsexist state, forms of prostitution that would service both men and women (by both men and women), performing sexual acts whose meaning no longer would construct sex as a weapon or a determinant of power, then the most reasonable approach to current practice is to develop a prostitution policy that forces the concept of the whore-prostitute to be radically reconstructed.

These policy recommendations are intended to delineate what I believe is the best approach to prostitution at this time. They are intentionally quite specific, because sometimes the capacity to generate different long-term goals rests on the specifics. In constructing these recommendations, I have been concerned with developing a policy that works neither to abolish nor to promote prostitution. I have therefore selected particular recommendations for a prostitution policy that I believe will be most effective at meeting the following criteria: (1) Does this overall policy improve the situation of working prostitutes and former prostitutes? Does it offer the appropriate protections in an industry riddled with abuse, while respecting the rights and dignity of all prostitutes, including those who choose to prostitute? (2) Does it effectively contribute to ending trafficking in women and children for prostitution? (3) Is it the policy that is most likely to facilitate reconstructing the "prostitute" as a heterogeneous category of diverse individuals, with full moral value and personhood,[1] who simply happen to be employed in a normalized sexual service industry? (4) Are these recommendations broad enough to reflect the complexity and diversity of the practice?

While I confess that I cannot imagine a sudden groundswell in contemporary American society supporting the immediate adoption of these recommendations, I am convinced that with the proper public relations and educational campaigns, particularly by feminists (including prostitute feminists), the American public can be brought, in the foreseeable future, to favor such a policy. A majority of Americans already favor legalization of prostitution.[2] Once the comparative data on the various options are adequately publicized, it will be a relatively small step to move the public to favor decriminalized prostitution and legalized prostitution facilitation.

I divide this discussion into three sections: recommendations for a decriminalized prostitution policy, recommendations for a legalized prostitution facilitation policy, and recommendations for an anti-trafficking policy.[3]

Recommendations for a Decriminalized Prostitution Policy

In general, much of what needs to be done for prostitutes is what needs to be done for *all* women, including the provision of social services and legal sanctions directed at improving our economic opportunities and providing support for those who are survivors of both sexual and nonsexual abuse. But what provisions must be made specific to prostitution?

Although some of the measures I recommend are quite costly, they can be financed, wholly or in part, by savings from the extraordinary amount currently expended attempting to enforce criminalized prostitution and from increases in tax revenues generated by prostitutes' taxable incomes under a decriminalized system. Additionally, some of these measures can be financed by diverting some of the resources currently directed at the general population to services specifically targeted toward prostitute populations. Therefore, in addition to decriminalizing prostitution,[4] I recommend the following measures:

A. The establishment of governance boards to recommend appropriate regulations, government services, and practices directed at increasing the well-being of prostitutes and the community at large. Such boards must include a preponderance of female members; significant representation of current and past prostitutes and prostitutes' advocacy groups, representing both prostitutes' rights and prostitute-victim organizations; and a proportionate diversity in the racial, ethnic, economic class, sexual orientation, physical and mental abilities, and so forth of both prostitute and nonprostitute members. This board must also include feminists concerned with the impact of any policy on the larger community of women. The governance board would be responsible for determining acceptable size, form, and content of advertising directed at both selling prostitute services and seeking prostitute employees. Additionally, this board would act as a mediator between conflicting groups, for example, neighborhood associations and streetwalkers.

Although time limitations do not allow a discussion of the precise needs and goals that justify each of my specific policy recommendations, my recommendation on the regulation of advertising is an excellent example of how ideal conceptions affect policy decisions. Abolitionists are unlikely to believe that any advertising of prostitution is legitimate, while those desiring to promote prostitution are unlikely to want any restrictions on advertising specific to prostitution. However, the desire to normalize prostitution requires that prostitutes and facilitators be permitted to advertise their services. Conversely, the belief that the current practice and conceptual construction of prostitution are potentially quite risky to prostitutes and embody various gender disparities and subordination requires appropriate protections with regard to advertising.

B. Foreign prostitutes must be permitted to migrate for work and be provided with the same protections and benefits as those who apply to be nonprostitute migrant workers. (According to current INS policy, prostitution requires automatic exclusion or deportation.) Prostitute facilitators (e.g., brothels) should be permitted to sponsor foreign prostitutes for short-term work visas.

C. Because runaway minors are a significant part of the streetwalking population, government programs for them must be established that neither return them to abusive homes nor place them in abusive government-supported living arrangements. Ongoing counseling for abused children, including sexually abused children, and significant economic and social support for emancipated minors must be provided. Much of the financing required for these provisions can be obtained by taking resources from budgets that are already in place to aid abused and runaway minors, and by tailoring some existing programs to the needs of minors who are or have been involved in prostitution. Government funds can also be used to support, expand, and tailor to the needs of prostitutes' existing shelters and programs organized by various nongovernmental organizations.

It shall be illegal for anyone below the legal drinking age to prostitute. If, in the opinion of a community, an individual is not sufficiently mature to drink alcohol responsibly, then the individual is surely not sufficiently mature to face the risks and dangers of prostituting. However, minors caught prostituting shall not be charged with a criminal offense but rather shall be provided with all necessary social service supports for them to survive without prostituting. (Their clients, however, will be subject to criminal charges.)

D. Government grants must be provided to encourage the development of prostitute unions and professional associations or guilds for those who wish to enter or to remain in prostitution. These women must have the opportunity for their voices to be represented.

E. Conversely, the government must fund and organize agencies to enable those who wish to leave prostitution to do so. These agencies would provide services as diverse as emergency shelters, counseling, medical care, and reeducation for alternative employment. Drug treatment programs directed at women in general and prostitute women in particular are essential. Drug treatment programs specifically designed for pregnant women must also be established. (Currently, pregnant women struggle to find any drug treatment programs that will serve them.)[5]

Most of the financing required for these provisions can be obtained by diverting funds from existing shelter, counseling, medical care, and employment training programs for the general population, and by tailoring some of these programs to the needs of prostitutes and former prostitutes.

F. The government must establish counseling agencies to apprise those considering entering prostitution of both the dangers and the potential advantages of prostituting. These agencies would be charged with neither promoting nor abolishing prostitution but simply presenting an unbiased, informed overview of the current situation.

G. The government must provide both needle-exchange programs and programs that subsidize the cost of condoms to help lower the spread of AIDS and other STDs.

H. A massive STD-prevention public education campaign must be instituted. We currently have a rather modest program directed at the general population. Not only does the existing program need significant expansion, but a campaign specifically targeting prostitutes must also be developed. In both cases, the discussion must normalize sexual behavior, and materials must be tailored to the diverse populations they are intended to address. Literature must be made available in as many languages as are necessary for the targeted population.

The costs of these programs, as well as those in G, should be more than offset by savings on medical treatment for those who would otherwise be infected.

I. Similarly, a public education campaign about prostitution and prostitutes, aimed at changing their conceptual constructions, must be instituted. Given how ingrained these representations are, it will take some time to overturn them. But since I sincerely believe that campaigns against violence against (nonprostitute) women have seriously undermined prevailing assumptions that such behavior is "normal" or legitimate, I can see no reason why the prevailing concept of "the prostitute" cannot be similarly addressed.

J. Sensitivity and support training for police must be instituted. Given both the historical global devaluation of prostitutes and the documented abuse of prostitutes by police, decriminalization is insufficient to change the incredibly negative relationship between the police and prostitutes. Because at present there is such clear evidence of police disinterest in pursuing crimes against prostitutes and suspected prostitutes, including rape and murder, it is necessary to establish an effective program to increase police sensitivity to dealing with such crimes, whether committed by the police or others.[6] Simply decriminalizing prostitution is altogether inadequate to address the depth of discrimination and harm prostitutes suffer under the current criminal justice system.

Costs for such programs will be offset many times over by savings on the current cost of arrests, trials, and incarceration of prostitutes.

K. Medical care represents a particular problem for prostitutes. The negative reaction of many medical personnel toward prostitutes often makes them reluctant to seek medical treatment or to reveal the sometimes relevant fact of their work when they do seek care. Significant issues regarding medical access, particularly for poorer prostitutes must be addressed. Clinics must be established to provide medical care to prostitutes and to do so anonymously if the patient so chooses.[7] Clinics must be open at hours appropriate for prostitutes and include mobile units to reach workers in outlying areas. Payment should be optional, since many prostitutes who need these services the most are not able to pay for them. Since many of these women are eligible for Medicaid, the greatest new costs to the community will be for training caretakers in treatment appropriate to the needs of the target population and in the purchase and equipping of mobile units.

General health and STD treatment and prevention services should be provided for all sex workers, including illegal immigrants. Clinic workers should be fairly compensated, nonjudgmental regarding sex work, have received the appropriate sensitivity training, and be sufficiently diverse to address the diverse population of prostitutes. Some existing government-funded health clinics could be designated to fulfill these functions. Clinics should provide free or low-cost condoms and actively pursue STD prevention education. These clinics must be governed by boards that include prostitutes and former prostitutes.

If, at the time of implementation, the United States does not have universal health coverage, governance boards or prostitute unions should be provided with "seed money" to organize insurance groups, which would allow prostitutes with sufficient income to obtain insurance coverage at reduced group rates. Seed money can also be used to encourage medical practitioners to receive the appropriate training to serve this target

158 | *Prostitution Policy Recommendations*

audience. These governance boards or prostitute unions can, in turn, make available information on "prostitute-friendly" physicians and medical practices.

    L. Streetwalking is a particularly difficult aspect of prostitution policy to address. As noted in Chapter 5, streetwalkers are, in general, sporadic or inexperienced sex workers who are the most likely to be victimized, especially violently. If I knew of any way to eliminate this form of prostitution, I would embrace it. Unfortunately, I do not. Approaches that may seem to be solutions often do not work. For example, when I began this project, I was searching for some way to remove automobiles from the practice, since getting into a car with a total stranger puts sex workers at terrible physical risk. But prostitutes have convinced me that this will not work. As long as our culture associates automobiles with sexuality, especially "dirty" sex, men will continue to demand to have sex in cars.[8] As long as some women are as vulnerable and powerless as many streetwalkers are currently, there will always be someone who will accede to that demand. The best solution I have been able to envision would use many but not all aspects of the Dutch "safe parks" described in Chapter 5. The United States should employ similar physical logistics to those in the Netherlands, including providing "living rooms" for such parks. However, given traditional differences in Dutch and U.S. police relations with the public, and with prostitutes in particular, I recommend a different approach to policing the parks. As in the Netherlands, one or two officers should be stationed to stand at the entrance to the parks during hours of operation. Special police units should be established for this duty—ones that have a disproportionately high percentage of women officers and that receive special training for the assignment. As in the Dutch projects, officers must be legally barred from recording license plate numbers and be required to come to the living rooms regularly to advise and encourage streetwalkers to report all criminal acts against them. Additionally, at least initially, these officers should be accompanied by prostitute union representatives, to ensure appropriate oversight and instill confidence that punitive measures will not be taken against either prostitutes or clients frequenting the parks.

Social workers and doctors must also visit the living rooms at least once weekly. Former prostitutes and addicts must be available to advise prostitutes on safe needle and condom use. Sitting rooms must provide a place to sit and rest, free or extremely inexpensive food, and inexpensive condoms. Some format for prostitute communications, especially regarding dangerous customers and union organizing, must be offered. This can be achieved by simply providing and maintaining a bulletin board for the purpose. Additionally, referrals for self-defense training and training for empowerment and/or for nonprostitute employment must be provided by these facilities. Referrals for domestic violence and drug counseling must be provided. These efforts can be undertaken with grant money from the government to social service organizations that include prostitute or prostitute union representation on their governance boards.

Unlike most Dutch parks, U.S. safe parks must be centrally located. An approach similar to that in the Hague could be adopted; however, given the difference in Dutch and American land use, I recommend that the parks be set discreetly within commercial shopping areas. Although their use should be limited to hours after the shops have closed, the surrounding area must have late-night foot traffic, easily accessible mass transit, and excellent street lighting. Ghettoizing streetwalking into low-income neighborhoods must be avoided by establishing a minimum average income for residents in areas selected for development of streetwalking parks. In this way we can avoid the problems demonstrated by Berlin's policy.

Although these parks would require governmental financing, the costs are not as great as one might expect. Stalls in the Netherlands are constructed with simple high metal dividers. The cost of garbage pails and minimal landscaping is relatively insignificant. The major cost would be for the living rooms. Wherever possible, however, existing structures can be used. Most U.S. cities would require only one such park. The living rooms should be staffed with at least some former prostitutes, who will require somewhat less training. And the cost for police to be stationed outside the parks will be far less than that currently budgeted for prostitution control.

Soliciting outside these parks should not be illegal. However, although it does represent an increase in risk to prostitutes, police must be permitted to insist that they or their clients "move along" if they are genuinely disturbing the peace. Some groups object to allowing the police this latitude because it reduces available negotiating time and thus lessens prostitutes' ability to assess clients and negotiate safer sex. I believe, however, that when prostitution creates genuine disturbances in neighborhoods, the animosity produced is legitimate and undermines the overall project of normalization. Hence, if prostitutes congregate and solicit in large numbers and thereby interfere with traffic flow, or if they solicit so aggressively or loudly that it becomes problematic, or if they engage in sexual acts publicly, the police must be permitted to intervene. We allow the police this latitude toward other forms of public nuisance, and if we are to avoid creating justifiable public hostility toward prostitution, the same latitude must obtain. To avoid abuse, however, police must be trained to distinguish legitimate instances of disturbing the peace. An oversight board including prostitutes must be established to hear complaints and determine sanctions when the police overstep established guidelines.

M. In Europe, under decriminalized systems of prostitution, "living off prostitutes' earnings" has sometimes been made a criminal offense. Such laws have been used to close down hotels and apartments rented by prostitutes, forcing them onto the street. These laws have also made it illegal for other adults to live with prostitutes; any commingling of resources becomes criminal. Pheterson cites an instance in Sweden in which "a prostitute's daughter was expelled from the [state] university because her tuition was paid by her mother."[9] Although such laws appear to constitute protection for prostitutes against abusive pimps, when they are written in such sweeping terms they serve only to further isolate and stigmatize prostitutes. They must therefore be forbidden from inclusion in any U.S. prostitution policy.

N. Finally, although I am opposed to zoning prostitution, I strongly favor restrictive zoning of pornographic bookstores, live sex shows, and the like. I am, for a variety of reasons, uncomfortable with government censorship of pornography; but what I saw in the red-light district in Amsterdam, where numerous pornography shops, movie theaters, and live sex shows were intermingled with prostitution windows, convinced me that it is essential to separate pornographic outlets both from unavoidable public view[10] and, particularly, from active prostitution. Because pornographic imagery is often especially misogynistic and violent, it is important to discourage conjoining such images with prostitute activity. It is reasonable to assume that if men are stimulated by these images immediately before or during their encounters with prostitutes, they may wish to engage in similar behavior. In addition, I think it worthwhile to zone these outlets in order to stigmatize such images as a matter of policy—a statement of their offensiveness in general. I see such an approach as temporary, necessary only as long as the majority of sexually explicit materials constitute hate speech against women. But until things change in this regard, I argue that there should be small areas given over to pornographic businesses—ones in which few, if any, other types of commerce are permitted.[11] Organized prostitution, like most other businesses, would not be permitted in zoned pornographic outlet areas. And the unwitting passerby would not have to be confronted by even "soft-core" imagery in windows.

Regulating Brothels and Other Prostitution Facilitation

Although many positions that defend decriminalization of prostitution do not discuss governance of brothels and other organized forms of facilitation, I am convinced this is essential to any prostitution policy. Unquestionably, most of the worst abuse suffered by prostitutes overall occurs at the hands of facilitators and their agents. Whether the abuse is physical, psychological, or economic, the existing literature consistently cites brothel owners, pimps, and other facilitators as the greatest source of harm to prostitutes. Systems that criminalize prostitution encourage this tendency by making it impossible for prostitutes to seek redress. In response to my open-ended questions during our interviews, however, even prostitutes in the legalized system in Nevada and decriminalized system in the Netherlands universally focused their complaints on abuse by employers.

Both historical and current legal and social factors, especially stigmatization, have given prostitute facilitators outrageous degrees of control over prostitute workers. Given the enormous disparity in power between prostitutes and their employers, decriminalizing prostitute facilitation would be extremely dangerous and highly unlikely to improve the lot of prostitutes. A laissez-faire approach to facilitation will, like other such forms of capitalism, only encourage greater power disparities. Since most prostitutes prefer to work in organized settings and, according to Vanwesenbeeck's study, are likely to fare better in them, brothels, massage parlors, and the like continue to be the predominant sites of prostitution, even when prostitution is decriminalized and facilitation is illegal (as was the case when I visited the Netherlands in 1996). Criminalized facilitation policies only force these organized operations underground, where, uncontrolled, they continue to engage in abusive practices. I therefore call for strictly enforced systems of legalized facilitation that *control facilitators but not prostitutes.*

Before describing the specifics of my proffered policy, I note what a good example facilitation policy constitutes of the need for feminists to offer fully developed policy recommendations rather than simple generalized stances. If one takes the position that prostitution should be decriminalized without speaking to the question of facilitation, one may actually worsen the situation of many women. Because decriminalization not only removes one of the barriers to prostituting but also communicates that prostituting is permissible, if not altogether de-stigmatized, it is likely that some women will enter prostitution who otherwise would not have done so, and that some women will enter with less concern and caution than they might otherwise have had. So unless one simultaneously puts in place restrictions on facilitators, one will increase the capacity of facilitators to exploit and abuse their prostitute employees.[12]

The legalized facilitation policy I favor includes the following features:

A. Legalized facilitation would be under the direct control of the same governance boards as those overseeing decriminalized prostitution.

B. Organized facilitators, including brothels, sex clubs, massage parlors, escort services, eros centers, and agencies, as well as pimps, would be required to register and pay licensing fees. However, fees would be kept low enough to allow prostitutes themselves to organize such services.

C. The size of these businesses would be limited to, for example, no more than ten prostitutes per brothel. Owners could own or have an interest in only one such business. This restriction is intended to lessen the traditional connection between sex work and organized crime, to lessen the potential for public nuisance, and to lessen the likelihood of exploitation and trafficking.

D. The government would set in place policies and programs that would encourage a shift from the traditional organization of facilitation to genuine self-employment, involving, for example, having prostitutes pay set amounts for rooms, client referrals, and supplies rather than pay a percentage of their fees to facilitators. This would both lessen economic abuse and provide prostitutes with far greater control over the conditions of their work. This model is not unlike the current arrangement of many hair stylists who pay a monthly fee for use of work stations, towels, and so forth and then set their own hours, fees, and many specifics of their contracts with clients.

The legal apparatus must distinguish between traditional facilitation and worker-controlled cooperatives. For example, the Dutch home-worker arrangement described in Chapter 5, where prostitutes coopera-tively rent an apartment and hire a receptionist, would constitute self-em-ployment, depending on such factors as who sets the rules and who pro-vides (what percentage of) the actual sexual services. Government support, including low-cost loans, should be provided to encourage the development of these cooperatives.

E. Conversely, traditionally organized facilitation must comply with existing regulations on self-employment. In legal brothels in Nevada, owners classify prostitutes as "independent contractors" when "they are, by legal definition, 'employees,'"[13] in order to avoid paying taxes and providing benefits for them. This classification, furthermore, al-lows facilitators to charge prostitutes otherwise illegal fees. Declaring an employee an independent contractor is an easy mechanism for worker exploitation.

F. These businesses would be subject to the same laws regarding em-ployee rights as any other businesses, including standards for maxi-mum lengths of shifts, freedom of movement, and so forth. Given the history of abuse in facilitator-prostitute arrangements, fair financial re-muneration would also be required. Prostitutes would be legally en-sured an appropriate percentage of the fees charged for their services. The proper percentage would be established by the governance board by determining the actual overhead for specific forms of facilitation and would allow facilitators a reasonable profit. Minimally, however, prostitutes should receive at least 60 percent of the income they gener-ate (as opposed to, for example, the 20 percent they currently receive in Nevada).

G. In addition to the safety regulations required of all businesses, prostitution requires safety regulations specific to the field. These must be established by the governance boards. Minimally, I would recommend that facilitators must either require client identification or control the comings and goings of clients (but not prostitutes) so that it is difficult for clients to escape prosecution if they engage in any abusive behavior. In addition, brothels, massage parlors, sex clubs, and the like must provide alarm buttons, similar to those in banks, on or near beds, stalls, and in other appropriate locations so security can be alerted to problem customers. Also escort and out-call services must provide drivers to bring prostitutes to clients: these drivers must meet the clients for identification purposes and remain nearby to ensure that the prostitute leaves safely after providing her (or his) services.

H. In addition to the health and hygiene standards that apply to any business, facilitators must provide and require the use of condoms. Notice of this health regulation must be publicly and prominently posted in the facilities. (In one rather clever campaign, the Dutch Ministry of Health distributed stickers for the windows in the red-light district that said, in Dutch, "I do it with," above a cartoon depicting a nearly naked woman dancing with a giant condom. I was struck by both their understanding of the value of a bit of humor and their recognition of the need to communicate with an international clientele.) Further, facilitators should provide clean, structurally supportive beds and clean showers, wherever beds and showers are used. They should also provide educational information on STDs to prostitutes and clients. Finally, they must adhere to regulations on safe sado-masochism, including the provision of safe devices and apparatuses. Appropriate time limitations for various forms of bondage must also be regulated.

I. Specific practices that are, in the view of the governance board, clearly misogynistic or that encourage disrespect of prostitutes specifically or women in general may be outlawed. I would suggest that both window prostitution and the brothel lineup are, because of their public nature and meaning, damaging to prostitutes and the class of women in general. There is nothing subtle about their messages of objectification. In window prostitution, women are displayed in the same way as wrenches in a plumbing store. Similarly, brothel lineups pose women as though they were mannequins or other inanimate objects. Although there are a variety of nonstigmatized professions in which people are selected explicitly on the basis of their appearance, few involve practices that so clearly communicate "this person is nothing but a piece of meat." Window prostitution and lineups symbolically depersonify more egregiously than, for example, streetwalking and bar prostitution do, because in the latter instances women both inhabit normal human environments and interact with clients as human agents. Given the propaganda value of window prostitution and brothel lineups, which publicly present and symbolize women as pure physical objects for the delectation of male lust, it is legitimate to oppose their permissibility.

Pornography is commonly used in prostitution. It is certainly available in most brothels. While I have already indicated the need for zoning pornographic outlets and live sex shows, the issue of pornographic materials in brothels is somewhat complicated. Because many clients appear to require sexually explicit materials for arousal or satisfaction, an outright ban on such materials would be problematic. Governance boards, however, can be charged with either establishing guidelines or censoring materials that are available in facilitation establishments, in order to eliminate the most violent or degrading imagery.

Sadomasochistic and bondage and dominance practices are sufficiently common to prostitution that many brothels have S&M rooms. Like pornography, these practices require guidelines or outright bans in order to weed out the most misogynistic, unhealthy, and violent activities.

The value of such legislation is threefold. First, it expresses a public consensus that banned behaviors and the values they communicate are not acceptable. It also provides a kind of "legal buffer zone," which I believe is essential to any prostitution policy. For many clients, part of prostitution's appeal is its taint and forbiddenness. Therefore, one runs the risk that by decriminalizing prostitution, one will encourage those behaviors that are not decriminalized because they are especially problematic. This is not sufficient reason to continue a policy of criminalization that causes so much harm. But the implications to child prostitution and similarly horrific practices is truly worrisome. I see regulations such as those against some pornography and some S&M or practices such as the lineup as allowing a certain "wiggle room"; they will unquestionably sometimes be violated, but their violation is less likely to cause the same degree of hardship as the violation of many other regulations. For this reason, governance boards may wish to draw the line on permissible materials and behaviors a bit more strictly than otherwise, thereby sending the "right message" while providing a buffer zone of acts that can be violated without horrendous results. But this would, correspondingly, require greater tolerance by law enforcement than in cases of more dangerous violations. Perhaps most important, such regulations provide prostitutes with the legal recourse essential to control more violative instances.[14]

J. Public employees would be charged with performing regular, surprise inspections of the facilities but not of the prostitutes. Inspections must cover health code regulations and ensure that no minor is permitted on the premises and no worker is there against her or his will. Examiners must be trained specifically for this employment, in accordance with the requirements detailed by the governance boards. They must be able to communicate in the languages of and, whenever possible, represent the various diverse racial, ethnic, and cultural populations of the prostitutes being interviewed.

Inspections, however, cannot be used to justify any required governmental registration of *prostitutes*. The success of enforcing regulations on legalized facilitation depends on the cooperation of prostitute workers. Given the stigma attached to prostitution even under decriminalized systems, prostitutes will come forward to report abuse, trafficking, and other violations only if they are assured anonymity. This requires that regulatory agencies develop methods for identifying prostitute workers without violating their anonymity. Systems of this sort have already been developed with regard to HIV testing, where code words or fictitious names are used to identify participants.

K. If inspections by the Immigration and Naturalization Service are required, these inspectors, too, would be subject to the mandate of anonymity for all U.S. citizens and legal immigrants described in paragraph J, above. Participation in prostitution by itself must not be sufficient to justify deportation, and no mention of such participation may appear on any documents in instances where an illegal immigrant is deported.

L. Severe penalties must be assigned and strictly enforced against any facilitator found to be using threats, extortion, deception or violence or engaging in the prostitution of children or trafficking.

M. All forms of zoning of facilitation establishments must be avoided. As discussed above, zoning codifies stigmatization and increases criminal activity in the area.[15]

Recommendations for an Anti-Trafficking Policy

The cases of trafficking in persons to the United States described in Chapter 5 underline the need for a responsive and humane U.S. anti-trafficking policy. As I indicated previously, the definition of trafficking I use allows that not all migrating prostitutes are trafficked and that non-sexual laborers, including men, may be trafficked. This point is critical in light of current U.S. anti-trafficking policy approaches[16] and their impact on women. As the "Human Rights Standards for the Treatment of Trafficked Persons" states, "When laws target typically 'female' occupations, they are usually overly protective and prevent women from making the same type of decisions that adult men are able to make. For example, anti-trafficking laws might prohibit women from migrating for work thereby throwing women into the hands of traffickers."[17] Additionally, allowing women and children to migrate while placing their movements under greater legal scrutiny than men's provides justification for discriminatory treatment by law enforcement. For example, several of the stipulations of article 8 of the "Proposed Convention Against Sexual Exploitation" (January 1994 draft) are problematic—including a provision that requires that "State Parties agree . . . to ensure supervision of railway stations, airports, seaports and en route, and of other public places, in order to prevent international traffic in women and children for the purpose of prostitution."[18] Since we know that men are trafficked for a variety of labors, focusing exclusively on trafficking in women and children for prostitution is likely to backfire. It will establish a sufficiently "chilly" climate for migrant women to constitute a virtual prohibition against migration, particularly for those women whose prior history or future intentions could be viewed as even slightly questionable.

Therefore, although any complete prostitution policy must be accompanied by an anti-trafficking policy, that policy should not be directed solely at prostitution. Indeed, the specific policy I support is fundamentally that proposed by the "Human Rights Standards for the Treatment of Trafficked Persons" (January 1999). In addition to accepting the definition of trafficking provided in Chapter 5, anti-trafficking legislation should include the following provisions:

A. The government may not discriminate against trafficked persons. They may not be placed in enforced confinement, including in INS detention camps.

B. We must recognize that trafficked persons are victims of serious rights abuses and therefore must not simply protect their rights but also protect them from reprisals.

C. The government shall ensure that its efforts to punish traffickers do not violate the rights of trafficked persons to privacy, dignity, and safety.

D. Victims must have the right to seek reparations from traffickers, and the government must provide the assistance necessary for them to do so.

E. Victims shall be provided with temporary visas, including work visas, until criminal cases against their traffickers are resolved. The government must provide appropriate health and social services, including psychological counseling, during this period.

F. Although some agencies—for instance, the San Francisco Task Force—suggest that victims should be granted permanent visas, this seems most unwise; it may encourage those desperate to immigrate to become involved with traffickers. However, trafficked persons must have the right to seek asylum, and grounds for asylum should include the possibility of retaliation as well as discrimination that may ensue if they are returned to their home countries. (For example, Alison Murray cites strong evidence that HIV-infected trafficked Burmese women were executed when they were returned to Burma.) Additionally, HIV-infected victims of trafficking must be granted asylum if treatment is unavailable in their home countries.

G. If trafficked persons want to return home, the government shall ensure that they are able to do so and shall provide transportation when necessary.

H. The United States shall adopt laws outlawing the practice of mail-order brides.[19]

I. The U.S. military will be charged with developing policies to lessen their role in the trafficking of women into the United States. Such policies will be barred from interfering with legitimate marriages with non–U.S. citizens.[20] Rather, emphasis will be placed on controlling the illegal activities of U.S. servicemen in foreign countries, for example, the purchasing of wives. Traditional U.S. military involvement in the regulation and control of native prostitutes near foreign U.S. military bases will cease. Appropriate counseling and social services must be provided to foreign-born wives of current or former U.S. military members who met and married while stationed abroad.

Conclusion

Clearly, this three-part proposed policy is incomplete. I have assuredly overlooked some valuable provisions, and some adjustments will be required to speak specifically to the needs of gay, transgendered, transsexual, and heterosexual male prostitutes. Further, this policy is a response to the specific social and cultural conditions that exist presently and will require revision in light of changing background conditions. Overall, however, I am confident that it constitutes a blueprint for a prostitution policy that normalizes prostitution and prostitutes. For I am convinced that women will never be normalized, will never cease being "other," until sex and sexual activity are normalized. And sex and sexual activity will never be normalized until the sale of sexual activity is normalized (and vice versa.) If sexual activity is normalized, then its sale is unremarkable. Even if one believes that sexual activity is, or involves, or should involve intimacy, its sale, like that of psychological counseling, massage, or professional physical aid for geriatric patients, should be unremarkable.

Prostitution must be normalized by eliminating those aspects of the practice that are venal. It must be normalized by understanding what it really is and who really is part of it and why. If a woman chooses to prostitute, she deserves the right to do so with dignity and the same protections the state guarantees to all its citizens. If a woman is prostituting because the circumstances of her life have made it a necessity, she should be assured access to state-funded programs that give her the resources necessary for her to find other alternatives. And if she opts to continue prostituting, she deserves the right to do so with dignity and the protections the state guarantees to all its citizens. If a woman is prostituting because she is being forced to by others, she should be guaranteed a well-developed and well-executed government apparatus to discourage, uncover and vigorously prosecute trafficking or other forms of coerced prostitution. She should further be assured access to state-funded programs that give her the resources necessary to provide her with other alternatives. And if she opts to continue prostituting, she deserves the right to do so with dignity and the protections the state guarantees to all its citizens.

If a child is prostituting, he or she must be removed from any prostitute facilitator and be provided with all necessary state support. That child must also be guaranteed a well-developed and well-executed government apparatus to discourage, uncover, and vigorously prosecute those engaged in facilitating child prostitution.

The specific recommendations of this chapter have been selected because they most effectively satisfy these functions, given the current context. These long-range goals of normalization are not the work of a lifetime but of many generations. But unless feminists find a way of eliminating the construct of the prostitute as "other of other," unless we begin fighting for the rights and dignity of prostitutes, until we recognize that "she" is "us," I despair for any long-term success in eliminating gender hierarchies.

Notes

NOTE TO THE PREFACE

1. For a discussion of this "protection" see Firestone, *Dialectic of Sex*, esp. 146–155.

NOTES TO THE INTRODUCTION

1. Firestone, *Dialectic of Sex*, 150.

2. See Hawkesworth, "Democratization: Reflections on Gendered Dislocations in the Public Sphere."

3. Or, more broadly, patriarchy subordinates those who are born female, become female, or act in accord with the traditional female role.

4. This is not to suggest that women are in a subordinate position in every possible instance.

5. The specific reference is to Carole Vance's *Pleasure and Danger: Exploring Female Sexuality*, but I intend the phase more broadly to include the many feminists who have focused on more positive aspects of heterosexuality and theorized ways radically to alter its practice and meaning.

6. In particular, I have researched the issue of for-profit surrogate mothering and state attempts to require the insertion of the birth control device Norplant as a condition of probation.

7. Although there are certainly male prostitutes, they constitute a relatively small percentage of the prostitute population.

8. This term is used to refer to, for example, Women's Studies, Black/African American Studies, Native American Studies, Latino/a Studies, Chicano/a Studies, Asian American Studies, Gay and Lesbian Studies, etc.

9. Flax, "Women Do Theory," 20.

10. I do not mean to suggest that these facts are pre- and atheoretical. As is clear from the work of deconstructionists and feminist epistemologists, what counts as a fact is determined by political-social-cultural constructs. But within these constructs, new 'facts' are discovered and must be explained and understood through some (probably less general) theory.

11. Traditional philosophy has often been remiss in taking this dictum seriously enough to do the social science research necessary for policy development, as well as failing to understand that philosophical analyses are contingent and historically situated.

12. I say "in the broadest sense" because there is a huge variation among possible policies in each of these categories, so that although one might, for example, favor certain forms of decriminalized prostitution, one might oppose other forms of decriminalization.

13. Brothel prostitution is legal in thirteen counties in Nevada. Each of these counties has its own self-regulatory system of legalization.

14. In speaking of 'heterosexual' prostitution, I mean prostitution between individuals who see themselves as engaging in heterosexual sexual activity. Societal determinations of gender, sex, and sexual orientation are extremely contradictory and murky. It would be quite difficult to establish a social criterion or "objective" standard for what constitutes heterosexual behavior, based on physiology or gender or sexual orientation or identity. For example is sex involving what are roughly categorized as a straight woman and a transgender or transsexual or gay or bisexual male, heterosexual sex? The subjective beliefs of the participants are, however, critical to my analysis because it is against the standard, the prevailing conceptual construction, that the participants presume obtains, that determines which conceptual constructions(s) is (are) relevant. Physical differences between heterosexual and nonheterosexual activity are not as important in this discussion. What makes me limit this discussion to heterosexual prostitution is that my expertise does not include knowledge of non-heterosexual prevailing conceptual constructions (nor of their corresponding practice.) (I am indebted to Talia Bettcher for suggesting this clarification.)

15. The three exceptions are male escort services (which often include sexual services as part of a larger service), a very small number of women who have begun to use massage out-call services, and the peculiar case among German women of sex tourism in Kenya.

NOTES TO CHAPTER 1

1. According to the U.S. State Department Web site, in 1997 the most credible estimate was that two hundred thousand Thai women and children were engaged in prostitution. A large number labor under debt bondage. Children as young as seven years old are prostituted; girls ranging in age from twelve to eighteen are increasingly trafficked from South China. And "there continue to be credible reports of involvement by some corrupt police, military and Government officials in trafficking schemes." In Thailand, however, trafficked women have no

right to legal counsel or health care if arrested and are not protected by the same amnesty offered to other illegal alien workers.

2. *Matichon*, October 18, 1980. Source: Siriporn Skrobanek, "Transnational Sexploitation of Thai Women."

3. For example, can we assert a woman's opportunity to make a genuinely "voluntary" choice given the lack of real options open to women and the narrowing effects of socialization on a woman's vision of her abilities and possible future?

4. This phrase is taken from Lorraine Code's *Rhetorical Spaces: Essays on Gendered Locations*.

5. Code, *Rhetorical Spaces*, 24, 29. See also Hartsock, *Feminist Standpoint Revisited*, and Haraway, "Situated Knowledges."

6. Code, *Rhetorical Spaces*, 10.

7. At the United Nations headquarters in Geneva, Switzerland, during a special seminar on "Trafficking and the Global Sex Industry: Need for Human Rights Framework," held June 21–22, 1999, this view was given voice by a variety of representatives of NGOs (see *Coalition Report*, Coalition Against Trafficking in Women 5–6 [1998–2000] page 8); it was also raised by Andrea Dworkin in an interview on San Francisco's KQED-FM *Forum*, (Michael Krasny, host) April 15, 1997.

8. Bell, *Reading, Writing*, 73.

9. Pheterson, *Vindication*, 3–4.

10. Murray, "Debt-Bondage," 61–62.

11. This has been particularly problematic because it has often been pursued by feminists whose other positions I have greatly admired.

12. hooks, *Feminist Theory*, 171. (italics added)

13. A 1984 study of street prostitutes in San Francisco indicated a 60 percent rate of child sexual abuse in the backgrounds of the subjects (Silbert and Pines, "Pornography"). In 1985, D.K. Weisberg, (*Children of the Night*) reported that, in American studies, the rate of intrafamilial childhood sexual abuse among juvenile prostitutes ranged between 31 and 66.7 percent. See also VanWesenbeeck, *Prostitutes' Well-Being*, 19.

14. Alder "'Passionate and Willful' Girls," 89.

15. See Chesney-Lind, "Women and Crime," esp. 87.

16. Barry, *Prostitution of Sexuality*, 305; italics added.

17. Delacoste and Alexander, eds., *Sex Work*, 291.

18. Pheterson, *Vindication*, 33.

19. Ibid., 340.

20. Alexander, "Prostitution," 189.

21. From an interview at the 1989 World Whores' Summit in San Francisco, in Carol Leigh's video *Outlaw Poverty, Not Prostitutes* (1992). Available through her website www.bayswan.org/sexworkers.html

22. Bell, *Reading, Writing*, 185.

23. Rawls, *Theory of Justice*.

24. See, for example, Fineman "Feminist Theory in Law," esp. 10–11; and Sherwin, "Feminist Ethics," esp. 283–284.

25. See, e.g., Pyne Addelson, *Impure Thoughts*; Fineman "Feminist Theory in Law"; Jacobs, "Adding Complexity to Confusion"; Jaggar, ed., *Living with Contradictions*; Rhode, "Feminist Critical Theories"; Sherwin, "Feminist Ethics."

26. See Kuo, "Secondary Discrimination," 910–913.

27. Halley, "Sexual Orientation," 551; see her whole article for a useful discussion of the varieties of essentialist and constructivist views.

28. Vance, as quoted in Jackson and Scott, *Feminism and Sexuality*, 11. Bordo, *Flight to Objectivity*, 283.

29. This discussion is not intended to be an exhaustive description of intrinsic qualities. As the example of selling china figurines suggests, there are nonbiological physical causes intrinsic to many behaviors, such as the fact that any activities involving china figurines carry with them the possibility of breakage.

30. See Butler, *Gender Trouble*, 1.

31. See Eagleton, *Literary Theory*; Adams and Ware, "Sexism and the English Language"; and Baker, "'Pricks' and 'Chicks.'"

32. As MacIntyre states, "The truth is . . . that all non-trivial activity presupposes some philosophical point of view and . . . not to recognize this is to make oneself the ready victim of bad or at the very least inadequate philosophy" ("Utilitarianism and Cost-Benefit Analysis," 217–237).

33. Yanow, *How Does a Policy Mean?* x–xi.

34. This failure is painfully common in philosophical analyses.

NOTES TO CHAPTER 2

1. From Atkinson, "Institution of Sexual Intercourse," 42.

2. This is a new twist for men and one unanticipated by Firestone and other second-wave radical feminists—and a phenomenon that surely testifies to the necessary consideration of capitalism in any feminist analyses.

3. Atkinson, "Institution of Sexual Intercourse," 42.

4. In the discussion that follows, I use Stevi Jackson and Sue Scott's broad definition of sexuality as "encompassing erotic desires, practices and identities" (*Feminism and Sexuality*). Furthermore, although not all heterosexual acts involve or lead to heterosexual intercourse, I generally include intercourse under this discussion simply because it is, along with fellatio and manual arousal, among the most common services that prostitutes provide.

5. See, e.g., Jackson and Scott, eds., *Feminism and Sexuality*, and LeMoncheck, *Loose Women*.

6. MacKinnon, "Feminism, Marxism, Method." 532.

7. Radical feminism can be traced to Kate Millett and, later, the Southern Women Writers' Collective and is most commonly associated with the work of Catharine MacKinnon, Andrea Dworkin, and Kathleen Barry.

8. Dworkin, *Intercourse*, 158.

9. Indeed, in *Intercourse*, Dworkin ascribes only two positive values to sexual acts: the possibility for true intimacy and communion, discussed in the context of the homosexual relationship in James Baldwin's *Another Country*, and what Dworkin calls "skinlessness" (see p. 100), but which is seen as a source of male violence against women in the current social-political context. Neither value is presented as a likely outcome of current heterosexual activity.

10. Jackson and Scott, eds., *Feminism and Sexuality*, 18.

11. Ibid., 18. The sex radical position, elaborated below, is most commonly associated with the works of Gayle Rubin and Carole Vance.

12. Bell, *Reading, Writing*, 81.

13. Ibid., 83.

14. Ibid., 86.

15. LeMoncheck, *Loose Women*, 41.

16. See ibid., 42.

17. Jackson and Scott, eds., *Feminism and Sexuality*, throughout.

18. For example, see Leidholdt, *Sexual Liberals*, throughout.

19. See Bell, *Reading, Writing*, 84.

20. Ibid., 85.

21. Some (e.g., Amber Hollibaugh) argue that we should not deny that the eroticization of power can be a real and legitimate source of pleasure.

22. See Hollibaugh, "Desire for the Future."

23. See Rubin, "Thinking Sex," 270.

24. See, for example, LeMoncheck, *Loose Women*; Jackson and Scott, eds., *Feminism and Sexuality*; Bell, *Reading, Writing*.

25. Jackson and Scott, eds., *Feminism and Sexuality*, 20.

26. The anthology then includes articles exemplifying both positions. I strongly recommend that readers interested in feminist analyses of sexuality read these sustained discussions.

27. Bell, *Reading, Writing*, I–II.

28. In Nanette Davis's anthology, *Prostitution*, for example, the contributors of the sixteen chapters were asked to begin with a social and legal definition for prostitution for their respective countries. The consensus among these discussions was that the term was ambiguous in each culture.

29. Prostitution may involve providing services without physical interaction or contact, for example, masturbatory acts performed for the client's viewing. If, however, one were to define prostitution as involving only verbal or visual inter-action, then the suggested definition would be too broad, including paid phone sex, stripping, appearing in pornographic films, and participating in live sex

shows. Indeed, the distinction between illegal prostitution and legal sex acts is at times decidedly muddy. While, in the United States, peep shows involving the private viewing of masturbation are legal, the same show would presumably constitute illegal prostitution if performed in a private hotel room by a streetwalker. Similarly, while private lap dancing is legal in the United States, a streetwalker performing a similar service in a private hotel room could face legal charges. The distinction appears to rest on the perceived willingness of the sex worker to go "beyond" these services at the client's request.

30. I use the phrase "implicit and explicit" because access to some body parts (e.g., the vagina or mouth) is almost always explicit in prostitution contracts, whereas access to many other body parts (e.g., the shoulder or back) is not. Furthermore, access to body parts is generally limited to access within specific acts (e.g., accessing her mouth for oral sex but not for kissing).

31. This definition should perhaps be qualified by the phrase "when such acts and access are agreed to for the purpose of 'sexual gratification' (in its broadest reading)." This condition is intended to exclude such acts as sexual encounters that occur as part of sex therapy, in which the major motivation is not immediate sexual gratification but rather the development of a "sexually functional" individual. I say "perhaps" because, although it does not seem appropriate to include acts such as those performed in sex therapy (with a licensed therapist) under the category "prostitution," the distinction between such instances and what sometimes occurs in prostitution becomes hard to determine.

32. See, for example, Bell, who calls phone sex and stripping forms of prostitution (*Reading, Writing,* 107), while in *Vindication,* Pheterson calls strippers and phone-sex workers "whores" (4).

33. The only exception I can envision to this claim is if the woman severely harms or kills her sexual partner through the sexual act. This is not to say that prostitution does not affect the moral character of the prostitute; it may do so in a variety of ways (including both positive and negative effects) and to greater or lesser degrees. But this is hardly equivalent to the claim that one sells one's moral character.

34. Shiatsu massage may require the use of the therapist's feet and back.

35. I imagine that someone may object that, although this is true, in these other cases the client/patient is passive; but this may also be the case in prostitution. Nor is it always the case in, e.g., physical therapy, where the patient is often asked to exert opposing pressure.

NOTES TO CHAPTER 3

1. At the moment, the jury is out with regard to whether, e.g., hetero- and homosexuality are socialized phenomena. Some evidence of genetic markers con-

nected to sexual orientation has emerged, although it is not clear what role, if any, they have in determining the actual sexual orientation of specific individuals.

2. I include "bodily state" because sexual pleasure and orgasm do not necessarily require physical *movement*. Both are often achievable by pure thought.

3. Whether or not, and the degree to which, such differences are intrinsic is highly controversial. Many feminists believe they are, at least in part, due to social construction—that is, different diets, physical training and activity, etc. are held to be responsible for some of the physical differences between male and female.

4. For example, I once knew a woman, a registered nurse and quite sexually active, who used birth control pills and two barrier methods to protect against pregnancy (and STDs).

5. This is the typical evaluative technique of virtually any teleological moral system, for example, utilitarianism and social contractarianism.

6. Dworkin, *Intercourse*, 135; italics added.

7. Ibid., 123.

8. Unless one could offer a case scenario in which heterosexual intercourse would be the least evil of the possible alternatives.

9. I am not suggesting that it is *currently* possible for any act of heterosexual intercourse to be altogether free of negative moral values, especially those relating to issues of power. Heterosexual activities are currently constructed as so grotesquely gendered that I believe all such contemporary acts will include aspects of dominance and subordination in accord with gendered classes.

NOTES TO CHAPTER 4

1. Bell, *Reading, Writing*, 2.

2. E.g., Baker ("'Pricks' and 'Chicks'") notes that a common slang term for penis is *prick*, as in "to prick with a needle."

3. See, e.g., Jeffreys, "Eroticizing Women's Subordination."

4. I commonly encountered this sort of convoluted reasoning when counseling battered women, whose "partners" often justified their violence with (unfounded) accusations of infidelity.

5. Clearly, "liking it" makes one more liable to "do it."

6. Dworkin, *Intercourse*, 134.

7. Indeed, such an imaging appears to occur to and disturb men—as evidenced by the frequent representation of the vagina with teeth.

8. How else can we understand the commonality of breast "augmentation," which generally destroys the erogenous capacity of the nipple?

9. Humm, *Dictionary of Feminist Theory*, 98.

10. Kostash, "Second Thoughts," 486.

11. Sheffield, "Sexual Terrorism," 46.

12. See Peterson, "Coercion and Rape."

13. Dworkin, *Intercourse*, 35.

14. Ibid., 27.

15. Ibid., 60.

16. In this discussion, I am particularly indebted to the work of Shannon Bell, whose groundbreaking *Reading, Writing* and *Rewriting the Prostitute Body* is a sustained scholarly feminist analysis of "the prostitute" as conceptual construct.

17. Bell offers a brief but interesting discussion of the relationship (*Reading, Writing*, 107–108).

18. Pheterson, *Vindication*, 4.

19. VanWeesenbeeck, *Prostitute's Well-Being*, 13.

20. Bell, *Reading, Writing*, 44.

21. Acton, *Prostitution Considered*, 39–40.

22. DuBois and Gordon, "Seeking Ecstasy."

23. Ibid., 33.

24. Bell, *Reading, Writing*, 71.

25. Doezma, "Forced to Choose."

26. LeMoncheck, *Loose Women*, 143.

27. Doezma, "Forced to Choose," 47.

28. Pheterson, *Vindication*, 81–82.

NOTES TO CHAPTER 5

1. Vance, ed., *Pleasure and Danger*, 5.

2. Dworkin, *Intercourse,* 125.

3. One may hold, as did John Stuart Mill, that "higher" pleasures exist that are ultimately more rewarding—that intellectual and moral pursuits lead to an even greater level of happiness and pleasure. But as one who has worked in ethical theory for numerous years and strived to lead a moral and intellectual life, I can only say that I am not convinced. Intellectual and moral pursuits, in my view, lead to complex pleasures that are rarely, if ever, pure. The complexity of the processes generally yield mixed feelings and sensations. Whatever ecstasy results from such endeavors is often more complicated than that experienced in sexual response. Intellectual and moral pleasure are also "located" elsewhere—removed from the viscerality and animality whose simplicity is part of the appeal of sexual activity. Most important, moral and especially intellectual pleasures often require a level of privilege beyond most people's reach. The ability to "ponder intellectual questions" depends on a socioeconomic situatedness beyond most human beings' capacity. Sexual pleasure is, at least in theory and often in practice, a more "de-

mocratic" outlet—even extremely poor and disadvantaged heterosexual individuals have the possibility of experiencing pleasure in heterosexual activity.

4. Vance, ed., *Pleasure and Danger*, 1.

5. Southern Women's Writing Collective, "Sex Resistance," 146–7.

6. Firestone, *Dialectic of Sex*, 147.

7. This privileged status is currently being contested by gay and lesbian domestic partnership legal arrangements, but even here the society is recognizing and privileging (theoretically) monogamous coupling.

8. Vance, ed., *Pleasure and Danger*, 2.

9. Ibid., 4.

10. Perhaps the more surprising change in this regard has been the evolving objectification of men as physical/sexual objects. Men now undergo far more plastic surgical procedures, hair-replacement therapies, exercise and diet regimens, and other practices than I, certainly, would ever have predicted only twenty years ago. Here it appears that capitalism has met feminist protests against female sexual objectification by "equalizing" objectification—an outcome that was not what most second-wave feminists had in mind. Even here, however, patriarchy is consistently on display. Women strippers, for example, earn less and work under poorer conditions than male strippers working in the same clubs. See Kempadoo and Doezema, eds., *Global Sex Workers*.

11. For example, condoms do not prevent the spread of syphilis when a lesion occurs above the condom line.

12. Dworkin, *Intercourse*, 166–167.

13. Until recently in the United States, this included exclusionary rules that exempted a man from being charged with rape when the victim was his wife, which, along with adultery laws, protected men's rights to exclusive sexual access and use of women. Despite legal abolition of these rules, the "law in action" continues, in practice, to exclude men who rape or assault their wives from legal sanctions as long as the wife remains in the same domicile. Although father-child incest has long been illegal in the U.S., prosecution was, until recently, exceedingly rare. Prosecution for child incest still lags far behind estimates of the commonality of the crime.

14. For useful overviews of these debates, see Ferguson, "Transitional Feminist Sexual Morality," and LeMoncheck, *Loose Women*.

15. Anechiarico and Kuo, "The Justified Scoundrel."

16. For the 1 percent figure, see Prostitutes' Education Network (PENET) (www.creative.net/~penet); for the 12 percent figure, see Fechner, "Three Stories."

17. Kosovski, "Brazil," 49.

18. See Miller, Romenesko, and Wondorkowski, "United States," 313. The Prostitutes Education Network (Penet) also estimates that while street prostitution constitutes 10 to 20 percent of prostitution in larger cities, in some smaller

cities, with few indoor options, it may constitute as much as 50 percent. (www.creative.net/~penet)

19. Miller, Romenesko, and Wondolkowski, "United States," 315.

20. Cultural differences of particular significance in comparing U.S. and Dutch policies are those that concern public policy (including police) administration. Often it is assumed that, unlike the United States, the Netherlands is a relatively homogeneous culture. As Anechiarico notes, however, "The Dutch political system is a complex balance of minority interests held together by a degree of trust and cooperation. . . . Instead of three or five elements in a coalition, there are dozens" ("Administrative Culture," 20).

21. Although all statistical information and generalizations about prostitution were obtained through published social science studies, this qualitative research made the social science data "real" by "putting a face" on their findings. The interviews also gave me insight into what social science research I needed to uncover.

I attempted to give these interviews as much of a conversational style as possible. I asked generally open-ended questions: for example, in interviews with prostitutes I asked about their job satisfaction; what, if any, abuse they felt they suffered in the industry; how they (or the brothel) dealt with clients who were too rough; what they wanted me to know about their experiences in prostitution. I then followed up on their responses until the topic appeared to be exhausted.

In Nevada, I spoke with five prostitutes who were working in brothels. All interviews were arranged by the representative of the Nevada Brothel Owners Association and conducted in the brothels. They ranged from twenty minutes to nearly two hours. In most instances I assume our conversations were monitored by "bugs," which one woman advised me were planted in all but one room (a TV viewing area) of the brothel. She, however, took me to the television room in order not to have to edit her parts of the conversation. And despite the bugs, women's comments were surprisingly critical of brothel management. In addition, I interviewed a former prostitute and then-manager of the Kit Kat Ranch; the manager of the Mustang II; the sheriff of Storey County, Nevada, at the time; the Nevada registered nurse responsible for health inspections for the Mustang Ranches; a professor of social work at the University of Nevada, Reno, whose research focused on prostitution in Nevada; and the president of the Nevada Brothel Association. I was also given tours of three brothels and permitted to observe interactions in the public areas of two of these for several hours.

I have interviewed three women who have worked in illegal prostitution in the United States. One is a spokeswoman for COYOTE (Call Off Your Old Tired Ethics, a prostitutes' rights organization), the second a spokeswoman for PONY (Prostitutes of New York, also a prostitutes' rights organization), and the third a former prostitute and prostitute victims' rights advocate whom I met through a meeting of the National Women's Studies Association. Additionally, I conducted a lengthy telephone interview with a manager of an escort service.

In the Netherlands, I met with three prostitutes. My contact with one, a self-employed home worker, was facilitated by the Mr. A. de Graaf Foundation. The second, a window prostitute, met with me as a representative of De Rode Draad. The third was a brothel prostitute introduced to me by the president of the Dutch brothel keepers' association. As in Nevada, I was provided with lengthy tours of two brothels and permitted to observe in public rooms for some time. I also interviewed the president of the brothel keepers' association as well as two other brothel owners; one brothel manager; a representative of the Foundation Against Trafficking in Women (STV in the Netherlands); a representative of the HAP Foundation (Huiskamer Aanloop Prostituées, an informational and AIDS prevention center for streetwalkers in Utrecht); two representatives of the Mr. A. de Graaf Foundation (the Dutch national center for research and documentation on prostitution matters); a representative of the HAJ Foundation, which ran the sitting room for the streetwalkers' park in Amsterdam; the head of the Amsterdam police Prostitution and Vice Unit; the head of the Amsterdam police unit that deals with streetwalkers; a Fulbright scholar and former employee of the Dutch Ministry of Health who was researching public health in prostitution; a professor of criminology at Erasmus University, Rotterdam, who was researching trafficking in women for prostitution between the Netherlands and Belgium; a professor of criminology at Utrecht University who was researching male prostitution; a professor of Women's Studies at the University of Amsterdam who was researching domestic violence and rape in the Netherlands; and a professor of business administration for the Free University, Amsterdam, and the University of Rotterdam, who had researched the business administration of brothels. When I met with the last professor again two years later, she had become the coordinator of the prostitution project on AIDS and STDs for the STD Foundation of the Dutch Ministry of Health.

None of the individuals I interviewed received any form of payment.

22. See Vanwesenbeeck, *Prostitutes' Well-Being*; James, "Motivations"; Davis, ed., *Prostitution*; and Wei and Wong "Five Hundred Prostitutes in Shangai."

23. Gebhard, "Misconceptions of Female Prostitutes."

24. See Wei and Wong, "Five Hundred Prostitutes in Shanghai," and Pillai, "Prostitution in India."

25. This may not be the case in Eastern European countries, which, since the breakup of the Soviet Union, have experienced periods where resources were sufficiently scarce as to have required women to prostitute for their (and their family's) survival.

26. Davis, ed., *Prostitution*, 50.

27. James, "Motivations," 178.

28. See Vanwesenbeeck, *Prostitutes' Well-Being*.

29. Although women hire male escorts, even when sexual services are provided they are usually part of a larger package, including taking the woman out, serving as a companion for the evening, and so forth. There is almost never an explicit sexual contract involved.

30. Vanwesenbeeck, *Prostitutes' Well-Being*, 126–128.

31. Sometimes the appearance of prostitutes plays into this desire: for example, some clients display a preference for "less attractive" or older prostitutes because they feel safer with them.

32. Germany is one of the few major jurisdictions where prostitution is legalized and regulated.

33. Enloe, *Bananas, Beaches and Bases*, 36.

34. Women's Leadership Institute, "Women, Violence and Human Rights"; and Enloe, *Bananas, Beaches and Bases*.

35. Indonesia, Sri Lanka, and Goa (a state in India) are also being developed by sex-tourist promoters.

36. "In 1986, Thailand earned more foreign currency from tourism—$1.5 billion—than it did from any other economic activity" (Enloe, *Bananas, Beaches, and Bases*, 37).

37. Enloe, *Bananas, Beaches, and Bases*, 36.

38. Ibid., 36.

39. Kim "Re-conceptualizing Immigration," 1.

40. Gay, "'Patriotic' Prostitute," 34.

41. See Enloe, *Bananas, Beaches, and Bases,* 82–84. It is not clear that this applies to all nationalities. Enloe notes that prostitution was not among the problems associated with bases of the former Soviet Union in Vietnam and Afghanistan.

42. Ibid., 86–87.

43. See Kim, "Re-conceptualizing Immigration."

44. Women's Leadership Institute, "Women, Violence and Human Rights."

45. Vanwesenbeeck, *Prostitutes' Well-Being*, 11.

46. Paris, "Skin Trade," 45. This figure is contested, especially by prostitute rights organizations, though I have encountered no one who denies a significant trade in women globally.

47. See esp. Kempadoo and Doezema, eds., *Global Sex Workers*.

48. Woolston, *Prostitution in the United States*, 25.

49. Reynolds, *Economics of Prostitution*, 21.

50. Decker, *Prostitution*, 14.

51. Janus, *Janus Report on Sexual Behavior*, 3.

52. Elkies, "Upper East Side Prostitution Ring Busted," 12.

53. Law, "Commercial Sex," 527.

54. Miller, Romenesko, and Wondolkowski, "United States," 320.

55. See ibid., 313; and San Francisco Task Force, *Final Report,* appendix.

56. Miller, Romenesko, and Wondolkowski, "United States," 313.

57. Ibid., 318–319.

58. An arrest without probable cause while she was not working was the stimulus for Catherine La Croix to organize COYOTE/Seattle. See "The Biography of Catherine La Croix," available at http://www.whoreact.net.

59. Miller, Romenesko, and Wondolkowski, "United States."

60. Based on inconsistencies in the officer's own incident report and the testimony of Dotson and of the parking attendant, a completely independent witness, the court found not only that Officer Yee's testimony about the reasons for the stop were not credible but even that he had fabricated those reasons. The judge announced that she would recommend the U.S. Attorney's Office investigate the officer for perjury. From letter from Fania E. Davis, attorney for Yvonne E. Dotson, to James A. Quadra, San Francisco Deputy City Attorney, September 11, 1995, in San Francisco Task Force, *Final Report,* appendix.

61. "Biography of Catherine La Croix," 1.

62. Norma Jean Almodovar, in Pheterson, *Vindication,* 81.

63. Silbert and Pines, "Pornography and Sexual Abuse," 333.

64. In an interview, Penelope Saunders, executive director of HIPS (Helping Individual Prostitutes Survive), an outreach service in Washington, D.C., reported that one-third of the streetwalkers her organization serves are women, one-third are gay men, and one-third are transgendered. She indicated that she believed this was representative of the U.S. streetwalking population in general (and significant to other prostitute venues as well).

65. The risks associated with other forms of prostitution appear to be tied to the same factors.

66. Reichert and Frey, "Organization of Bell Desk Prostitution," 519.

67. Some agencies in Nevada employ drivers who require that a client provide a driver's license, credit card, and other identification before they will drop the escort off.

68. This is unverifiable and, from my experience with management insensitivity on this matter, I believe it somewhat suspect.

69. Brody, "Diary of a Prostitute" 197.

70. Miller, "Prostitution," 208.

71. Bosworth, "Prostitution Funded 'Sex Mall.'"

72. Bosworth, "Parlor Workers."

73. See Haberstroh, "Around the Island."

74. Bosworth, "Parlor Workers."

75. Farmer, "Collingsville Police Turn to Expert."

76. Miller, "Prostitution," 208.

77. Bosworth, "Prostitution Funded 'Sex Mall.'"

78. Ibid.

79. Bosworth, "U.S. Court Learns."

80. *The Chicken Ranch* (1982) Nicholas Broomfield and Sandy Sissel producers in assoc. with Churchill Films. Stamford, CT: Vestron Video and *We're Here Now* (1983) prod/dir-Dawn Wieking. Sanford/Pillsbury Productions. NY. (35)

81. Though I spoke with many people, the most extensive interviews were conducted with several prostitute women, especially "Pepper"; with George Flint, president of the Nevada Brothel Owners Association; with "Bridgit," a seventy-year-old former prostitute and then manager of the Kit Kat Ranch; with Alberta Nelson, the registered nurse who performed medical examinations for the Mustangs; and with then Storey County sheriff Robert Delcarlo.

82. See esp. Pillard, "Legal Prostitution."

83. Flint was not himself a brothel owner. Rather, he owned wedding chapels (an interesting connection, given my discussion of marriage and prostitution).

84. See Barry, *Female Sexual Slavery*, 131.

85. Prostitute "nude dancers" or "nude entertainers" are plentiful and easily accessed through glossy pamphlets ubiquitous in hotels and casinos, as well as through the yellow pages, internet, and newspapers. Streetwalking, bar and hotel prostitution, and escort services are also plentiful and illegal.

86. A similar justification was offered to Pillard to "explain" Winnemuca's policy; see her "Legal Prostitutes."

87. Nevada *Revised Statutes*. Pillard, "Legal Prostitution," 43.

88. NRS 244.342 (1971).

89. *Nye County v. Plankinton*, 94 Nev. 739 (1978).

90. See Pillard, "Legal Prostitution," for additional information on the specifics of different county regulations.

91. Ibid., 45.

92. It is sometimes difficult to determine whether a particular restriction on prostitutes constitutes an instance of "regulation by custom" or is simply a rule of brothel management, who are clearly concerned with keeping a low profile with the police and avoiding greater state interventions.

93. Prostitutes are required to eat on the grounds.

94. This was, however, more than my income as an associate professor of philosophy at that time.

95. This criticism was raised by Carol Leigh of COYOTE during a public panel discussion held at University of Nevada, Las Vegas.

96. Levy, "Brothel Regulation Criticized."

97. E.g., they indicated that they would regularly hold onto the man's testicles while engaging in intercourse, making the client particularly vulnerable and thereby ensuring that he "stayed in line." Several talked of throwing unwieldy clients off of themselves, while one woman told me that she had had a customer

thrown out because he tried to draw blood while sucking her nipple. Interestingly, his justification for his behavior was that his wife let him do so.

98. Pillard, "Legal Prostitution," 45.

99. The nearest brothel is eighty-five miles away.

100. Vanwesenbeeck, *Prostitutes' Well-Being*, 3.

101. This is evidenced by the difficulty Dutch officials have had establishing "safe parks" for streetwalking (discussed below).

102. Visser, "Legalisation of the Exploitation," 12.

103. In the case of prostitution, this involves accepting the apparent inevitability of prostitution. The Dutch focus on lessening the harms of the practice rather than on engaging in a (futile) attempt to eliminate it.

104. Visser, "Selling Private Sex," 2.

105. Visser, "Selling Private Sex," 1.

106. The exceptions are Belgium, which has laws on the books against prostitution, and Spain, which by practice (law in action) does not tolerate prostitution.

107. Visser, Oomens, Venicz and Nencel, "Research," 1, 3.

108. Art. 250b of the Dutch Penal Code, passed in 1911.

109. Art. 432 of the Dutch Penal Code.

110. See Chapter 1 for a description of the window prostitution.

111. Visser, Oomens, Venicz and Nencel, "Research," 2. "Legalisation of the Exploitation," 3.

112. I found the same contradictions in the attitude toward prostitution among the police as in the general population. When I objected that a then-existing procedure was stigmatizing, Verhees argued that the police were trying to eliminate stigma by normalizing prostitution, but a few sentences later she referred to prostitution as "vice." While the official police position is that oversight and restriction of prostitution are motivated purely by a desire to control abuse and trafficking, in my interview with Vanwesenbeeck, she suggested that the problematic procedure was really an attempt to control illegal immigrants and not trafficking.

113. Visser, "Selling Private Sex," 4.

114. Paralleling this frustration among U.S. police forces, the captain of the Omaha, Nebraska, vice squad added in an interview that many of the uniformed officers were extremely uncomfortable negotiating with prostitutes, finding it morally problematic.

115. Visser, "Selling Private Sex," 5.

116. Ibid., 8.

117. Ibid.

118. Visser, "Legalisation of the Exploitation," 2.

119. Visser, "Selling Private Sex," 8. According to Hilda Blank of the Stichting HAJ, 75 percent of streetwalkers in Amsterdam are addicted to heroin or

cocaine and some to alcohol. Some transsexuals are also drug addicts, but many are working to pay for their surgeries.

120. Vanwesenbeeck, *Prostitutes' Well-Being*, 6.

121. One important note: As Vanwesenbeeck states, the study is not totally representative of the prostitute population of the Netherlands; specifically, those "working under extremely negative conditions are probably under-represented" (since these women are far less likely to respond to questionnaires), and specific forms (e.g., street prostitution versus window prostitution) may be somewhat over- or underrepresented. There is also an underrepresentation of Southeast Asian, African, Eastern European, and ex-Soviet prostitutes in the immigrant prostitute population. Despite these stated shortcomings, the author estimates "that overall both our samples provide a reasonable reflection of the total population of women working in prostitution in The Netherlands"(*Prostitutes' Well-Being*, 72).

122. She uses deRidder's analysis of the concept. See *Determinanten van Psychische Gezondheid*, Utrecht: Nederlands Centrum Geesteljke Volksgezondheid, 1990.

123. Vanwesenbeeck, *Prostitutes' Well-Being*, 43.

124. She was able to do so with varying success. See table 4.2 in ibid., 71.

125. Ibid., 147–148.

126. Ibid., 147.

127. Ibid., 147–149.

128. Ibid., 69–70.

129. Ibid., 149.

130. Ibid., 149–150.

131. Ibid., 31.

132. Ibid., 102.

133. This attitude is consistent with my findings in Nevada.

134. Vanwesenbeeck, *Prostitutes' Well-Being*, 150.

135. Ibid., 149.

136. Ibid., 43.

137. Ibid.

138. Ibid., 45.

139. Ibid., 150.

140. In a private conversation I had with Kelly Holsopple, outreach program manager of Breaking Free, an anti-prostitution organization in Minneapolis—St. Paul (June 14, 1998), she emphasized the intensity and commonality of dissociation in the prostitute experience.

141. Vanwesenbeeck, *Prostitutes' Well-Being*, 150–151. I am not convinced that many of the examples she suggests, e.g., police work and surgery, do not also require emotion work, i.e., "acting in a way that is known to be false or that actually transforms one's feelings." Further, I maintain that this, as well as the de-

gree of intrusiveness that occurs in prostitution, is also shared with most women's experiences as wives.

142. Vanwesenbeeck, *Prostitutes' Well-Being*, 151.

143. Ibid., 152.

144. Ibid., 46.

145. Rubin, "Thinking Sex," 279.

146. Vanwesenbeeck, *Prostitutes' Well-Being*, 46.

147. Typical of this phenomenon is the case of the murder of Melissa Short, a Bay Area streetwalker, killed on December 24, 1996. Her boyfriend, Freddie Houston, reported her missing, informing the police of her last scheduled appointment with Dale Anthony Holmes. The police questioned the man and his brother but refused to search their home. On May 16, 1997, Shelly Morrow, also a Bay Area streetwalker, disappeared. Morrow's boyfriend, while searching for her, connected with Houston. He also contacted the Sheriff's Department "and asked them to search the house" of Holmes and his brother. But it was not until May 29, 1997, after "an unidentified informant told San Pablo police about the bodies and the suspects" that the police arrested the two Holmes brothers for murder. Short's body was found in a shallow pit at the end of the street on which the Holmeses lived. Houston was quoted as saying: "It was like I was the only one investigating. Why did it take this other girl to die before they went in there? The police didn't care about the girl because she was a prostitute" (Fernandez, "Tale of Love, A12).

148. See, for example, the handling of the infamous Hillside Strangler case in Los Angeles in the early 1980s; police showed little interest until a schoolgirl was murdered.

149. Chesney-Lind, "Women and Crime"; 82. Alder, "'Passionate and Willful' Girls," 82.

150. Alder, "'Passionate and Willful' Girls," 88.

151. Burns, "Once Widowed," 1, 12.

152. Murray, "Debt Bondage," 53. Note that some (e.g., Kathleen Barry) allow that nonprostitute immigrants may be trafficked, while others (e.g., the Dutch government) at times appear to have a narrower focus. Dutch legislation defines trafficking as "forcing a person, by violence or threat of violence, by abuse or by ascendancy, to prostitution or to undertake actions thereto." Brusa, "Survey on Prostitution," 12.

153. I want to make it clear, to those unfamiliar with current feminist anti-trafficking debates, that this claim is not just highly controversial but is at the core of disagreement among feminist anti-trafficking advocates. In the 1994 draft of the "Proposed Convention against Sexual Exploitation," a very different position is taken. There, by appeal to the 1949 "Convention for the Suppression of Traffic in Persons and the Exploitation of the Prostitution of Others," the authors maintain that "prostitution and the accompanying evil of the traffic in persons for

the purpose of prostitution are incompatible with the dignity and worth of the human person and endanger the welfare of the individual, the family, and the community" (see Barry, *Prostitution of Sexuality,* 324) and that "sexual violence and prostitution are not inevitable but are forms of sexual exploitation" (Ibid., 325). Therefore, article 6 of the document holds that "State Parties [must] reject any policy or law that legitimates prostitution of any person, female or male, adult or child; that legalizes or regulates prostitution in any way including as a profession, occupation, or as entertainment; and agree to adopt appropriate legislation that recognizes prostitution as an acute form of sexual exploitation, including . . . punishment of any person who procures, entices, or leads away by any means for the purposes of prostitution, another person, even with the consent of that person" (Ibid., 328–329).

154. As Narayan indicates, "One study reports that 77 percent of women with dependent immigrant status are battered" ("'Mail Order' Brides," 145).

155. "STV background information in the application to the Phare Democracy Programme," 1. 1991. Published by and available through STV. Post Bus 97799, 2509GD Den Haag the Netherlands.

156. Kempadoo and Doezema, eds., *Global Sex Workers,* 55.

157. Murray, "Debt Bondage," 59.

158. Ibid., 58–59.

159. Frank E. Loy, testimony before the U.S. Justice Department, *Congressional Testimonies,* February 22, 2000.

160. Ibid.

161. In 2001, these workers agreed to a $1.2 million settlement with one of the manufacturers whose garments were produced in this sweatshop, bringing their total legal settlements to $4 million.

162. Bonk, "Study Launched," 3.

163. Ibid., 3.

164. Global Survival Network, "Trapped."

165. Kim "Re-conceptualizing Immigration," 5; see also Haberstroh, "Around the Island."

NOTES TO CHAPTER 6

1. Unplanned pregnancies can be problematic due to natural conditions (e.g., naturally occurring famine) or socially constructed conditions (e.g., the construction of the family unit, which may make some pregnancies contextually problematic).

2. I don't mean to suggest that the forms of birth control currently available are unproblematic. I have argued elsewhere that many forms of birth control are dangerous to women and that research and development of these technologies has

been a deeply biased and misogynistic process (Kuo, "Secondary Discrimination," 919–926).

It is also interesting that some people argue for programs to encourage abstinence as an appropriate approach to AIDS prevention rather than for an aggressive "safe-sex" educational program and general availability of condoms, since the latter approach has proven far more effective in controlling the spread of AIDS (as evidenced by the comparative success rates in the United States and the Netherlands).

3. See, for example, Vance, ed., *Pleasure and Danger*, and Jackson and Scott, eds., *Feminism and Sexuality*.

4. For example, Belinda Cooper maintains, "The project created by feminism, . . . is that of finding, developing, validating and ultimately instituting a 'woman's voice,' a value system grounded in women's experience. . . . A 'female' approach to sex may well, in some ways, resemble the romantic vision that conservative moralists have extolled and liberal theorists rejected. . . . Responsibility towards others—'connectedness'—plays a strong part in the 'female' value system" ("Prostitution," 116).

5. For example, see Baldwin, "Split at the Root," and Kostash "Second Thoughts."

6. See Cooper, "Prostitution."

7. Kostash, "Second Thoughts," 485. This is, while a particularly powerful description of the view, one that Kostash had defended earlier in her career but rejects in the article.

8. I am *not* advocating a return to the ideology behind the "sexual revolution" (sometimes termed "sexual liberalism"), where the view was that we should all participate freely in sexual activities since "there is nothing wrong with sex and sexual behavior except society's morally ungrounded stigma and mystification of it." Indeed, as should be apparent, I am convinced there is a good deal wrong with sexuality and sexual activity as currently constructed and practiced. They are, among other things, weapons of sexism, and as such, their meaning (including mystification and stigma) cannot be dismissed as irrelevant to one's behavior. As many women learned rather painfully in the 1960s and 1970s, "free sex" in this context becomes just another patriarchal mechanism for men to gain sexual access to women—simultaneously continuing to objectify women while maintaining the social stigmatization of women who engage in nontraditional or nonexclusive sexual behavior.

Although much of my view of ideal sexuality dovetails with that of Gayle Rubin, my view departs from hers on some essential points. For example, I am not convinced that serious acts of sadomasochism, ones that produce significant pain or are significantly demeaning, would exist in an ideal world because (1) I doubt that the desire to cause or to receive pain or demeaning behavior would exist at all, and (2) given the history of sexuality, I especially doubt that pain or demeaning others or oneself would be associated with sexuality.

9. I intend this description to be broad enough to include noncapitalist economies. Indeed, I am convinced that in an ideal world, economic organization would not fit a capitalist model. However, barring a fully technologized society in which all labor is performed by automatons, as long as labor is necessary, its provision by those who are capable of performing it would fit my broad definition.

10. Brownmiller, *Against Our Will*, 440.

11. I have qualified "all sexual orientations" with "nearly" both because of my concern with sadomasochism (see n. 8, above) and my concern with pedophilia. I do not believe that children, especially younger ones, should be used in any labor force, given their incapacity for genuine consent, their vulnerability to abuse, and their physical, emotional, and mental limitations.

12. Different regulations, e.g., on what specific health and safety measures are to be used, obviously would apply. But this is the case for most industries. Different health and safety measures are employed, for instance, by meat cutters and hair cutters.

13. The pleasure of the prostitute would be no more significant than the pleasure of the massage therapist or psychologist.

NOTES TO CHAPTER 7

1. For an excellent extended discussion of this issue, see Feinberg's, *Harm to Self*, vol. 1–4.

2. Ibid., ix.

3. For feminists, this claim is highly problematic, both because it emerges from a social contractarian, rights-based, individualistic tradition and because Mill presumed the public/private sphere distinction, with no apparent understanding of the political nature of "the personal." Unfortunately, length limitations do not allow me to address these issues here.

4. I accept Feinberg's suggestion that we adopt the following two corollaries to the broader Offense Principle: *a.* The Standard of Universality—"For the offensiveness (disgust, embarrassment, outraged sensibilities, or shame) to be sufficient to warrant coercion, it should be the reaction that could be expected from almost any person chosen at random from the nation as a whole, regardless of sect, faction, race, age, or sex." *b.* The Standard of Reasonable Avoidability— "No one has a right to protection from the state against offensive experiences if [s/]he can effectively avoid those experiences with no unreasonable effort or inconvenience." See Feinberg, *Harm to Self*, vol. 1–4, 20–22.

5. See, e.g., *Muller v. Oregon* (U.S. 1908), in which the court permitted restricting the working hours of women while having earlier (*Lochner v. New York*)

(1902) rejected a similar limitation on the working hours of males. The court held that "limitations upon personal and contractual rights may be removed by legislation, there is that in [women's] disposition and habits of life which will operate against a full assertion of rights." Woman is "properly placed in a class by herself, and legislation designed for her protection may be sustained, even when like legislation is not necessary for men and could not be sustained" (cited in Hill, "Protection of Women Workers," 253).

6. I am hesitant to be more absolute on this point largely because it is not clear, short of entering the legal morass involved in claiming that animals have rights, how to prevent individuals from torturing their own animals in the privacy of their own homes.

7. Much of this material comes from my paper "Who Owns Women's Bodies? Bodily Autonomy, Bodily Integrity and the State" presented at the National Women's Studies Association Annual Conference, Simmons College, Boston, Massachusetts, June 2000.

8. The concept of bodily autonomy is embedded in that of personal autonomy, "the question of what it is to know what one really wants—to discern the desires of one's authentic self—and to act in accordance with those desires" (Meyers, *Self, Society and Personal Choice,* xii). There is clearly a question about the degree to which my desires are a reflection of my "authentic self" rather than merely a reflection of my acculturation. So while one may have the right to governmental noninterference (bodily autonomy) regarding breast augmentation, it is far from clear that I have *personal* autonomy in making such a decision. Furthermore, the right of bodily autonomy is not independent of the social-historical context. Different contemporary cultures view the limits of bodily autonomy differently (e.g., some permit rather severe physical punishment), and historically, interference with bodily autonomy was more acceptable in the United States (e.g., forced lobotomies and sterilization of the mentally ill were legal in the early twentieth century).

9. See Kuo "Secondary Discrimination."

10. See esp. Devlin, *Enforcement of Morals.*

11. See, e.g., Lynch and Neckes, *Cast Effectiveness.*

12. See esp. Pillard, "Rethinking Prostitution."

13. Pheterson, *Vindication,* 8.

14. As one worker pointed out to me, if prostitution is not illegal, prostitutes are more likely to report illegal and abusive practices in their competitors' organizations (thereby eliminating some competition) as well as in their own situations.

15. Chesney-Lind, "Women and Crime," 80.

16. Ibid., 89.

17. Weitzer, "Prostitutes Rights," 25. See also Vanwesenbeeck, *Prostitutes' Well-Being,* 3.

18. See, e.g., Weitzer, "Prostitutes Rights."

19. Chesney-Lind, "Women and Crime," 78.

20. As I discuss below, like legalization, criminalization also constitutes a form of secondary discrimination.

21. This is not to suggest that required medical tests occur only under legalization. Even under criminalization, some jurisdictions require convicted prostitutes to undergo such exams. See Bell, *Reading, Writing*, 179, on mandatory HIV testing in California; and Pheterson, *Vindication*, 5, on prostitutes being required to wait in jails for the result of involuntary gonorrhea tests in San Francisco. See also San Francisco Task Force, *Final Report*.

22. Stock, "When Older Women."

23. In fact, a Las Vegas prostitute was "the first person to ever be convicted under a law making it a felony to solicit sex after testing HIV positive" (San Francisco Task Force, *Report Final*, appendix D: "The "New" Prostitution: New Cases Nationwide").

24. Rather bizarrely, this is common even with prostitutes who are known to be at high risk for HIV. In Amsterdam, the population most likely to be offered bribes for sex without condoms (and most likely to agree) are HIV-infected and severely drug-addicted prostitutes who work behind the railroad station.

25. This three-month lag occurs with the Elisa test. There is also a PCR test currently available (Amplicor HIV-1 or Viral Load test) that has only a thirty-day lag, but as of the date of this writing, it cost $500.

26. San Francisco Task Force, *Final Report*, appendix A: "Models of Prostitution Regulation," 21.

27. In the Philippines, where registration was combined with mandatory medical exams, the unhygienic methods used for testing became a serious source of STD transmission (paralleling the difficulty with mandatory testing experienced in England in the 1860s and Paris in the 1830s). See San Francisco Task Force, *Final Report*.

28. Pillard, "Legal Prostitution," 45.

29. Leigh, a San Francisco prostitute, performance artist, and COYOTE spokesperson, repeated this sentiment several times in my interviews with her in April 1997.

30. See Fechner, "Three Stories," 42.

31. Vanwesenbeeck, *Prostitutes' Well-Being*, 29.

32. This includes the lack of policies directed at lessening gender differentials in income.

NOTES TO CHAPTER 8

1. See, for example, Fechner, "Three Stories."

2. My approach here is more linear/analytic than previously in this text. I use somewhat traditional methodologies, which, to some extent, reflect the dominant

male epistemic and ethical methodologies in the Anglo-American analytic tradition. I do so because many of the positions I disagree with are themselves presented in this manner and because positions are both logically and practically more compelling if it can be demonstrated that they are the most plausible by employing both traditional and nontraditional methodologies. Furthermore, law and policy makers are most likely to respond to traditional argumentation; such methodologies are currently privileged.

3. See Alison Jaggar, "Contemporary Western Feminist Perspectives." I specify that this is a particularly American position because it was consistently at variance with the views of the numerous Western European feminists, of virtually every ilk, with whom I met. They were, I think, too influenced by postmodernism to be comfortable with the absoluteness of this perspective.

4. Overall, "What's Wrong with Prostitution?" 721 and 723.

5. Ibid., 724. This is a citation from a British author that Overall (a Canadian) includes in her conclusion.

6. The social contract is key to a political theory that initially gained popularity during the Enlightenment, a time in which the legitimate power of the state could no longer be justified by appeal to divine right of kings. Briefly, according to this theory, without a commonwealth individuals exist in a "state of nature." They band together to form a state in order to preserve themselves (their lives, welfare, and, depending on the author, their property). In so doing, they agree to a contract, laying down many of the freedoms they have in a state of nature in exchange for greater security. The social contract theory is generally conceptually embedded in the creation of modern democratic states, including the United States. Pateman argues convincingly that, in effect, it constitutes the embedding of state-sanctioned patriarchy as well.

On Pateman's view (and in my experience), what is almost always ignored in discussions of the social contract is that the authors of this theory, generally explicitly, did not include women as "individuals"; i.e., the social contract was conceived of as a contract between men because contractual agreements can only occur between equals and women were judged to be inferiors.

7. Pateman, *Sexual Contract*, 2.

8. Ibid., 203.

9. This is not because prostitution is a site where patriarchy and capitalism intersect, for Pateman recognizes that capitalism depends on the marriage contract and that the marriage contract depends on and interacts with capitalist structures, so control over women's bodies would not be a distinguishing feature of prostitution. In fact, often her attempts to distinguish prostitution from marriage or other labor appear forced and rather bizarre; for example:

> If a prostitute were merely another worker, the prostitution contract, too
> would always involve a capitalist, yet very frequently the man who enters into

the contract is a worker. . . . The capitalist has no intrinsic interest in the body and self of the worker, or, at least, not the same kind of interest as the man who enters into the prostitution contract. The employer is primarily interested in the commodities produced by the worker; that is to say, in profits. (Pateman, *Sexual Contract*, 202–203)

But these claims apply to most service providers; workers as well as capitalists get their hair cut, undergo surgery, and hire kids to mow the lawn, and in none of these cases are profits made for the person using the service. It seems Pateman confuses two senses of "hiring"; individuals can hire a service worker to provide them with a personal service or hire employees who provide services to others as laborers (and profit makers) for their company. Further, as Pateman seems at other times to recognize, "the worker" she is envisioning is male; for although it may be true that "the capitalist has no *intrinsic* interest in the body and self of the [female] worker," the ubiquitous occurrence of work-related sexual harrassement testifies to the capitalists' interest in the body and self of the female worker, whether intrinsic or not.

10. Pateman, *Sexual Contract*, 204.

11. Ibid., 205–206.

12. Ibid., 206; italics added.

13. Bell, *Reading, Writing*, 78.

14. Although reproduction generally requires sexual intercourse, it is the reproduction of (male) children and not sexual activity that is valued in these instances.

15. Although Pateman recognizes that other forms of domination exist, her analysis of prostitution generally appears to overlook this fact.

16. Pateman, *Sexual Contract*, 207–208.

17. Ibid., 208.

18. Ibid., 209.

19. Ibid., 148–149.

20. Ibid., 209.

21. Millett, "Prostitution," 42.

22. One of the more disturbing scenes I witnessed with regard to window prostitution in Amsterdam involved an incident where three young Dutch men were being very disrespectful to a heavy-set, dark-skinned African prostitute. I was appalled by both the misogyny and the racism evident in the encounter, particularly by the behavior of the ringleader. But when I mentioned the incident to several different sex workers and to representatives of the de Graaf, I consistently received the same response: The African prostitute tolerated it because she knew that the fellow was likely to return later without his friends to purchase her services—and would not be likely to "act out" then. To impress

one another men will engage in behavior that they would not consider acting on privately.

23. The practice of dominance prostitution is highly psychologically complex. Who has real control in these situations is currently a matter of debate, but men do pay to be demeaned and degraded in these arrangements.

24. Even nonpublic sex work in which no physical contact occurs may be a far more effective source of patriarchal propaganda than prostitution—because in the case of phone sex, the worker can play *to* the client's misogynistic fantasies without having to play *out* those fantasies as a physical, embodied being. Thus the paid phone-sex worker is far more likely to go along with the client's misogyny than is the prostitute, who may physically suffer if she does so.

25. Satz, "Markets in Women's Sexual Labor," 80–81. See also Barry, *Prostitution of Sexuality*.

26. Who suffers more violence is particularly unclear if one is discussing secretaries in their roles as wives or significant others—a role many prostitutes do not take on. Similarly, Barry states, "Beating, rape, and even murder are generally considered merely 'occupational hazards' of prostitution" (*Prostitution of Sexuality*, 36), but the studies on which these claims are based rely solely on the testimony of former prostitutes who have been victimized by and are attempting to escape prostitution.

27. Indeed, when Satz maintains that prostitutes are "far more likely to be victims of violence" ("Markets in Women's Sexual Labor," 81), she cites figures on street prostitutes despite having previously acknowledged that they are unrepresentative of the industry as a whole.

28. Similarly, policies directed at LPNs, secretaries, and other paid nurturant providers must include protections corresponding to the objectification, subordination, and degradation associated with these traditional female roles.

29. Bell, *Reading, Writing*, 135.

30. See Rubin "Thinking Sex," and Astuto and Califia, "Being Weird."

31. Ferguson, "Transitional Feminist Sexual Morality," 499.

32. Ibid., 500.

33. Jeffreys, "Sadomasochism," 241.

34. Califia, "Feminism and Sadomasochism," 232–233.

35. LeMoncheck, *Loose Women*, 93.

36. Ferguson, "Transitional Feminist Sexual Morality," 501.

37. For example, Fechner quotes Selma James's speech before the House of Commons (March 5, 1979) in which she maintained, "We want to make it clear that if there were no poor women, there would not be one woman on the game, not one" ("Three Stories,"42).

Notes to Chapter 9

1. This is intended as a general, prima facie claim since a specific prostitute may, like a specific nonprostitute, behave in ways that lessen her or his moral status (e.g., by murdering another).

2. Although they may not be familiar with the distinction between legalization and decriminalization, they generally express the belief that if prostitution were legalized, then prostitutes could be required to be tested for STDs; thus they clearly favor legalization.

3. Most of these suggestions are culled from a wide variety of sources.

4. This would, of course, entail no government systems of registration or mandated medical tests.

5. Although I would strongly prefer inclusion of Vanwesenbeeck's call for a "free drug supply" along the lines of those successfully attempted in experimental programs in Liverpool and Amsterdam, or at least of a policy decriminalizing drug usage (which significantly lowers the cost of illegal drugs), given recent U.S. history, including the supposed "drug wars," I see such approaches as currently politically impossible today.

6. When I worked at Haven House, the value of such sensitivity programs for police handling of domestic violence was constantly demonstrated. Pasadena's police chief had publicly affirmed his commitment to improving police service to victims of domestic violence and had instituted a required program of sensitivity training provided by Haven House staff. When a client from Pasadena required police help or support, the Pasadena police were, almost universally, at least minimally appropriate and responsive. However, whenever the shelter had a client who required support from the Los Angeles police, the situation was generally a nightmare; we were regularly dismissed or worse. (I particularly remember one instance when, after attempting to kill our client, her "partner" returned to the apartment where her children were asleep. The L.A. police refused to go in and remove the children because they didn't want to wake the woman's partner.) The difference between the two departments was truly dramatic.

7. This medical care should be part of a larger policy ensuring medical coverage for all U.S. residents. However, the vulnerability of prostitutes, including lives of severe poverty among many, makes their medical needs especially compelling. Further, medical care for prostitutes should be a particular priority since their well-being is likely to impact significantly on the larger population. But in this recommendation, I am laying out a need not simply for the provision of medical services but for services that address the special needs of various prostitute populations.

8. I think it significant that, in the recent past, at least two world-famous actors have been caught having sex with streetwalkers in their cars in Los Angeles. Clearly they didn't choose streetwalkers because they couldn't afford "higher-

end" prostitutes. Men, or at least Western men, do seem to find sex in cars erotic.

9. Pheterson, *Vindication*, 16.

10. This would be justified by a limited-offense principle. (See Chapter 6.)

11. Perhaps coffee shops or the like could be permitted in these zones.

12. Not only would this be the case with more naive potential prostitutes, but because decriminalization is likely to increase the number of women willing to prostitute, competition for employment with facilitators will increase and thus further the power disparities between prostitutes and facilitators.

13. San Francisco Task Force, *Final Report*, 17.

14. The issue of legalized prostitution facilitation once again exemplifies my purpose in defining prostitution narrowly, to include only private sexual acts. Because I believe that public commercial sex acts as currently performed, (including live sex shows and striptease) generally constitute a communal affirmation of misogyny, their status as hate speech targeting both female performers and women in general makes them legally far more problematic than prostitution.

15. See also discussion of the West German policy, which established a "state approved apartment block" with rooms rented for prostitution (Yondorf, "Prostitution as a Legal Activity," 417–433); and the report of the Southern Australia Committee to Decriminalise Prostitution, Prostitution Act Draft 5 (1996), in San Francisco Task Force, *Final Report*, appendix D.

16. See the January and March 1999 drafts submitted by the United States to the United Nations Commission on Crime Prevention and Criminal Justice for the "Protocol on Trafficking in Women and Children," to be attached to a new "Convention Against Transnational Crime"—documents titled, respectively, "Draft Protocol to Combat International Trafficking in Women and Children Supplementary to the Draft Convention on Transnational Organized Crime" and "Draft Protocol to Prevent, Suppress, and Punish Trafficking in Women and Children Supplementing the Convention Against Transnational Organized Crime." Available at http://www.uncjin.org.

17. "Human Rights Standards for the Treatment of Trafficked Persons," 11. Developed by the Global Alliance against Traffic in Women (Thailand), the Foundation against Trafficking in Women (STV-The Netherlands) and the International Human Rights Law Group (U.S.A.) Jan 1999. Available at http://www.inet.co.th/org/gaatw/shr99.htm.

18. Barry, *Prostitution of Sexuality*, 330.

19. A weak version of such laws exists in the Philippines. See Barry, *Prostitution of Sexuality*, 158.

20. This occurred historically and was often motivated by racist concerns.

Bibliography

Achilles, Rona. "The Regulation of Prostitution: Background Paper." In *San Francisco Task Force on Prostitution: Final Report*, appendix D. San Francisco: Board of Supervisors, 1995.

Acton, William. *Prostitution Considered in Its Moral, Social, and Sanitary Aspects*. London: Frank Cass, 1870.

Adams, Karen, and Norma C. Ware. "Sexism and the English Language: The Linguistic Implications of Being a Woman." In *Women: A Feminist Perspective*, ed. Jo Freeman, 331–346. Mountain View, CA: Mayfield, 1995.

Alder, Christine M. "'Passionate and Willful' Girls: Confronting Practices." *Women and Criminal Justice* 9, 4 (1998): 81–101.

Alexander, Priscilla. "Prostitution: Still a Difficult Issue for Feminists." In *Sex Work: Writings by Women in the Sex Industry*, ed. Frederique Delacoste and Priscilla Alexander, 184–230. San Francisco: Clies, 1998.

———. "Registration, Mandatory Testing and Health Certificates: The Record." In *San Francisco Task Force on Prostitution: Final Report*, appendix D. San Francisco: Board of Supervisors, 1996.

Anechiarico, Frank. "Administrative Culture and Civil Society: A Comparative Perspective." *Administration and Society* 30, 1 (March 1998): 13–34.

——— and Lenore Kuo. "The Justified Scoundrel: The Structural Genesis of Corruption." *Journal of Social Philosophy* 25, 1 (Spring 1995): 147–161.

Astuto, Cynthia, and Pat Califia. "Being Weird Is Not Enough: How to Stay Healthy and Play Safe." In *Coming to Power: Writings and Graphics on Lesbian SM*, ed. Members of Samois, a Lesbian/Feminist S/M Organization. Boston: Alyson Publications, 1987.

Atkinson, Ti-Grace. "The Institution of Sexual Intercourse." In *Notes from the Second Year: Women's Liberation: Major Writings of the Radical Feminists*. ed. Ann Koedt and Shulamith Firestone. New York: Radical Feminism, 1970. 42–47.

Baker, Robert. "'Pricks' and 'Chicks': A Plea for 'Persons.'" In *Philosophy and Sex*, ed. Robert Baker and Frederick Elliston. Buffalo, NY: Prometheus Books, 1984. Reprinted in *Feminist Philosophies*. ed. Janet A. Kourany, James P. Sterba and Rosemarie Tong, 34–45. Upper Saddle River, NJ: Prentice Hall, 1999.

Baldwin, Margaret A. "Split at the Root: Prostitution and Feminist Discourses of Law Reform." *Yale Journal of Law and Feminism* 5, 47 (1992). 49–120.

Balos, Beverly, and Mary Louise Fellows. "A Matter of Prostitution: Becoming Respectable." *New York University Law Review* 74, 5. (November 1999): 1220–1303.

Barry, Kathleen. *Female Sexual Slavery.* New York: New York University Press, 1985.

———. *The Prostitution of Sexuality.* New York: New York University Press, 1995.

Bell, Shannon. *Reading, Writing and Rewriting the Prostitute Body.* Bloomington: Indiana University Press, 1994.

Benn, S. I. "Freedom, Autonomy, and the Concept of a Person." *Aristotelian Society Proceedings* 76 (1975): 109–130.

Bergen, R. K. *Wife Rape: Understanding the Response of Survivors and Service Providers.* Thousand Oaks, CA: Sage, 1996.

Boles, Jacqueline, and Charlotte Tatro. "Legal and Extralegal Methods of Controlling Female Prostitution: A Cross-Cultural Comparison." *International Journal of Comparative and Applied Criminal Justice* 2, 1 (Spring 1978): 71–85.

Bonk, Denise. "Study Launched on Trafficking of Women and Children in the Americas." *Congressional Testimonies,* April 12, 2000 (Archives). Available at http://secretary.state.gov/

Bordo, Susan. *The Flight to Objectivity.* Albany: State University of New York Press, 1987.

———. *Unbearable Weight: Feminism, Western Culture, and the Body.* Berkeley: University of California Press, 1993.

Boston Women's Health Book Collective. *Our Bodies, Ourselves; A Book by and for Women.* New York: Simon and Schuster, 1973.

Bosworth, Charles, Jr. "Parlor Workers Say They Didn't Tell of Sex Employees, Testify They Assumed Owner Knew of Prostitution; St. Louis Man Is on Trial." *St. Louis Post-Dispatch* November 5, 1998. B1.

———. "Prostitution Funded 'Sex Mall': Jury Is Told Massage Parlors Served as Fronts, Prosecutor Charges." *St. Louis Post-Dispatch,* October 23, 1998.

———. "U.S. Court Learns About Inner Financial Workings of Metro East Massage Parlors." *St. Louis Post-Dispatch,* June 21, 1998. C1.

Brody, Liz. "Diary of a Prostitute." *Glamour,* April 2001, 194–197.

Brownmiller, Susan. *Against Our Will: Men, Women and Rape.* New York: Bantam, 1976.

Brusa, Licia. "Survey on Prostitution, Migration and Traffic in Women: History and Current Situation." Survey prepared for human rights seminar on action against traffic in women and forced prostitution. Council of Europe,

European Committee for Equality between Women and Men, Strasbourg, Sept. 25–27 1991.

Bureau of Municipal Research. "Prostitution in Our Cities." *Civic Affairs* (February 1983): 9–10.

Burns, John F. "Once Widowed in India, Twice Scorned." *New York Times*, Sunday, May 29, 1998, 1 and 12.

Butler, Judith. *Gender Trouble: Feminism and the Subversion of Identity.* New York: Routledge, 1990.

Caldwell G., S. Galster, and N. Steinzor. "Crime and Servitude: An Expose of the Traffic in Women for Prostitution from the Newly Developed Independent States." *Report of the Global Survival Network.* Available at http://www.witness.org. Date unavailable.

Califia, Pat. "Feminism and Sadomasochism." In *Feminism and Sexuality: A Reader*, ed. Stevi Jackson and Sue Scott, 230–237. New York: Columbia University Press, 1996.

Chapkis, Wendy. *Live Sex Acts: Women Performing Erotic Labor.* New York: Routledge, 1997.

Chesney-Lind, Meda. "Women and Crime: The Female Offender." *Signs: Journal of Women in Culture and Society* 12, 1 (1986): 78–96.

Code, Lorraine. "Is the Sex of the Knower Epistemologically Significant?" *Metaphilosophy* 12 (1981): 267–276.

———. *Rhetorical Spaces: Essays on Gendered Locations.* New York: Routledge, 1995.

Cole, Eve Browning. *Philosophy and Feminist Criticism: An Introduction.* New York: Paragon, 1993.

Cooper, Belinda. "Prostitution: A Feminist Analysis." *Women's Rights Law Reporter* 11, 2 (Summer 1989): 99–120.

Davis, Nanette J., ed. *Prostitution: An International Handbook on Trends, Problems, and Policies.* Westport, CT: Greenwood Press, 1993.

Decker, John F. *Prostitution: Regulation and Control.* Littleton, CO: Fred B. Rothman & Co., 1979.

Delacoste, Frederique, and Priscilla Alexander, eds. *Sex Work: Writings by Women in the Sex Industry.* San Francisco: Cleis, 1987.

Devlin, Patrick. *The Enforcement of Morals.* London: Oxford University Press, 1965.

Doezema, Jo. "Forced to Choose: Beyond the Voluntary v. Forced Prostitution Dichotomy." In *Global Sex Workers: Rights, Resistance, and Redefinition*, ed. Kamala Kempadoo and Jo Doezema, 34–50. New York: Routledge, 1998.

DuBois, Ellen Carol, and Linda Gordon. "Seeking Ecstasy on the Battlefield: Danger and Pleasure in Nineteenth-Century Feminist Sexual Thought." *Feminist Studies* 9, 1 (Spring 1983). Pagination from reprint in *Pleasure and*

Danger: Exploring Female Sexuality, ed. Carole S. Vance, 31–49. Boston: Routledge and Kegan Paul, 1984.

Dworkin, Andrea. *Intercourse*. New York: Free Press, 1987.

Eagleton, Terry. *Literary Theory: An Introduction*. Minneapolis: University of Minnesota Press, 1983.

Elkies, Lauren A. "Upper East Side Prostitution Ring Busted: DA Says That Up-and-Coming Musician Ran $2 Million-a-Year Call Girl Business." *Our Town* (New York City), March 1, 2001, 12, 18.

Ellis, Havelock. *Sex in Relation to Society: Studies in the Psychology of Sex*. Vol. 6. Philadelphia: F. A. Davis, 1910.

Enloe, Cynthia. *Bananas, Beaches and Bases: Making Feminist Sense of International Politics*. Berkeley: University of California Press, 1989.

Ensler, Eve. *The Vagina Monologues*. New York: Villard, 1998.

Farmer, Christine M. "Collingsville Police Turn to Expert on Prostitution." *St. Louis Post-Dispatch*, April 11, 1998. Five Star Lift edition, 16.

Fechner, Holly B. "Three Stories of Prostitution in the West: Prostitutes Groups, Law and Feminist 'Truth.'" *Columbia Journal of Gender and Law* 4 (1994): 26–72.

Feinberg, Joel. *Harm to Self: The Moral Limits of the Criminal Law*, 3 vols. New York: Oxford University Press, 1986.

Ferguson, Ann. "A Transitional Feminist Sexual Morality." In *Feminist Frameworks: Alternative Theoretical Accounts of the Relations between Women and Men*, ed. Alison M. Jaggar and Paula S. Rothenberg, 496–503. New York: McGraw-Hill, 1993. Reprinted from Ferguson, Ann. *Blood at the Root: Motherhood, Sexuality and Male Dominance*. London: Pandora/Unwin Hyman, 1989.

Fernandez, Elisabeth. "Tale of Love, Mystery and Murder." *San Francisco Examiner*, June 1, 1997, A1 and 12.

Fineman, Martha Albertson. "Feminist Theory in Law: The Difference It Makes." *Columbia Journal of Gender and Law* 2, 1 (1992): 3–23.

Finstad, Liv, and Cecilie Hoigard. "Norway." In *Prostitution: An International Handbook on Trends, Problems, and Policies*, ed. Nanette Davis, 206–224. Westport, CT: Greenwood Press, 1993.

Firestone, Shulamith. *The Dialectic of Sex: The Case for Feminist Revolution*. New York: Bantam Books, 1972. Originally published New York: William Morrow, Inc., 1970.

Flax, Jane. *Thinking Fragments: Psychoanalysis, Feminism and Post-Modernism in the Contemporary West*. Berkeley: University of California Press, 1989.

———. "Women Do Theory." *Quest* 5, 1 (Summer 1979): 20–26.

Foucault, Michel. *Discipline and Punish: The Birth of the Prison*. Translated by Alan Sheridan. New York: Pantheon, 1979.

————. *The History of Sexuality: An Introduction.* Vol 1. Translated by Robert Hurley. New York: Vintage Books, 1980.

Fraser Committee (Special Committee on Pornography and Prostitution). *Pornography and Prostitution in Canada.* Vols. 1 and 2. Ottawa: Ministry of Supply and Services, 1985.

Gay, Jill. "The 'Patriotic' Prostitute." *The Progressive,* February 1985.

Gebhard, P. H. "Misconceptions of Female Prostitutes." *Medical Aspects of Human Sexuality* 3(3) 1969. 24–30.

Giobbe, Evelina. "Confronting the Liberal Lies about Prostitution." In *Sexual Liberals and the Attack on Feminism,* ed. Dorchen Leidholdt and Janice Raymond, 67–82. New York: Pergamon, 1990.

Global Survival Network. "Trapped: Human Trafficking for Forced Labor in the Commonwealth of the Northern Mariana Islands (a U.S. Territory)." 1999. Available at http://www.globalsurvival.net.

Haberstroh, Joe. "Around the Island, Crime and Courts Cracking Down on Parlor Prostitution." *Newsday,* November 2, 1994, A33.

Halley, Janet E. "Sexual Orientation and the Politics of Biology: A Critique of the Argument from Immutability." *Stanford Law Review* 46, 3 (February 1994): 503–568.

Haraway, Donna. "Situated Knowledges." In *Simians, Cyborgs, and Women: The Reinvention of Nature.* New York: Routledge, 1990.

Hartsock, Nancy C. M. *The Feminist Standpoint Revisited and Other Essays.* Boulder, CO: Westview, 1998.

Hawkesworth, Mary. "Democratization: Reflections on Gendered Dislocations in the Public Sphere." Paper presented to the New York Society for Women in Philosophy, November 1999.

Hill, A. C. "Protection of Women Workers and the Courts: A Legal Case History." *Feminist Studies* 5, 2 (1979).

Hollibaugh, Amber. "Desire for the Future: Radical Hope in Passion and Pleasure." In *Pleasure and Danger: Exploring Female Sexuality,* ed. Carole Vance, Boston: Routledge and Kegan Paul, 1984.

hooks, bell. *Feminist Theory: From Margin to Center.* 1984. Excerpt reprinted as "Black Women: Shaping Feminist Theory," in *Women and Values: Readings in Recent Feminist Philosophy,* ed. Marilyn Pearsall, 162–173. Belmont, CA: Wadsworth, 1993.

Hulse, James W. *Forty Years in the Wilderness: Impressions of Nevada 1940–1980.* Reno: University of Nevada Press, 1986.

Humm, Maggie. *The Dictionary of Feminist Theory.* Columbus: Ohio State University Press, 1990.

Jackson, Stevi, and Sue Scott, eds. *Feminism and Sexuality: A Reader.* New York: Columbia University Press, 1996.

Jacobs, Leslie Gielow. "Adding Complexity to Confusion and Seeing the Light:

Feminist Legal Insights and the Jurisprudence of the Religious Clauses." *Yale Journal of Law and Feminism* 7, 1 (1995): 137–72.

Jaggar, Alison M. "Contemporary Western Feminist Perspectives on Prostitution." *Asian Journal of Women's Studies* 3, 2 (1997): 8–29.

———. "Prostitution." In *Philosophy of Sex*, ed. Alan G. Soble. Totowa, NJ: Littlefield, Adams, 1980.

———, ed. *Living with Contradictions: Controversies in Feminist Social Ethics.* Boulder, CO: Westview, 1994.

Jaggar, Alison M., and Susan Bordo, eds. *Gender/Body/Knowledge: Feminist Reconstructions of Being and Knowing.* New Brunswick, NJ: Rutgers University Press, 1989.

Jaggar, Alison M., and Paula S. Rothenberg, eds. *Feminist Frameworks: Alternative Theoretical Accounts of the Relations between Women and Men.* 3d ed. New York: McGraw-Hill, 1993.

James, J. "Motivations for Entrance into Prostitution." In *The Female Offender*, ed. L. Crites, 177–205. Lexington: Lexington Books, 1976.

Janus, S. S., and C. L. Janus. *The Janus Report on Sexual Behavior.* New York: John Wiley and Sons, 1993.

Jeffreys, Sheila. "Eroticizing Women's Subordination." In *The Sexual Liberals and the Attack on Feminism*, ed. Dorchen Leidholdt and Janice G. Raymond, 132–135. New York: Pergamon, 1990.

———. "Sadomasochism." In *Feminism and Sexuality: A Reader*, ed. Stevi Jackson and Sue Scott, 238–244. New York: Columbia University Press, 1996.

Jenness, Valerie. *Making It Work: The Prostitutes' Rights Movement in Perspective.* Hawthorne, NY: Aldine de Gruyter, 1992.

Kempadoo, Kamala, and Jo Doezema, eds. *Global Sex Workers: Rights, Resistance, and Redefinition.* New York: Routledge, 1998.

Kim, Hyun Sook. "Re-conceptualizing Immigration: Circulation of Women, Sex and Capital." In *Third Women's Policy Research Conference Proceedings— Exploring the Quincentennial: The Policy Challenges of Gender, Diversity and International Exchange.* Washington, DC; Institute for Women's Policy Research, January 1, 1994.

Kosovski, Ester. "Brazil." In *Prostitution: An International Handbook on Trends, Problems and Policies*, ed. Nanette Davis. Westport, CT: Greenwood, 1993

Kostash, Myrna. "Second Thoughts." In *Feminist Frameworks: Alternative Theoretical Accounts of the Relations between Women and Men*, ed. Alison Jaggar and Paula S. Rothenberg, 484–489. 3d ed. New York: McGraw-Hill, 1993.

Kuo, Lenore. "Coerced Birth Control, Individual Rights, and Discrimination." In *Biomedical Ethics Reviews: 1992.* 101–125. Totowa, NJ: Humana, 1993.

———. "The Morality of Non-Altruistic Surrogate Mothering." *Southern Journal of Philosophy* 27, 3 (Fall 1989): 361–380.

———. "Secondary Discrimination as a Standard of Feminist Ethics: Norplant, a Case Study." *Signs: Journal of Women in Culture and Society* 23, 4 (Summer 1998): 907–944.

Law, Sylvia A. "Commercial Sex: Beyond Decriminalization." *Southern California Law Review* 73, 3 (March 2000): 526–610.

Leigh, Carol, producer and distributor. *Outlaw Poverty, Not Prostitutes*. 1992. Videocassette. 20 min.

Leidholdt, Dorchen, and Janice G. Raymond. *The Sexual Liberals and the Attack on Feminism*. New York: Pergamon Press, 1990.

LeMoncheck, Linda. *Loose Women, Lecherous Men: A Feminist Philosophy of Sex*. New York: Oxford University Press, 1997.

Levy, Rachael. "Brothel Regulation Criticized: Sex Industry Advocate: Restrictions Excessive." *Las Vegas Sun*, April 2, 1997, 8A.

Loy, Frank E. "Testimony before the U.S. Justice Department." Appearance of Under-secretary for Global Affairs before U.S. Senate Committee on Foreign Relations, Subcommittee on Near Eastern and South Asian Affaires. Hearings on International Trafficking of Women and Children. *Congressional Testimonies*, February 22, 2000 (Archives). Available at http://secretary.state.gov

Lynch, Theresa, and Marilyn Neckes. *The Cost Effectiveness of Enforcing Prostitution Laws*. San Francisco: Unitarian Universalist Community Service Committee, 1978.

MacIntyre, Alasdair. "Utilitarianism and Cost-Benefit Analysis: An Essay on the Relevance of Moral Philosophy to Bureaucratic Theory." In *Values in the Electric Power Industry*, ed. Kenneth Sayre. 217–237. Notre Dame, IN: Notre Dame University Press, 1977.

MacKinnon, Catharine. "Feminism, Marxism, Method, and the State: An Agenda for Theory." *Signs: Journal of Women in Culture and Society* 5,3: (1982): 515–544.

———. *Toward a Feminist Theory of the State*. Cambridge, MA: Harvard University Press, 1989.

"Maria." "Testimony before U.S. Senate Foreign Relations Committee, Near Eastern and South Asian Affairs Subcommittee Hearings on International Trafficking of Women and Children." *Congressional Testimonies*, April 4, 2000 (Archives). Available at http://secretary.state.gov

Meyers, Diana T. *Self, Society, and Personal Choice*. New York: Columbia University Press, 1989.

Mill, John Stuart. *On Liberty*. Reprint, New York: Liberal Arts Press, 1956.

Miller, Eleanor M., Kim Romenesko, and Lisa Wondolkowski. "The United States." In *Prostitution: An International Handbook on Trends, Problems, and Policies*, ed. Nanette J. Davis. Westport, CT: Greenwood Press, 1993.

Miller, Laura. "Prostitution." *Harper's Bazaar*, March 1, 1995, 208.

Millett, Kate. "Prostitution: A Quartet for Female Voices." In *Woman in Sexist Society: Studies in Power and Powerlessness*, ed. Vivian Gornick and Barbara K. Moran, 60–125. New York: Signet, 1971.

Murray, Alison. "Debt-Bondage and Trafficking: Don't Believe the Hype." In *Global Sex Workers: Rights, Resistance, and Redefinition*, ed. Kamala Kempadoo and Jo Doezema, 51–64. New York: Routledge, 1998.

Narayan, Uma. "'Mail Order' Brides: Immigrant Women, Domestic Violence and Immigration Law." In *Feminist Ethics and Social Policy*, ed. Patrice Diquinzio and Iris Marion Young, 143–158. Bloomington: Indiana University Press, 1997.

Oakly, Ann. *Sex, Gender and Society*. London: Maurice Temple Smith, 1972.

Overall, Christine. "What's Wrong with Prostitution? Evaluating Sex Work." *Signs: Journal of Women in Culture and Society* 17, 4 (Summer 1992): 705–724.

Paris, Margot Hornblower. "The Skin Trade: Poverty, Chaos and Porous Borders Have Turned Prostitution into a Global Growth Industry, Debasing the Women and Children of the World." *Time*, June 21, 1993, 44–47.

Pateman, Carole. *The Sexual Contract*. Stanford, CA: Stanford University Press, 1988.

Pearsall, Marilyn, ed. *Women and Values: Readings in Recent Feminist Philosophy*. Belmont, CA: Wadsworth, 1986.

Peterson, Susan Rae. "Coercion and Rape: The State as a Male Protection Racket." In *Feminism and Philosophy*, ed. Mary Vetterling-Braggin, Frederick A. Elliston, and Jane English, 360–371. Totowa, NJ: Rowman and Littlefield, 1977.

Pheterson, Gail. *The Prostitution Prism*. Amsterdam: Amsterdam University Press, 1996.

———, ed. *A Vindication of the Rights of Whores*. Seattle: Seal Press, 1989.

Pillai, T. V. "Prostitution in India." *Indian Journal of Social Work* 43, 3 (1982): 313–320.

Pillard, Ellen. "Legal Prostitution: Is It Just?" *Nevada Public Affairs Review* 1983 (2). 43–47.

———. "Rethinking Prostitution: A Case for Uniform Regulation." *Nevada Public Affairs Review* 1991 (1). 45–49.

Pyne Addelson, Kathryn. *Impure Thoughts: Essays on Philosophy, Feminism, and Ethics*. Philadelphia: Temple University Press, 1991.

Rawls, John. *A Theory of Justice*. Cambridge, MA: Harvard University Press, 1971.

Reichert, Loren D., and James H. Frey. "The Organization of Bell Desk Prostitution." *Sociology and Social Research* 69 (1984): 516–526.

Reynolds, Helen. *The Economics of Prostitution*. Springfield, IL: Charles C. Thomas, 1986.

Rhode, Deborah L. "Feminist Critical Theories." *Stanford Law Review* 42 (1990): 617–638.

Roerink, Hans. "Orientation on Possibilities of Care/Treatment and Aids Prevention for Drug Addicts of Turkish and Moroccan Origin in the Netherlands." Paper presented to Thirty-fifth International Institute on the Prevention and Treatment of Alcoholism and the Eighteenth International Institute on the Prevention and Treatment of Drug Dependence (organized by the International Council on Alcohol and Addictions, Lausanne, Switzerland). Berlin, June 10–15, 1990.

Rosen, Ruth. *The Lost Sisterhood*. Baltimore: Johns Hopkins University Press, 1982.

Rubin, Gayle. "Thinking Sex: Notes for a Radical Theory of the Politics of Sexuality." In *Pleasure and Danger: Exploring Female Sexuality*, ed. Carole S. Vance, 267–319. Boston: Routledge and Kegan Paul, 1984.

San Francisco Task Force. *San Francisco Task Force on Prostitution: Final Report*. San Francisco: Board of Supervisors, 1996.

Satz, Debra. "Markets in Women's Sexual Labor." *Ethics* 106, 1 (October 1995): 63–85.

Sheffield, Carole. "Sexual Terrorism." In *Feminist Philosophies*, ed. Janet A Kourany, James P. Sterba, and Rosemarie Tong, 45–60. Englewood Cliffs, NJ: Prentice-Hall, 1999.

Sherwin, Susan. "Feminist Ethics and in Vitro Fertilization." *Canadian Journal of Philosophy,* 13 (1987): 276–284.

Shrage, Laurie. "Should Feminists Oppose Prostitution?" *Ethics* 99 (January 1989): 347–361.

Silbert, Mimi H., and Ayala M. Pines. "Pornography and Sexual Abuse of Women." *Sex Roles* 10, 11/12 (1984): 857–868.

Silver, R. L., and C. B. Wortman. "Coping with Undesirable Life Events." In *Human Helplessness: Theory and Applications*, ed. J. Garber and M. E. P. Seligman, 279–340. New York: Academic Press, 1980.

Sion, Abraham. *Prostitution and the Law*. London: Faber and Faber, 1977.

Skrobanek, Siriporn. "The Transnational Sexploitation of Thai Women." Research paper, the Hague, March 1983. On file at the Mr. A. de Graaf Foundation.

Southern Women's Writing Collective. "Sex Resistance in Heterosexual Arrangements." In *The Sexual Liberals and the Attack on Feminism*, ed. Dorchen Leidholdt and Janice G. Raymond. 140–147. New York: Pergamon, 1990.

Stock, Robert W. "When Older Women Contract the AIDS Virus." *New York Times*, July 31, 1997, B1.

Stock, Wendy. "Toward a Feminist Praxis of Sexuality." In *The Sexual Liberals and the Attack on Feminism*, ed. Dorchen Leidholdt and Janice G. Raymnond, 148–156. New York: Pergamon, 1990.

Tong, Rosmarie. *Women, Sex, and the Law*. Totawa, NJ: Rowman and Little-field, 1984.

Vance, Carole, ed. *Pleasure and Danger: Exploring Female Sexuality*. Boston: Routledge and Kegan Paul, 1984.

Vanwesenbeeck, Ine. *Prostitutes' Well-Being and Risk*. Amsterdam: Free University Press, 1994.

Visser, Jan. "The Legalisation of the Exploitation of Prostitution." Background paper presented in Helsinki, November 13, 2000. Available through the Mr. A. de Graaf Foundation.

———. "Selling Private Sex in Public Places: Managing Street-Prostitution in The Netherlands." Conference paper for "Changing Perspectives on Female Prostitution," Liverpool, February 6, 1998. Available through the Mr. A. de Graaf Foundation.

Walkowitz, Judith. *Prostitution and Victorian Society: Women, Class, and the State*. Cambridge: Cambridge University Press. 1980.

Wei Y., and A. Wong. "A Study of Five Hundred Prostitutes in Shanghai." *International Journal of Sexology* 2 (1949): 234–238.

Weisberg, D. K. *Children of the Night: A Study of Adolescent Prostitution*. Toronto: Lexington, 1985.

Weitzer, Ronald. "Prostitutes Rights in the United States: The Failure of a Movement." *Sociological Quarterly* 32, 1 (1991): 23–41.

Whoreact.net. "The Biography of Catherine La Croix." Available at http://www.whoreact.net//catherinebio.

Women's Leadership Institute. "Women, Violence and Human Rights." Contemporary Women's Issues Collection. 1991. (www.womensleadership.com)

Woolston, Howard B. *Prostitution in the United States*. Montclair, NJ: Patterson Smith, 1969.

Yanow, Dvora. *How Does a Policy Mean? Interpreting Policy and Organizational Actions*. Washington, DC: Georgetown University Press, 1996.

Yondorf, Barbara. "Prostitution as a Legal Activity." *Policy Analysis* 5, 4 (1979): 417–433.

Index

Abstinence, 189n. 2
Abuse, of prostitutes: in childhood, 22–24, 95–96, 173n. 13; by customers, 84–85, 184–85n. 97; by facilitators, 82–83, 84, 161
Acquired immune deficiency syndrome. See HIV/AIDS
Addiction, sexual, 124, 126
Advertising, of prostitution, 154
African Americans, 84, 122
AIDS. See HIV/AIDS
Alder, Christine, 103
Almodovar, Norma Jean, 61, 75
Amsterdam: number of prostitutes in, 90; red-light district of, 15–16; streetwalking in, 92, 185–86n. 119; window prostitution in, 15–16
Analytic philosophy, 9
Anderson, Laura, 78
Animals, liberty-limiting principles and, 191n. 6
Anti-abolitionist prostitutes, 19–27; arguments for inclusion of, 22–27; definition of, 21–22; pathologization of, 22–24; prevalence of, 22; traditional exclusion of, 20–21
Arrests, for prostitution: harm caused by, 125–26; in United States, 73–75
Asia: motivation for prostitution in, 69; U.S. military in, 72. See also specific countries
Asylum, for trafficked persons, 168
Atkinson, Ti-Grace, 6, 37
Attractiveness, sexual, 64
Australia, exploitation of prostitutes in, 106
Austria, prostitute registration in, 9
Automobiles, sex in, 158, 196–97n. 8
Autonomy: bodily, 122–23, 128–29, 136–37, 191n. 8; personal, 191n. 8
Avoidability, Standard of Reasonable, 190n. 4

Baker, Robert, 54
Barry, Kathleen, 105, 174n. 7
Bartky, Sandra, 6
Belgium, criminalized prostitution in, 185n. 106
Bell, Shannon, 6, 20, 22, 27, 39, 41, 51, 140–41
Bell-desk prostitution, 76–77
Biology: and intrinsic characteristics, 29–30; of sexual activity, 44–47; of sexual dimorphism, 38; and sexual orientation, 44, 176n. 1
Birth control, 47, 188–89n. 2
Black Americans, 84, 122
Black feminism, on sexuality, 39
Blank, Hilda, 91, 185–86n. 119
Bodily autonomy: vs. bodily integrity, 122, 136–37; under criminalized prostitution, 128–29; under decriminalized prostitution, 136–37; definition of, 122; government interference with, 122, 123; in legal policies, 122–23; personal autonomy and, 191n. 8

Bodily integrity: vs. bodily autonomy, 122, 136–37; under decriminalized prostitution, 136–37; definition of, 122; in legal policies, 122–23
Body(ies): control of, in patriarchy, 6; and intrinsic characteristics, 29, 45–46; selling of, 42–43, 140
Bondage and dominance, 150–51, 165
Bordo, Susan, 6, 29
Boston, Massachusetts, zoning for prostitution in, 132
Britain. See Great Britain
British feminist socialism, 151
Brothel prostitution: cooperative, 93–94, 163; current practice in, 78–87; dominance of, 68; lineup in, 79, 83–84, 164–65; in Netherlands, 93–94; in Nevada, 79–87, 133, 172n. 13; recommendations for policy on, 161–67
Bunch, Charlotte, 6
Burma, trafficked women from, 168
Burnes, Walter, 73

California, trafficked women in, 108
Call Off Your Old Tired Ethics. See COYOTE
Camp Casey (South Korea), 72
Canadian Fraser Committee, 132
Cars, sex in, 158, 196–97n. 8
CASE. See "Convention against Sexual Exploitation"
Cash, Carmen, 78
Chesney-Lind, Meda, 103, 128
Children: in prostitution, 170, 172n. 1; trafficking of, 172n. 1. See also Minor(s)
Child sexual assault: and prostitutes, 22–24, 95–96, 173n. 13; and well-being, 95–96
Chiropractors, 43
Church and state, separation of, 128
Cities, harm caused by criminalized prostitution in, 125, 127–28
Citizenship status, of prostitutes, 26
Clients. See Customers
CNMI. See Commonwealth of the Northern Mariana Islands (CNMI), trafficked workers in
Coalition Against Trafficking in Women, 24–25
Coercion, as motivation for prostitution, 69
Commonwealth of the Northern Mariana Islands (CNMI), trafficked workers in, 108–9
Communion, in heterosexuality, 55–56
Conceptual construction, 51–61; in contexualization of policy, 30–32; current practice and, 34; definition of, 31–32; definitions in, 30; of heterosexuality, 51–57, 115–16; vs. intrinsic characteristics, 34; political meaning/value of, 31–32; of prostitution, 57–61
Condoms: education campaigns on, 131, 156; in Netherlands, 131; recommendations for policy on, 164; and STDs, 46, 130

208

Constructivism, 29
Consummation hostesses, 109
Contagious Diseases Act (Great Britain), 58, 59, 129
Contextualization, 27–33; and data collection, 28–33; intrinsic characteristics in, 29–30; role of, 27–28; *vs.* theoretical approach to policy, 27
Contract(s): marriage, 140, 143, 193n. 9; prostitution, 42, 49–50, 140–43, 193–94n. 9; sexual, 139–43; social, 139, 193n. 6
"Convention against Sexual Exploitation" (CASE), 24–25
"Convention for the Suppression of Traffic in Persons and the Exploitation of the Prostitution of Others," 187n. 153
Cooper, Belinda, 189n. 4
Cooperative brothels, 93–94, 163
Coping mechanisms, and well-being, 97–99
Counseling agencies, for potential prostitutes, 156
COYOTE (Call Off Your Old Tired Ethics), 21, 25, 183n. 58
Crime(s): against prostitutes, 60–61, 76, 102–3, 187n. 147; rates of, legalized prostitution and, 132
Criminality: child sexual abuse and, 24; intention in, 28
Criminalization, definition of, 65
Criminalized prostitution, 124–29; arguments against, 125–29; arguments for, 124–25; economic costs of, 127–28; harm to customers under, 124, 126–27; harm to prostitutes under, 125–26; ineffectiveness of, 125; *vs.* legal sex acts, 175–76n. 29; medical testing under, 192n. 21
Current practice, 62–110; conceptual construction and, 34; in contextualization of policy, 32; definition of, 32; of heterosexuality, 62–65; *vs.* intrinsic characteristics, 33–34; misconceptions about, 32; of prostitution, 65–110
Customers: abuse by, 84–85, 184–85n. 97; behavior of, 85; female, 70, 172n. 15; harm to, 124, 126–27; interactions with, and prostitute well-being, 99–100; motivation for, 69–71, 117–18; refusal of, 84; teenage, 150

Dancing, nude, 184n. 85
Data collection: contextualization and, 28–33; focus on streetwalking in, 2, 26, 68
Davis, Angela, 6
Deconstructionism, and sexuality, 38
Decriminalization, definition of, 12, 66
Decriminalized prostitution, 134–37; arguments for, 134–37; in Netherlands, 12, 88–104; recommendations for policy of, 153–61; in Western Europe, 71, 88, 185n. 106
Definitions, in conceptual construction, 30
De Graaf Foundation, Mr. A, 13, 88, 89
Delcarlo, Robert, 81, 83, 87
Denmark, prostitution venues in, 75
Desire, sexual, 44–45, 55
Discrimination: gender, 74, 127; in law enforcement, 74–75, 127; racial, 74–75; secondary, 123, 136; sexual stigmatization and, 102
Dissociation, as coping response, 98–99, 186n. 140
Divorce, 143
Doezema, Jo, 22, 60
Domestic violence, NGOs and, 4
Domestic workers, trafficking of, 105, 106
Dominance and bondage, 150–51, 165
Dominance prostitution, 151, 195n. 23

Dotson, Yvonne Elizabeth, 75, 183n. 60
Drug use: decriminalization of, 196n. 5; and streetwalking, 92, 97, 185–86n. 119; treatment programs for, 155
Dutch National Center for the Fight Against AIDS, 95
Dworkin, Andrea, 6, 38, 39, 48–49, 54, 55–56, 64–65, 174n. 7, 175n. 9

Eastern Europe: motivation for prostitution in, 181n. 25; women trafficked from, 104
Economic motivation, for prostitution, 24, 59, 69, 85, 134–35, 151
Economic situation, and well-being, 96
Education campaign, public: about prostitution, 156; for STD prevention, 131, 156
Ellis, Havelock, 59
El Monte, California, 108
Emotional connection, in heterosexual activity, 63
Emotional vulnerability, 115, 116
Emotion-focused reactions, and well-being, 97–99
Empowerment, prostitution as source of, 104
England. *See* Great Britain
English Collective of Prostitutes, 151
Enloe, Cynthia, 6, 71
Ensler, Eve, 113
Epistemology: feminist, 19–20; postmodern, 19–20; traditional, 7–8, 19
Escort services: current practice in, 77–78; female, 75, 77–78; male, 172n. 15, 182n. 29
Essentialism, 29
Europe: decriminalized prostitution in, 71, 88, 185n. 106; motivation for prostitution in, 181n. 25; women trafficked from, 104. *See also specific countries*
Exploitation: all prostitutes as victims of, 24–26; community stigmatization and, 26; legal status and, 26

Facilitation, prostitution: abuse in, 82–83, 84, 161; coercion in, 69; criminalization of, 161–62; decriminalization of, 161; definition of, 124; legalization of, 162–67; legal status of, 66; in Netherlands, 89; recommendations for policy on, 161–67
Facts, in theory development, 9, 171n. 10
False consciousness theory, 20, 23, 24–25
Federal government, prostitution policy role of, 124
Feinberg, Joel, 120, 190n. 4
Female, construction *vs.* biology of, 38
Feminist(s): American, 139–49; black, 39; British socialist, 151; context in, 27–28; epistemology of, 19–20, 27–28; global, 6; on heterosexuality (sex wars), 38–41; liberal, 5; libertarian, 40; Marxist, 5; multicultural, 6, 39; on patriarchy, 5–6; perspective in, 27–28; on prostitution, 138–51; radical, 5, 38–39, 174n. 7; sex radical, 39–40, 149–51
Ferguson, Ann, 149–50, 151
Fijnaut, Cyrille, 111
Financial motivation, for prostitution, 24, 59, 69, 85, 134–35, 151
Firestone, Shulamith, 6
Flax, Jane, 9
Flint, George, 80, 82, 83, 84, 86
Forced prostitution: all prostitution as, 25; as sexual assault, 25; *vs.* voluntary prostitution, 25, 60
Foucault, Michel, 38, 51
Foundation against Trafficking in Women, 105

France, prostitutes in, 61, 192n. 27
French, Diane, 73
Freud, Sigmund, 59

GAATW. *See* Global Alliance Against Trafficking in
 Women
Gebhard, P. H., 69
Genital mutilation, female, 103
Germany, legalized prostitution in, 132, 182n. 32
Global Alliance Against Trafficking in Women
 (GAATW), 105
Global feminism, emergence of, 6
Globalization, of prostitution, 71–73
Global Survival Network, 109
Governance boards, 154, 162, 163, 164, 165, 166
Great Britain: feminist socialist view in, 151; prosti-
 tution in, 58, 59, 129, 192n. 27
Greece, prostitute registration in, 132
Guatemala, prostitute registration in, 132
Guilt, moral, of customers, 124, 126

Hague (Netherlands), 92–93
HAP Foundation, 91
Harm: under criminalized prostitution, 124,
 125–27; as intrinsic risk of heterosexuality,
 46–47
Harm Principle, 120–21
Haven House, 7, 23, 196n. 6
Hawkesworth, Mary, 4
Health: public, legalized prostitution and, 129–31;
 sexual activity and, 37
Health standards, in brothels, 164
Herleen (Netherlands), 92
Heterosexism, 55, 114
Heterosexual activity(ies): conceptual construction
 of, 51–57, 115–16; current practice of, 62–65;
 ideal practice of, 111–17; as institution, 37; intimacy in, 46, 50, 52, 56–57, 63, 114–16; intrinsic
 characteristics of, 44–47, 48–49; negative values
 of, 46–47, 48, 64; positive values of, 51–52,
 55–56, 62–63; stigmatization of, 52, 55, 112,
 113–14
Heterosexuality: complexity of, 40–41, 62; contradictions of, 40–41, 62; criteria for analysis of,
 40–41; cultural values in, 37; feminist sex wars
 over, 38–41; mystification of, 113; patriarchy
 and, 37–38, 112, 141, 144–45; power in,
 38–39, 55; and sexism, 52; sexual dimorphism
 and, 38
Heterosexual practice: current, 62–65; ideal,
 111–17
Hillside Strangler case, 187n. 148
Hindu widows, 103–4
HIV/AIDS: approaches to prevention of, 131, 156,
 189n. 2; as intrinsic risk of heterosexuality, 46;
 in Netherlands, 131; in Philippines, 72; prostitutes with, 72, 130, 131, 192n. 23; testing methods for, 130, 192n. 25; trafficked persons with,
 168
Holland. *See* Netherlands
Holmes, Dale Anthony, 187n. 147
Holsopple, Kelly, 186n. 140
Homophobia, 55
hooks, bell, 6, 21
Hotel prostitution, 76–77
Houston, Freddie, 187n. 147
Human immunodeficiency virus. *See* HIV/AIDS
Human Rights Convention of the European Com-
 munity, 26

"Human Rights Standards for the Treatment of
 Trafficked Persons," 104–5, 167
Hygiene standards, in brothels, 164

Ideal, in philosophy, 10
Ideal practice, 111–18; in contextualization of pol-
 icy, 32–33, 34; definition of, 32; formation of vi-
 sion of, 33, 34; of heterosexual activity, 111–17;
 of prostitution, 117–18
Identity, sexuality and, 36–37, 140–41
Identity studies, emergence of, 8
IIAV. *See* Internationaal Informatiecentrum en
 Archief Voor de Vrouwendeweging
Immigration: illegal, and trafficking, 104–6; by
 prostitutes, 104, 154
Immigration and Naturalization Services (INS),
 108, 154, 166
India, Hindu widows in, 103–4
Indonesia, prostitute registration in, 132
INS. *See* Immigration and Naturalization Services
Inspections, of brothels, 166
Integrity, bodily, 122–23, 136–37
Intellectual pleasure, 178n. 3
Intention, and criminality, 28
Intercourse (Dworkin), 38, 48–49, 175n. 9
Interdisciplinary research: emergence of, 8; in pub-
 lic policy, 9
Intergenerational sexual activity, 149–50
Internationaal Informatiecentrum en Archief Voor
 de Vrouwendeweging (IIAV), 13, 17
International Conference on Traffic in Persons, 105
International Human Rights Law Group, 105
Intimacy, in heterosexuality: conceptual construc-
 tion of, 52, 56–57, 115–16; in current practice,
 63; definition of, 114–15; feminist view of, 114;
 as intrinsic characteristic, 50; vulnerability and,
 46, 115–16
Intrinsic characteristics, 44–50; *vs.* conceptual construction, 34; *vs.* current practice, 33–34; definition of, 29–30; of heterosexuality, 44–49; of
 prostitution, 49–50
Islam, sexual purity in, 103

Jackson, Stevi, 40, 41
James, Selma, 195n. 37
Jones, Lee, 134

Kempadoo, Kamala, 22
Kenya: prostitute registration in, 132; sex tourism
 in, 70, 172n. 15
Kim, Hyun Sook, 109
Kim, Luther, 78
Kit Kat Ranch, 79, 82, 85, 86
Korea: trafficked women from, 78, 109; U.S. mili-
 tary in, 72, 109
Kosovski, Ester, 67

Labor Commission, U.S., 108
Labor Department, U.S., 108
La Croix, Catherine, 183n. 58
Language, political meaning/value of, 31–32
Las Vegas, Nevada, bell-desk prostitution in, 76
Las Vegas Sun (newspaper), 83
Law(s): in heterosexual practice, 64–65; on living
 off prostitutes' earnings, 89, 160; in Netherlands,
 89–90; on prostitution, 73, 80–82, 89–90,
 132–34; on prostitution facilitation, 89
Law enforcement: under criminalized prostitution,
 125–26, 127–28; in current prostitution practice,

66, 73–75; economic costs of, 127–28; gender discrimination in, 74, 127; in Netherlands, 88; police assault of prostitutes and, 75; racism in, 74–75; sensitivity training for police in, 156–57, 196n. 6; toleration of prostitution in, 66, 74, 88; visibility of prostitution and, 74
Legalization, definition of, 12, 65–66
Legalized prostitution, 129–34; arguments against, 129–34; arguments for, 129; in Nevada, 79–87, 172n. 13
Legal policy(ies): bodily autonomy/integrity in, 122–23; extralegal supports with, 3–4; liberty-limiting principles in, 120–21; *vs.* public policy, 3; secondary discrimination in, 123; standards for evaluation of, 119–23
Legal status: of prostitutes, 26, 81–82; of prostitution, 65–66
Leigh, Carol, 79, 134, 184n. 95, 192n. 29
LeMoncheck, Linda, 41, 60
Liberal feminism, on patriarchy, 5
Libertarian feminism, on sexuality, 40
Liberties, individual, legal policies limiting, 120–21
Lineup, in brothels, 79, 83–84, 164–65
Living arrangements, shared, in heterosexuality, 63
Living rooms, for streetwalkers: in Netherlands, 90–93; in United States, 158–60
Logic, and intrinsic characteristics, 30
Loose Women, Lecherous Men (LeMoncheck), 41
Lyon, France, 61
Lyon County, Nevada, 87

MacKinnon, Catharine, 6, 28, 38, 39, 174n. 7
Madonna-whore bifurcation, 52–53, 127, 135, 148
Mail-order brides, 105, 169
Male, construction *vs.* biology of, 38
Marriage, positive values of, 148
Marriage contract, 140, 143, 193n. 9
Marxist feminism, on patriarchy, 5
Massachusetts: prostitution law in, 73; zoning for prostitution in, 132
Massage out-call services, 70, 172n. 15
Massage parlors, current practice in, 78–79
Massage therapy, 43, 176n. 34
Masturbation, 175–76n. 29
Meaning: definition of, 10; determination of (*see* Conceptual construction); in philosophy, 10; in public policy, 10, 31–32
Medical care, for prostitutes, 157–58, 196n. 7
Medical testing, required: under criminalized prostitution, 192n. 21; under legalized prostitution, 129, 130–31
Metaphor, prostitution as, 42
Methodology: anti-abolitionist prostitutes and, 19–27; contextualization in, 27–28; data collection in, 28–33; of feminist public policy, 18–19; interdisciplinary, 8; multicultural, 8–9; of philosophy, 9–10, 27; of women's studies, 8–9
Mexico: prostitute registration in, 132; trafficking of women from, 107–8
Meyers, Diana, 122
Military, U.S., and trafficking, 71–72, 109, 169
Mill, John Stuart, 120–21, 178n. 3, 190n. 3
Miller, Eleanor, 74
Millett, Kate, 143–44, 174n. 7
Minor(s): as customers, 150; as prostitutes, 149–50, 154–55; recommendations on, 154–55; runaway, 154–55
Minority feminism, on sexuality, 39
Misogyny, 37, 144

Mitchell, Juliette, 6
Moral character, sexual activity and, 42, 176n. 33
Moralism, legal: and criminalization of prostitution, 125, 128; definition of, 120; problems with, 121
Moral pleasure, 178n. 3
Morrow, Shelly, 187n. 147
Motivation: for customers, 69–71, 117–18; for prostitutes, 24, 59, 69, 85, 86, 134–35, 151
Muller v. Oregon, 190–91n. 5
Multicultural feminism: emergence of, 6; on sexuality, 39
Multiculturalism: in public policy, 9; in women's studies, 9
Murder, of prostitutes, 61, 102, 187n. 147, 187n. 148
Murray, Alison, 105, 106, 168
Muslim communities, sexual purity in, 103
Mustang I and II, 79, 80, 82, 83–84

National Task Force on Prostitution (COYOTE), 25
Nelson, Alberta, 84
Netherlands: approach to social problems in, 12–13, 88; brothel prostitution in, 93–94; current prostitution practice in, 12, 87–104; HIV in, 131; number of prostitutes in, 90; streetwalking in, 90–93, 185–86n. 119; trafficking in, 106, 187n. 152; window prostitution in, 15–16
Network of Sex Work Projects, 20–21
Nevada: bell-desk prostitution in, 76; brothel prostitution in, 79–87, 133, 172n. 13; laws in, 80–82, 132–34; nude dancing in, 184n. 85
New York City, prostitution arrests in, 73
Nongovernmental organizations (NGOs), 4
Normalization: of prostitution, 111, 117, 169–70; of sexuality, 111–12, 117; of women, 111
Nude dancing, 184n. 85
Nye County, Nevada, 81, 129, 130

Objectification: of men, 179n. 10; of prostitutes, 146–47
Objectivity, in traditional epistemology, 19, 27
Offense Principle, 120–21, 190n. 4
Olongapo (Philippines), 72
Oppressed, disciplines of, emergence of, 8
Orgasm, 52, 62, 113
"Orientation on Possibilities of Care/Treatment and Aids Prevention for Drug Addicts of Turkish and Moroccan Origin in the Netherlands," 131
Our Bodies, Ourselves, 113

Parent-Duchatelet, Alexander John Baptiste, 129
Parks, for streetwalkers: in Netherlands, 90–93; in United States, 158–60
Partnerships, sexual, 37
Pateman, Carol, 139–43
Paternalism, legal: definition of, 120; problems with, 121
Patriarchy: criminalization of prostitution and, 128; definition of, 5; feminisms on, 5–6; and heterosexuality, 37–38, 112, 141, 144–45; origins of, 5–6; selling acceptance of, 143–44; and stigmatization, 112, 141
Pedophilia, 190n. 11
Personal autonomy, 191n. 8
Perspective, in legal/moral analysis, 27–28
Peru, prostitute registration in, 132
Pheterson, Gail, 20, 22, 26, 160

Philippines: number of prostitutes in, 72; regulation of prostitution in, 192n. 27; U.S. military in, 72
Philosophy, 9–10; conceptual analysis in, 30; methodology of, 9–10, 27
Phone sex, 195n. 24
Physical vulnerability, 46–47, 115–16
Pillard, Ellen, 81, 87, 134
Pines, Ayala, 76
Pleasure: of customer *vs.* prostitute, 118, 190n. 13; intellectual, 178n. 3; moral, 178n. 3; sensual, 113–14; sexual, 62, 178–79n. 3
Police: assault of prostitutes by, 75; sensitivity and support training for, 156–57, 196n. 6. *See also* Law enforcement
Politically correct terminology, 31
Pornography: in brothels, 165; zoning for, 160–61
Postmodernism, 19–20
Power: female, 55; in heterosexuality, 38–39, 55; male, 38–39; sale of, prostitution as, 143–44; stigmatization and, 111, 112–13
Practice. *See* Current practice; Ideal practice
Pregnancy: drug treatment programs during, 155; as positive value of heterosexuality, 63; unintended, 47, 63–64, 188n. 1
Privacy, and sexual activity, 47, 65, 116
Problem-focused reactions, and well-being, 97–98
Professional associations and guilds, 155
"Proposed Convention against Sexual Exploitation," 167, 187–88n. 153
Prostitutes' rights organizations, 20–21, 22
Prostitutes' Well-Being and Risk (Vanwesenbeeck), 94–102
Prostitution: ambiguity of term, 30, 41–42; definition of, 41–43, 172n. 14; number of women in, 67
Prostitution (Davis), 175n. 28
Prostitution practice, current, 65–110; customer motivation in, 69–71; global, 71–73; legal status in, 65–66; in Netherlands, 12, 87–104; prostitute motivation in, 69; research context for, 67–68; trafficking in, 104–10; in United States, 73–87, 107–10
Prostitution practice, ideal, 117–18
Public education campaigns: about prostitution, 156; for STD prevention, 131, 156
Public health, legalized prostitution and, 129–31
Public policy: definition of, 3; extralegal supports in, 3–4; interdisciplinary approach to, 9; *vs.* legal policy, meaning in, 10, 31–32; multicultural approach to, 9
Purity, female sexual, 103–4

Racism, in law enforcement, 74–75
Radical feminism: origins of, 174n. 7; on patriarchy, 5; on sexuality, 38–39. *See also* Sex radical feminism
Rape: blaming victim for, 61, 85; institutional support after, 102; in Netherlands, 91; by police, 75; spouse, 179n. 13; of streetwalkers, 76, 91, 102
Rawls, John, 27
Reading, Writing and Rewriting the Prostitute Body (Bell), 20
Reasonable Avoidability, Standard of, 190n. 4
Recommendations, policy, 152–70; audience for, 11–12; criteria for, 152–53; for decriminalized prostitution, 153–61; for facilitated prostitution, 161–67; limitations of, 14; for trafficking, 167–69
Red-light district, of Amsterdam, 15–16

Red Thread, The, 21
Registration, prostitute, 132, 166, 192n. 27
Reno, Janet, 110
Reproduction, and oppression of women, 112
Reputation, sexual, 103
Research, context for, 2, 26, 67–68
Rietberger, Andrea, 90
Rights: of prostitutes, 26, 133; sexual purity and, 103–4
Rode Draad, De, 21
Roerink, Hans, 131
Rojanasathien, Boonchu, 17
Romenesko, Kim, 74
Rubin, Elaine, 6
Rubin, Gayle, 102, 189n. 8
Runaway minors, 154–55

Sadomasochism, 150–51, 189–90n. 8
Sadomasochistic prostitution, 151, 165
Safety regulations, recommendations for, 163–64
Safe parks, for streetwalking: in Netherlands, 90–93; in United States, 158–60
San Francisco Task Force, 168
Satz, Debra, 145–46
Saunders, Penelope, 183n. 64
Scent, and sexual desire, 45
Scott, Sue, 40, 41
Secondary discrimination, 123, 136
Secretarial work, 146–47
Self-employment, 163
Selling: of acceptance of patriarchy, 143–44; of bodies, 42–43, 140; in definition of prostitution, 42–43; of self, 42, 141–42; of sexual services, 42–43
Sensual pleasure, 113–14
Sexism: construction of sexuality and, 51, 52; and sexual stigmatization, 112
Sex radical feminism: critique of, 149–51; on prostitution, 149–51; on sexuality, 39–40, 149–51
Sex therapy, 176n. 31
Sex tourism: current practice of, 71; in Kenya, 70, 172n. 15; in Thailand, 17
Sexual assault: child, 22–24, 95–96, 173n. 13; forced prostitution as, 25. *See also* Rape
Sexual attractiveness, 64
Sexual contract, 139–43
Sexual Contract, The (Pateman), 139–43
Sexual desire: biology of, 44–45; and female power, 55
Sexual dimorphism, 38
Sexual harassment, 28
Sexuality: backlash in, 36–37; definition of, 174n. 4; and identity, 36–37, 140–41; as institution, 37; mystification of, 113; normalization of, 111–12, 117; sexism and, 51, 52. *See also* Heterosexuality
Sexually transmitted diseases (STDs): approaches to prevention of, 156; under decriminalized prostitution, 135; and heterosexuality, 46, 47, 64; under legalized prostitution, 129–31; required testing for, 129, 130–31
Sexual orientation, biology and, 44, 176n. 1
Sexual pleasure, 62, 178–79n. 3
Sexual purity, female, 103–4
Sexual reputation, 103
Sexual revolution, 52, 189n. 8
Shiatsu massage, 176n. 34
Short, Melissa, 187n. 147
"Significant others," 37
Silbert, Mimi, 76

Silver, R. L., 97
Singapore, prostitute registration in, 132
Skinlessness, 56
Social contract, 139, 193n. 6
Socialist feminism, British, critique of, 151
Social services, with decriminalized prostitution, 135
Social vulnerability, 115, 116
Solanas, Valerie, 36
Southern Women Writers' Collective, 174n. 7
South Korea: trafficked women from, 109; U.S. military in, 72, 109
Spain, prostitution in, 185n. 106
Sports, bodies in, 140
Spousal rape, 179n. 13
Statistical studies, streetwalking in, 2, 26, 68
STDs. *See* Sexually transmitted diseases
Stichting HAJ, 90–91
Stichting Tegen Vrouwenhandel (STV), 105
Stigmatization: by community, 26; criminalized prostitution and, 128; decriminalized prostitution and, 136; of heterosexual activity, 52, 55, 112, 113–14; patriarchy and, 112, 141; and power, 111, 112–13; of prostitution, 26, 101–4, 117, 136; and vulnerability, 115–17; and well-being, 101
Storey County, Nevada, 81
Streetwalking: decriminalization of, 92; drug use and, 92, 97, 185–86n. 119; impact on neighborhoods, 125, 127; law enforcement and, 74–75; in Netherlands, 90–93; prevalence of, 26, 68, 179–80n. 18; recommendations for policy on, 158–60; risks of, 75–76; in statistical studies, 2, 26, 68; violent crime and, 76, 91, 102
STV. *See* Stichting Tegen Vrouwenhandel
Subic Bay Naval Base (Philippines), 72
Subjectivity: definition of, 19–20; in feminist epistemology, 19–20, 27–28
Survival strategies, and well-being, 97–99
Switzerland, prostitute registration in, 132
Syphilis experiment, Tuskegee, 122

Technology, and intrinsic characteristics, 29–30, 34
Teenagers, prostitution and, 149–50, 154–55
Thailand: prostitution in, 17, 72, 172n. 1; trafficking in, 108, 172n. 1; U.S. military in, 72
Theory, in philosophy, 9–10, 27
Theory of Justice, A (Rawls), 27
Touch, and sexual desire, 45
Tourism, sex. *See* Sex tourism
Trafficking: in Asia, 72, 172n. 1; and brothels, 78, 86; child, 172n. 1; current practice of, 104–6; definition of, 104–6, 167, 187n. 152; escalation of, 72–73; of men *vs.* women, 167; in Netherlands, 106, 187n. 152; prevalence of, 106; recommendations for policy on, 167–69; in United States, 106, 107–10; U.S. military and, 71–72, 109, 169
Tuskegee syphilis experiment, 122

UN. *See* United Nations
Unions, prostitute, 155

United Nations (UN), 20, 21, 71, 110
United States: current prostitution practice in, 73–87, 107–10; feminist view on prostitution in, 139–49; number of prostitutes in, 73; trafficking in, 106, 107–10
Universality, Standard of, 190n. 4
University of Nevada–Reno, 67
Uruguay, prostitute registration in, 132

Vagina Monologues, The (Ensler), 113
Vance, Carole, 6, 29, 62
Vanwesenbeeck, Ine, 13, 94–102, 161, 185n. 112, 186n. 121
Verhees, Hordine, 90, 185n. 112
Victim(s), prostitutes as: conceptual construction of, 59–60; and exclusion from policy making, 20; and false consciousness theory, 20, 23, 24–25; and nonprostitute heterosexuality, 148; and objectification, 146–47; of sexual exploitation, 24–26
Victimizer, prostitutes as: conceptual construction of, 60–61, 146; in legalized prostitution, 133
Vietnam War, 72
Vindication of the Rights of Whores, A (Pheterson), 20
Violence: and heterosexual activity, 47, 55; against prostitutes, 60–61, 76, 102–3, 187n. 147
Visas, for trafficked persons, 168
Visibility, of prostitution, 74, 125
Visser, Jan, 88, 92
Voluntary prostitution, 25, 60
Vulnerability: emotional, 115, 116; with heterosexual activity, 46–47, 48–49; intimacy and, 46, 115–16; physical, 46–47, 115–16; social, 115, 116; stigmatization and, 115–17

Wages, recommendations for policy on, 163
Well-being, of prostitutes, 94–101
Whore(s): definition of, 57; *vs.* madonna, 52–53, 127, 135, 148; paradigm of, 57–58; *vs.* prostitute, 57–58, 135
Widows, Hindu, 103–4
Window prostitution: in Netherlands, 15–16; recommendations for policy on, 164–65
Women Against Violence, 7
Women's issues, privatization of, 4
"Women's situation": generalizations about, 8–9; interdisciplinary approach to, 8; multicultural approach to, 9, 101
Women's studies, 7–9; interdisciplinary nature of, 8; methodology of, 8–9; multicultural approach to, 9
Wondolkowski, Lisa, 74
Woodhull, Victoria, 48
Worker Exploitation Task Force, 110
Working conditions, and well-being, 96–97
World Charter for Prostitutes Rights, 25
World Whores Congresses, 20, 21, 25
Wortman, C. B., 97

Zoning: for pornographic outlets, 160–61; for prostitution, 132, 160, 167

About the Author

Lenore Kuo is professor of Women's Studies and Philosophy and chair of the Women's Studies Program at California State University at Fresno.